Principia Iuris

Principia Iuris

A Historical and Comparative Introduction to the English Common Law

Geoffrey Samuel

Professor Emeritus, Kent Law School, UK

Edward Elgar
PUBLISHING

Cheltenham, UK · Northampton, MA, USA

Cover image: Harris Brisbane Dick Fund, 1941, *Portraits of Roman Jurisconsults*, from *Speculum Romanae Magnificentiae* (The Mirror of Roman Magnificence)

Published by

Edward Elgar Publishing Limited
The Lypiatts
15 Lansdown Road
Cheltenham
Glos GL50 2JA
UK

Edward Elgar Publishing, Inc.
William Pratt House
9 Dewey Court
Northampton
Massachusetts 01060
USA

Authorised representative in the EU for GPSR queries only: Easy Access System Europe – Mustamäe tee 50, 10621 Tallinn, Estonia, gpsr.requests@easproject.com

A catalogue record for this book
is available from the British Library

Library of Congress Control Number: 2025937362

This book is available electronically in the **Elgar**online
Law subject collection
https://doi.org/10.4337/9781035350575

MIX
Paper | Supporting
responsible forestry
FSC
www.fsc.org   FSC® C013604

ISBN 978 1 0353 5056 8 (cased)
ISBN 978 1 0353 5057 5 (eBook)
ISBN 978 1 0353 7076 4 (ePub)

Printed and bound by CPI Group (UK) Ltd, Croydon, CR0 4YY

Contents

List of abbreviations

AC	Appeal cases (Third Series)
AJCL	American Journal of Comparative Law
All ER	All England Law Reports (Butterworths & Co)
App Cas	Appeal Cases (Second Series)
C	Code of Justinian
CA	Court of Appeal
CC	Code civil (French civil code)
Ch	Chancery Division (Third Series)
Ch D	Chancery Division (Second Series)
CJQ	Civil Justice Quarterly
CLJ	Cambridge Law Journal
CLP	Current Legal problems
CLR	Commonwealth Law Reports
CPC	French Code of Civil Procedure
CPR	Civil Procedure Rules
D	Digest of Justinian
DCFR	Draft Common Frame of Reference
EHRLR	European Human Rights Law Review
EHRR	European Human Rights Reports
ER	English Reports
FLR	Family Law Reports
G	Institutes of Gaius
HL	House of Lords
ICLQ	International and Comparative Law Quarterly
IECL	International Encyclopedia of Comparative Law
J	Institutes of Justinian/Justice (High Court)
KB	King's Bench (Third Series)
KBD	King's Bench Division
LC	Lord Chancellor
LJ	Lord Justice (Court of Appeal)
LJCP	Law Journal Common Pleas
LJ Ex	Law Journal Exchequer
LJQB	Law Journal Queen's Bench

Ll Rep	Lloyd's List Law Reports
LQR	Law Quarterly Review
LR...CP	Common Pleas Cases (First Series)
LR...Eq	Equity Cases (First Series)
LR...Ex	Exchequer Cases (First Series)
LR...HL	English and Irish Appeals (First Series)
LR...QB	Queen's Bench Cases (First Series)
LS	Legal Studies
LT	Law Times Reports
MJ	Maastricht Journal of European and Comparative Law
MLR	Modern Law Review
NILQ	Northern Ireland Legal Quarterly
OJLS	Oxford Journal of Legal Studies
OUP	Oxford University Press
P	Probate Division (Third Series)
PC	Privy Council
PECL	Principles of European Contract Law
PL	Public Law
QB	Queen's Bench (Third Series)
QBD	Queen's Bench (Second Series)
RIDC	Revue Internationale de Droit Comparé
RSC	Rules of Supreme Court
SC	UK Supreme Court
SLR	Statute Law Review
UNIDROIT	Principles of International Commercial Contracts
WLR	Weekly Law Reports

Preface

This book is offered as an updated replacement for my *A Short Introduction to the Common Law* (Elgar, 2013) and, to a much lesser extent, for my *Law of Obligations* (Elgar, 2010). It differs from the 2013 book in that it is longer and organised in terms of legal maxims (*principia, regulae iuris*). These maxims are themselves organised, not alphabetically, but along the traditional institutional structure, inherited from Roman law, of public law, the law of persons, the law of property, the law of obligations and the law of actions (remedies). There are also separate chapters on law as a discipline, the historical development of the courts, procedure, taxonomy and theory, and legal reasoning. Books of legal maxims are by no means a novelty (quite the opposite), yet I hope they will act as a useful vehicle for presenting contemporary law and legal institutions from an historical and comparative angle. Maxims offer something of a comparative approach, but I am not intending this book as some kind of sophisticated work on comparative law. It is aimed both at those starting out on a law degree and at those just interested in knowing something about law's rich intellectual history.

To be honest, I had grave doubts about going ahead with publishing the manuscript because a new book on legal maxims, whatever its merits, can hardly be described as an original project. There have been many over the centuries. However, the project received serious support from my comparative law and legal historian colleague Luca Siliquini-Cinelli, from some of the anonymous referees (others were not damning but shared some of my reservations) and from colleagues at Elgar. I would like to thank them profusely for their support.

Perhaps one other reason for producing this book is in memory of the late Peter Stein (1926–2016) whose own academic monograph on the subject, published in 1966, remains the seminal work on the topic. I was Peter's Roman law student both at undergraduate and at post-graduate level (his only Roman law student that year), and he once told me how the late Walter Ullmann (1910–1983) – one of the leading historians on the history of public law in Europe – had urged younger colleagues to do serious research on the *regulae iuris*. I am not, of course, offering my book as serious research (although chasing the medieval origins of some of the maxims proved a challenge), but if it encourages others to build on Peter Stein's foundation, so much the better.

Geoffrey Samuel
Blean, Kent
May 2025

Table of cases and practice directions

Table of statutes

Introductory remarks

A new book on legal maxims, whatever its merits, can hardly be described as an original project. It is probably no exaggeration to say that there has been one or more in every century during the last millennium. The original source was the last title of Justinian's *Digest*, which has a list of over two hundred of such maxims described as *regulae iuris* (D.50.17). This last title, together with Justinian's *Institutes*, became the starting point for legal education in the sixteenth century in continental Europe. In the three centuries that followed, there were many works on this title, several of which laid the foundations for the French *Code civil* of 1804. One work from the eighteenth century describes these *regulae iuris* as "the base and the foundation of the edifice [of law]" (Dantoine 1710: Preface). And even during the late medieval era, one of the leading jurists of the time, Baldus de Ubaldis (1327–1400), wrote that if one wanted to have knowledge of something, one had to have knowledge of its foundational principles (see maxim 2). It is not surprising, therefore, that many of the leading maxims (*brocadica, principia, regulae*), in addition to those coming directly from Roman law, were formulated by the Commentators on Roman law (Post-Glossators) and canonists of the late Middle Ages. Indeed, in addition to the Roman *regulae*, canon law produced its own list of eighty-eight *regulae iuris* in a thirteenth-century work (*Liber Sextus*).

During the last century, books of maxims still appeared – one thinks in particular of a two-volume work by two French authors (Roland & Boyer 1999) – and this century has seen the publication of a small book of one hundred legal principles by a Belgian specialist on legal argumentation (Goltzberg 2018). Such books were not confined to the continent. Francis Bacon (1561–1626), who held the office of Lord Chancellor (1618–1621), was equally taken with what he considered to be the scientific importance of legal maxims, and the nineteenth century saw many published collections of legal maxims in England and in the United States. A leading academic monograph on *regulae iuris* was published in 1966 by Peter Stein (1926–2016) who a year later became the Regius Professor of Civil Law at Cambridge. Stein's book remains a scholarly classic, but it is not the last word on the subject. Writing in 2016, Ian Williams notes how maxims "provided the means to establish claims that the common law was a 'science'" in that they could be seen as the principles underpinning the common law. And demonstrating "that the common law was a science was a means to establish the common law's equivalence or even superiority over other bodies of learning" (Williams 2016: 204). Be that as it may, one might say today. Yet whatever the influence of maxims on legal practice, concludes Williams, the role of legal maxims in legal education "achieved some success" (*ibid*) in the early modern common law. Some today might regard maxims as little more than abstract rhetoric of little actual legal value, yet recently James Gordley has written:

> One might think that legal principles of this sort are useless. I disagree, despite everything I have just said. Such principles capture a truth, or more accurately, an aspect of the truth, that makes sense to us intuitively, regardless of its intellectual pedigree and independently of its specific applications (2022: 207; see also Doria 2016).

One is not, it must be said at once, looking for some kind of 'basic principle' of success for maxims in the present or late common law. Moreover, one is certainly not going to claim that the *regulae juris* are the *principia* that endow law with a scientific status. But do they still have relevance for legal education? The late Peter Birks (1941–2004) thought that all they did was provide a child's eye view of law; they were simplistic statements torn from their context (2014: 258) – or as an Italian jurist has put it, *la banalizzazione estrema del fenomeno giuridico* (Doria 2016: 1). It is difficult to deny that he has a point. Moreover, most have also been torn from their historical and cultural context as well, with the result that what they mean today can be very different from what they meant to those who formulated them. Yet such a child's eye view of the law – if that is what the *regulae iuris* represent – has a more powerful legacy than one might think. The European codes, or most of them, can be seen as nothing more than a systematised set of *principia* or *regulae* – introductory 'nutshells' as Alan Watson once described them (Watson 1994) – and these codes can hardly be written off as meaningless. Indeed, Birks himself thought that the Roman introductory textbooks (*Institutes*) were maps of the law that were as relevant for the common law as for the civilian systems (Birks 1997). And these *Institutes* consisted largely of general *regulae iuris*. Presenting the maxims within the structured system of the *Institutes* (see maxim 41) might, then, raise the *regulae iuris* from a child's eye view to a bird's eye one that could provide a valuable introduction to law.

The introduction could be valuable for several reasons. First, because these maxims or *regulae* have a transnational flavour in that many (if not all) are relevant for all the Western traditions of law. They might not have exactly the same meaning in each individual legal tradition, but they are as likely to be cited on the continent as in the United Kingdom and North America. In saying this, it is not implied that these maxims represent some kind of transnational law. They do not. At best, what they represent are shared legal ideas and values expressed in succinct forms of words, for the most part in Latin. Each legal culture will interpret these words in terms of its own cultural mentality. Yet, while there is not a system of transnational law, there is, arguably, a Western legal tradition with a shared historical vision, and that this vision is partly captured by the *regulae iuris* and the structural categories in which they can be arranged, many of which have come from Roman sources.

This suggests a second reason why maxims might form a valuable introduction to law. They have a certain comparative dimension which permits those coming to law to appreciate differences, especially between the civil and the common law traditions. One is not talking here of a sophisticated comparative exercise designed to elicit new knowledge; the comparison is more of a 'chiaroscuro' effect – that is to say, the use of contrast to emphasise an object through, in art for example, light and dark (used to great effect by the artist Caravaggio and the Hollywood film director Robert Siodmak). One can, arguably, learn more about, say, English contract law by emphasising the important differences (rather than similarities) between 'contract' and *'contrat'* (see e.g., Legrand 2022: 257–258 fn 99). These differences, it must be admitted, will not be central to this introductory work, but they will on occasions be important. Moreover, studying English law in isolation from other legal traditions is, arguably, a barren exercise intellectually. One might add that approaching the common law from a top-down perspective, although not the common law way (see maxim 122), is valuable for civil law students coming to Anglo-American law for the first time.

The comparative element takes one on to a third reason why maxims can be valuable. They emerge out of history and thus emphasise the deep historical roots of law. One of the side effects that comes from treating law as some kind of science is that the discipline, as a body of knowledge, is able to transcend its history and present itself as a timeless corpus of textbook knowledge. Accordingly, just as one can be an expert in chemistry or mathematics without a knowledge of the history of chemistry or mathematics, one can be a competent lawyer without ever having studied legal history or Roman law. Yet surely this is to be regretted. Those jurists who do have a profound knowledge of the writings of jurists from Roman to modern times can reflect on the number of so-called original ideas to be found in the modern academic law journals that are not so original. Much of what is said today has been said before. Of course, it is difficult to read Bartolus, Baldus, and some of the canonists without a profound knowledge not just of Latin but of the abstruse abbreviations to be found in medieval manuscripts. And so one is rightly hesitant to assert that these jurists need to be read, at least not without some massive investment in translations, which is unlikely to happen soon. What can be studied is the *regulae iuris* which, if properly sourced (not always easy or possible), can give a sense that contemporary legal thought is constructed upon a two millennia (or more) tradition. This is not serious legal history. But it at least opens a window (if not a door) to the past.

The plan of this book is itself based upon a maxim concerning the structure or taxonomical plan of Roman law (maxim 41). The plan is from an obscure, but talented, jurist who went by the name of Gaius and who wrote a textbook for students commonly called the *Institutes* of Gaius (probably published in the middle of the second century AD). The textbook, clearly written and structured, was so successful that it remained in use up until Justinian ordered a second edition, which was officially published in 534 AD (*Institutes* of Justinian). An original edition of Gaius, which was known to exist because of extracts in Justinian's *Digest*, was discovered only in 1816. However, Justinian continued to use the plan in his edition of the *Institutes* and it is also set out in the *Digest* of Justinian (D.1.5.1). In using the Gaius plan, it is not being implied that English law conforms to its structure; it does so in part, but equally, there are parts that cannot be made to conform. Nevertheless, the plan is convenient, especially for law students from the continent and from some South American countries who are interested in learning about the common law.

1. Law as a discipline

What is it to study law? What is it to have legal knowledge? What is law? These are the questions that will be investigated – if only in outline – in this opening chapter. Just how much insight the existing principles and maxims actually provide is an interesting question in itself, and one reason for this difficulty is that even within the Western tradition of law there exists more than one legal tradition with different legal mentalities and cultures. Latin maxims have, nevertheless, tended to dominate partly because of the influence of the Latin Church, and while there has long been a strict separation between law and religion at one level, there is, at another level (historical and philosophical), a close interrelationship.

1. IUS EST ARS BONI ET AEQUI

Law is the art of goodness and fairness.

(Ulpian D.1.1.1pr)

This definition, if it can be called that, is, in one sense, not much more than a piece of rhetoric deriving, as the jurist Ulpian (AD 170-223/8) tells us, from an earlier jurist, Celsus (circa AD 67–130). That said, Ulpian also makes the point that the actual word *ius* (law) is derived from *justitia* (justice), and this is interesting in that it illustrates a direct linguistic relationship between law and justice that does not exist in many contemporary languages. It needs hardly to be said, however, that a close association between law and justice remains for many a fundamental feature of contemporary law. What, then, is meant by justice? This is a question that takes one well beyond the discipline of law, even if the Roman jurists provided their own definition of justice (maxim 8).

Yet Ulpian's comment does, of itself, raise some fundamental issues. What if a law is one that is unfair and not good? One can think of the Nazi laws permitting the most awful and murderous discrimination against Jewish people. Are such laws not law? As will be seen, Ulpian makes a distinction between 'civil law' (*ius civile*) and 'natural law' (*ius naturale*) and this could be regarded – and has been regarded – as implying that any civil law that contravenes natural law is not law (see maxim 44). This, of course, assumes that natural law is one based on moral as well as legal foundations, which certainly became the case once the Church adopted Roman law (see maxim 51). One problem with this law-as-morality view is that it simply does not accord with empirical reality: there exist laws, even in the Western tradition itself, which for many are regarded as neither good nor fair, and yet they are seen, certainly by the authorities and many lawyers, as valid law. In addition, there is the problem of actually defining 'good' and 'fair'; laws that are unfair for some might be regarded as fair for others. Perhaps the only thing that can be said at this stage is that the law and morality issue is one that has generated much jurisprudential literature and is a topic normally studied in courses on jurisprudence (legal philosophy and legal theory).

Another issue raised by Ulpian's statement is the meaning of the word *ars*. A dictionary might simply translate it as 'art' but this just begs a question about what Ulpian and other jurists of the time might have had in mind when employing this word. What is meant by the 'art' of law? As will be seen, *ars* can be contrasted with *scientia* – the expression *scientia iuris* being found in the Roman sources – and when 'science' began to assume its modern meaning, the civil law tradition developed the idea of legal science. In the Roman sources, *scientia* meant knowledge, and so *scientia iuris* in Roman law just meant knowledge of law; but after the Renaissance, it began to acquire a meaning closer to that of the natural sciences. Law is a science to be ranked alongside mathematics, zoology, and chemistry (see further Samuel 2022: 121–127). Yet whatever the situation, *ars* suggests that a definition of law as a body of knowledge includes a skill that has to be learned. As to the nature of this skill, Ulpian says that it is the ability to distinguish between what is fair and iniquitous (*aequum ab iniquo separantes*) and what is licit and illicit (*licitum ab illicito discernentes*). It is, he concludes, a real philosophy (*veram philosophiam*) and not some pretended discourse (*simulatam affectantes*) (D.1.1.1.1). Again, it has to be said that this is little more than lightweight rhetoric, although this does not mean that there are not important skills that a lawyer needs to acquire in order to be competent.

2.　　QUI VULT SCIRE REI, DEBET SCIRE PRINCIPIA REI

> *He who wishes to know about something must first know its principles.*

> (Baldus, Comment on D.1.1.1)

In noting that law was founded upon principles, the medieval jurist Baldus de Ulbaldis (1327–1400) was not furnishing a definition of law as such, but he was providing insight into what he (and others) thought was the knowledge foundation of law. Law as a 'thing' (*res*) was a matter of *principia*. One development that had given rise to this late medieval view was the circulation in Europe of the works of Aristotle after they had been translated into Latin; there was now a new logic (*logica nova*) through which law could be known and applied. This logic was the syllogism (Errera 2006: 31ff). This method consisted of two propositions, the major and the minor premise, from which it was possible to infer a third proposition, the conclusion. 'All men are mortal' (major premise), 'Socrates is a man' (minor premise), therefore 'Socrates is mortal' (conclusion). The importance of this logic was that it permitted the medieval Italian Roman lawyers to extend the law as found in the Roman texts (*Corpus Iuris Civilis*) to factual situations – new cases if you will – not themselves contemplated in the Roman *Corpus*, for medieval society was not the same as that of Ancient Rome. What the jurist needed to do was to induce out of the Roman law texts a *principium* and then use this principle as a major premise in a legal syllogism to be applied to a factual situation that was similar or analogous to the ones in the *Corpus* from which the principle had been induced. The idea that law is a matter of searching for principles remains a fundamental characteristic of contemporary legal thought (see e.g., Goff 1999 reprint); and a good example of this form of reasoning in the modern common law can be found in a judgment of Lord Simon (see Maxim 125). One might note that the existence or not of principles would also determine if a discipline such as law or theology was an 'art' (*ars*) or a 'science' (*scientia*): *Si in theologia non essent principia, non esset ars vel scientia* (if there are no principles in theology it is neither an art nor a science), wrote a 13th century theologian (quoted in Errera 2006: 83).

3. OMNIA IN CORPORE IURIS INVENIUNTUR

Everything [that you need to know about law] is in the corpus of [Roman] law.

(Accursius Gloss on D.1.1.10)

The assertion that everything that the law student needs to know is to be found in the Roman law texts might seem a most odd maxim for the debuting student of English law. However, the assertion is more important than it might seem. If one goes back to Ulpian's view on law, he says of the art (*ars*) of law that jurists can justly call themselves 'priests' (*sacerdotes*) (D.1.1.1.1). Later, he adds that to have knowledge of law (*iuris prudentia*) is to have knowledge of things divine and human (*divinarum atque humanarum rerum*) (D.1.1.10.2). This begged a question for the early interpreters of the rediscovered Roman law, who themselves were clerics: must knowledge of law include a knowledge of theology? Accursius replied *non, iam, omnia in corpore iuris inveniuntur.*

As an Italian legal historian has noted, this phrase "not only expresses the idea that the civil law must be separate from theology, from morality, and from what was by that time considered extraneous to the *scientia iuris* but also expresses faith in the idea that a discipline for human actions is always and in every instance found in positive norms, taken as a whole, and in the idea of positive law as a *systema legum* (system of laws)" (Bellomo 1995: 180). Such a closed system view is not, of course, confined to medieval Roman lawyers; it is a widespread 'paradigm' to be found in contemporary Western legal systems, including the common law. It is one of the foundations of what is called a 'positivistic' or doctrinal view of law. Another jurist from this same medieval period criticised a student for citing a non-legal work: *non licit allegare nisi Iustiniani leges* (it is not permitted to cite anything other than what is in Justinian's laws). Law, in short, was seen as a self-enclosed body of material, and this remains a powerful view amongst today's lawyers.

4.   LE JUGE TRANCHE LE LITIGE CONFORMÉMENT AUX RÈGLES DE DROIT QUI LUI SONT APPLICABLES

> *The judge decides the litigation in conformity with the rules of law that are applicable to it.*

> (French *Code de procédure civile*, article 12)

The idea that this body of material consists of rules is very clearly stated in this French code provision. Law is an abstract (although usually expressed in texts) set of rules to be applied by a judge to any factual situation that comes before him or her, and this implies in turn that legal knowledge itself consists of knowing rules. Such an epistemological (knowledge) thesis finds solid support in the work of some legal theorists. The late Herbert Hart (1907–1992) thought that law was to "be characterized by a union of primary rules of obligation with … secondary rules," these latter being concerned with "the ways in which the primary rules may be conclusively ascertained, introduced, eliminated, varied, and the fact of their violation conclusively determined" (Hart 1994: 94). Jurists and others convinced that law will one day be dispensed by AI machines equally tend to think that legal knowledge is a matter of rules. As one specialist once put it: "*rules* do and should play a central role in legal science, legal knowledge representation, and in legal reasoning." And "authority for this proposition can be found in legal theory, and even a philosopher such as Dworkin, who has questioned the sufficiency of rules for legal decision-making, does nevertheless himself seem to presuppose a predominant place for them, as MacCormick has shown" (Susskind 1987: 78–79). Others are not so convinced by this rule-model view (see maxim 10).

5. IUS AUTEM CIVILE EST, QUOD EX LEGIBUS, PLEBIS SCITIS, SENATUS CONSULTIS, DECRETIS PRINCIPUM, AUCTORITATE PRUDENTIUM VENIT

> *Civil law arises from legislation, plebiscites, enactments of the Senate, decrees of the emperor and the authority of learned jurists.*

(Papinianus, D.1.1.7pr)

However, assuming (at least for the moment) that the rule-model is the dominant one, the next question is this: how are legal, as opposed to non-legal, rules to be identified and distinguished? As the statement from the Roman jurist Papian (142–212 AD) indicates, it is a matter of various official sources. One of the direct sources of law that remains valid today – indeed it is the principal source of law in continental systems – is legislation. In the United Kingdom, this is written law (statutes) enacted by Parliament. The opinions of jurists are regarded as an important indirect source of law, at least in continental law, while the decisions of the courts are, in theory at least, again only an indirect source in continental law. However, in the common law tradition, the decisions of the courts are a direct source of law, cases being regarded as precedents.

Custom is often seen as a source of law as well, but, despite a considerable amount of writing on the topic (for a summary see Jolowicz 1963: 195–218), it is probably, for those involved with legal education and legal practice, of little relevance today as a direct formal source of law in the United Kingdom. Indeed, much of it has been absorbed by case law (*ibid*: 207). This said, there is one topic where custom in the guise of cultural norms existing as a sub-system within a national legal system is impacting upon the way Western jurists think about law. This is the theory of legal pluralism. How is a national legal system to cope with cultural norms or practices of a sub-group living within the national system, especially if these cultural norms or practices conflict with the positive national law? With difficulty, it would seem (see further Provost 2017).

6. CONSUETUDINEM AUT RERUM PERPETUO SIMILITER IUDICATARUM AUCTORITATEM VIM LEGIS OPTINERE DEBERE

Custom or the authority of a line of similar legal decisions ought to be given the force of legislation.

(Callistratus D.1.3.38)

Precedent, as well as custom, seemed to have been a source of law in Roman times, according to this statement from the Roman jurist Callistratus (late second and early third century AD). However, this is not actually to suggest that Roman law recognised a doctrine of precedent – that is to say, a doctrine asserting that previous decisions are binding. At best, it probably gives expression to the idea that similar cases should be decided alike on an analogy that such a line of decisions is equivalent to a custom. In fact, precedent as a *formal* source of law is not generally a feature of the civil law, and it is actually prohibited for judges in France to give general rulings (*réglements*) which could be regarded as legal rules (CC art. 5). This said, it would be wrong to think that in France, decisions of the courts are not of importance; they act as arguments of authority and are now considered, at the very least, to be indirect sources of law (Rouvière 2023: 56–59).

In England, the formal position is different. Precedent is a direct source of law in the United Kingdom, and thus previous decisions act as the basis of the law to be applied in situations not regulated by statute. This doctrine of precedent can be summarised as follows: "In the hierarchical system of courts which exists in this country, it is necessary for each lower tier, including the Court of Appeal, to accept loyally [as binding] the decisions of the higher tiers" (Lord Hailsham LC in *Broome v Cassell & Co Ltd* [1972] AC 1027, 1054). The necessity for precedent is in turn rooted in the need for certainty (see e.g., Practice Direction [1966] 1 WLR 1234).

The impression is often given that the doctrine of precedent is something as old as the common law itself. Yet this cannot be the case. Before the 16th century, there was little substantive law because the whole trial process was centred on the jury verdict; the judge was little more than a referee, and questions of pure law rarely surfaced (see maxim 15). And even up to the 19th century, there was no proper hierarchical system of courts; decisions of fact (in common law courts) were still decided by a jury who never gave reasons for their verdicts, and there were few reliable law reports. It is really only during the 19th century, especially with the establishment of official law reports in 1866 and the reorganisation of the courts into a proper hierarchy in 1875, that one sees a formalised theory of precedent establishing itself (Jolowicz 1963: 230).

And this theory only lasted just over a century before it began to break down, or at least to retreat back into the older idea of a search for principle (Practice Direction [2001] 1 WLR 194). Thus, some common law judges, in the last few years, have indicated their reservations about precedent even if they refuse to go as far as saying that it is now extinct and should be avoided.

The first major step in this retreat from strict precedent was the Practice Direction ([1966] 1 WLR 1234) issued by the House of Lords indicating that a "too rigid adherence to precedent may lead to injustice in a particular case and also unduly restrict the proper development of the law"; the Law Lords proposed therefore "to depart from a previous decision when it appears right to do so". A second step was Lord Goff's 1983 lecture where he said the "answer must lie both in not adopting too strict a view of the doctrine of precedent, and yet according sufficient respect to it to enable it to perform its task of ensuring not merely stability in law, but consistency in its administration". He went on to note that in the past "there appeared to exist some judges who saw the law almost as a deductive science, a matter of finding the relevant authorities and applying them to the facts of the particular case". This, he said, is no longer the case; judges cannot disregard or ignore precedents, but they see themselves at liberty to adapt or qualify them to ensure a legally just result on the facts before them (Goff 1999). Perhaps, then, "the enduring strength of the common law is that it has been developed on a case-by-case basis by judges for whom the attainment of practical justice was a major objective of their work" (Lord Steyn in *Att-Gen v Blake* [2001] 1 AC 268, 292).

As for the actual operation of precedent, it is not cases that bind but "their rationes decidendi do" (*R (Kadhim) v Brent Housing Board* [2001] QB 955, para 16). Yet discovering the ratio, as Lord Denning MR once pointed out, can be a difficult task, especially as the *ratio* has to be distinguished from any *obita dicta* (things said by the way) which are not binding (*The Hannah Blumenthal* [1983] 1 AC 854, 873–875). As Leggatt LJ has put it:

> The doctrine of precedent, which is a structuring principle of the common law, presupposes that what a court decides extends beyond the particular dispute before it and that, from analysis of a past case, a general proposition can be derived which has the force of law in later cases. Such a proposition is known as the *ratio decidendi* (or *ratio*) of the case. Statements made by judges in the course of giving reasons for their decisions which do not form part of the *ratio*, known as *obiter dicta*, may be strongly persuasive – particularly when they are the carefully considered observations of eminent judges. But it is generally accepted that the *ratio decidendi* is alone binding as a precedent: see e.g., 11 *Halsbury's Laws* (5th edn) (2015) para 25. Hence the ability to identify the *ratio* of a case and to distinguish it from *obiter dicta* is an indispensable skill for any common lawyer (*R v Parole Board* [2019] 3 All ER 954, para 40; and see further paras 42–59).

What, then, is meant by the expression in terms of method? The most important point to stress is that the *ratio decidendi* of a case is not an abstract rule or principle to be induced out of a case subsequently to be applied in a deductive fashion as if the rule were a code provision. This is not to say that induction, deduction and the syllogism have no formal (or ideological) role (see maxim 125). But the *ratio* "is almost always to be ascertained by an analysis of the material facts of the case" (*Lupton v FA & AB Ltd* [1972] AC 634, 658 per Lord Simon). It is this notion of the 'material facts' of a case that holds the key to the application of a precedent in that a comparison must always be made between the facts of the case in hand and the facts of any precedent (see Lloyd LJ in *Frozen Value Ltd v Heron Foods Ltd* [2012] 3 All ER 1328, paras 117–120). As to the actual reasoning associated with precedent, this is as much part of legal knowledge as is precedent itself, for how a precedent is to be found, interpreted and applied is by no means straightforward (see e.g., maxims 122, 126).

7. LEX EST COMMUNE PRAECEPTUM, VIRORUM PRUDENTIUM CONSULTUM, DELICTORUM QUAE SPONTE VEL IGNORANTIA CONTRAHUNTUR COERCITIO, COMMUNIS REI PUBLICAE SPONSIO

A statute is a universal command, a decree of learned men in response to wrongs committed either voluntarily or in ignorance of a communal covenant of the state.

(Papinianus, D.1.3.1)

7A. LEGIS VIRTUS HAEC EST IMPERARE VETARE PERMITTERE PUNIRE

The characteristic of a statute is this: to command, to prohibit, to permit, to punish.

(Modestinus, D.1.3.7)

Nevertheless, the importance of precedent as a fundamental characteristic of the common law tradition should be treated with caution. Whatever may have been the position in the past, the primary source of law today in the UK is legislation, and this reflects itself in the case law in that nine out of ten cases heard by the English appeal courts involve the interpretation of a statutory text. (In addition to interpreting these public law texts, the courts often have to decide upon the meaning of words or phrases in private texts such as contracts, leases and wills.) Traditionally, this interpretative function of the courts in common law jurisdictions has given rise to its own set of methods, rules, presumptions and principles (see maxims 127–130).

In the civil law world, legislation is in theory the only formal source of law, and its traditional textual form is the code (private law) and the constitution (public law). All case law (*jurisprudence*) is, then, a matter of statutory interpretation. However, codes are very abstract in their language, which in turn means that judges have considerable interpretative liberty. In the English common law, in contrast, there is not just something of an anti-codification spirit but also a traditional lack of partnership between the judiciary and the legislator. This latter tendency may well belong more to the past than the present, but it has resulted in a particularly opaque legislative style that remains a characteristic of UK legislation. Some statutory provisions are so opaque that even the judges despair (see e.g., Animals Act 1971 s 2(2); *Mirvahedy v Henley* [2003] 2 AC 491). (See further maxim 127)

8. IUSTITIA EST CONSTANS ET PERPETUA VOLUNTAS IUS SUUM CUIQUE TRIBUENDI

Justice is the constant and perpetual wish to give each his legal entitlement.

(Ulpian, D.1.1.10pr)

Is law, then, just a matter of rules emanating from particular formal sources? Certainly, this seems the dominant model (see e.g., Lord Hope in *Sanatan Dharma Maha Sabha of Trinidad and Tobago Inc v Att-Gen of Trinidad and Tobago* [2009] UKPC 17, para 38). Yet there remain some further fundamental questions. What is the relationship, identified by Ulpian, between law (*ius*) and justice (*justitia*) (D.1.1.1pr)? This of course begs the question of what is meant by justice. Ulpian's definition of giving each his legal entitlement might seem just another piece of general rhetoric, but the French legal historian and philosopher Michel Villey (1914–1988) argued that it was narrow in its scope and simply described the *métier* of the judge when faced with a dispute about property, money, tutorship of a child, the legal status of someone, or some other litigation issue. The judge must attribute to each person what is legally due to them (Villey 1986: 62–63). There may well be something in this view since Ulpian later says: *Totum autem ius constitit aut in adquirendo aut in conservando aut in minuendo: aut enim hoc agitur, quemadmodum quid cuiusque fiat, aut quemadmodum quis rem vel ius suum conservet, aut quomodo alienet aut admittat* (And so all law is about acquiring or conserving or diminishing: indeed it is about how something becomes someone's, or how some thing or right is conserved or how he can transfer it or lose it) (D.1.3.41).

Justice, then, was, for the Romans (the cynic might say), just about keeping what you have and getting (legally) your hands on another's property.

This said, when Roman law, Christian thinking and the works of Aristotle came together in the late medieval period, the notion of justice started to receive serious consideration at a more abstract level by jurists and canonists. Of particular importance was the Aristotelian distinction, brought into the medieval world in particular by Saint Thomas Aquinas (1225–1274), between distributive and commutative justice. Distributive justice consists of rules by which society distributes rewards and punishments and imposes obligations on its members; commutative justice is made up of the rules which govern the relations between individuals, comprising, for example, the rule not to injure or cause loss to another as reflected in debt or compensation claims by one person against another (Porter 2007: 742). This distinction might be old, but it still has modern relevance as a senior common law judge indicated:

> My Lords, to explain decisions denying a remedy for the cost of bringing up an unwanted child by saying that there is no loss, no foreseeable loss, no causative link or no ground for reasonable restitution is to resort to unrealistic and formalistic propositions which mask the real reasons for the decisions. And judges ought to strive to give the real reasons for their decision. It is my firm conviction that where courts of law have denied a remedy for the cost of bringing up an unwanted child the real reasons have been grounds of distributive justice. That is, of course, a moral theory. It may be objected that the House must act like a court of law and not like a court of morals. That would only be partly right. The court must apply positive law. But judges' sense of the moral answer to a question, or the justice of the case, has been one of the great shaping forces of the common law. What may count in a situation of difficulty and uncertainty is not the subjective view of the judge but what he reasonably believes that the ordinary citizen would regard as right (Lord Steyn in *McFarlane v Tayside Health Board* [2000] 2 AC 59, 82).

At a philosophical level, the notion of justice is the subject of a vast literature. With the coming of the modern age, the whole topic became more complex as new disciplines emerged under the general heading of social sciences. Accordingly, there is now not just literature on the abstract notion of justice but much scholarship on political justice, economic justice, and social justice. When one talks, then, of justice and law, what kind of justice is one talking about? Is it to be determined by some abstract conceptual model or by utilitarian considerations? In terms of the law itself, the different kinds of justice can reflect themselves from time to time in the comments of judges. And often, justice becomes intermingled with other notions such as the public interest and policy, as the following extract illustrates:

> That public interest can therefore be seen as reflecting choices of social and economic policy and of social justice in Wales which may be different to the views of

social and economic policy and social justice reasonably held in other parts of the United Kingdom or by other people. As these choices are being exercised in matters within the primary legislative competence of the democratically elected Welsh Assembly, the Welsh Assembly is, in my view, reasonably entitled to adopt such choices and views for Wales (*Recovery of Medical Costs for Asbestos Diseases (Wales) Bill: Reference by the Council General for Wales* [2015] 2 All ER 899, 934).

In the end, Ronald Dworkin (1931–2013) was probably right in observing that "it is difficult to find a statement of the concept [of justice] at once sufficiently abstract to be uncontroversial amongst us and sufficiently concrete to be useful" (Dworkin 1986: 74). For the aspiring doctrinal lawyer, then, it is probably better to stay with Villey's view of the Roman expression *suum cuique tribuere.*

9.   UBI SOCIETAS IBI IUS

> *Where there is society there is law.*
>
> (Henri de Cocceji, Commentary on Hugo Grotius'
> *De jure belli et pacis*, 1744, attached to the
> *Prolegomena* § VIII)

One dominant idea about the source and nature of law is – or was – the thesis that law and society were intimately intertwined. Where there is society, there is necessarily law and vice versa. Or, put another way, society is a real 'thing' (*res*) which is bound together by law; if there was no law, there would be no society. Some have thought that the maxim *ubi societas* is Roman – it has even been attributed to Ulpian – and one reason for this is that it seems to have been the Roman attitude (see e.g., D.1.1.9). In fact, the expression is not Roman at all and neither is it medieval; it seems to have appeared only in the 18th century, although there are some similar references a century earlier. What was important about the maxim was that it provided an axiom upon which the existence and justification of law could be founded, in turn furnishing a theory as to why people were under an obligation to obey the law. If law was part and parcel of society itself as an empirical fact, then, being a member of society, one could not escape being under an obligation to obey. It was, however, a holistic view of humanity – that is to say that, as mentioned, society was a thing that existed as an empirical reality.

In the late medieval era, this thesis was undermined by what is sometimes called the nominalist revolution. This change in ontological (what exists) outlook, associated in particular with the philosopher William of Ockham (1285–1347), seriously challenged the view that collectivities (*universalia*) such as forests and society existed as realities; they were simply names (*nomina*) and as such nothing but metaphysical entities (see Lesaffer 2009: 248). What existed were just trees and individual humans. This nominalist revolution had a profound effect on legal thinking since it destroyed the existing philosophical theory as to why individuals should obey the law or the ruler. The response to this philosophical crisis was to replace the *ubi societas* vision with social contract theory. This thesis was based on the idea – seemingly given support by a text in Roman law (D.1.4.1) – that the *populus* had by contract transferred all their inherent power and sovereignty to the ruler who in turn would guarantee their security (Jones 1940: 109–110). One had started to move into the age of individualism, which in recent times was given its full expression by the UK prime minister Margaret Thatcher (1925–2013) who declared that 'there is no such thing as society' (Thatcher 1987). As for social contract theory, it did not survive – or fully survive – the rise of the social sciences in the 19th century. Where was the sociological evidence for such a contract? The only response was a return to more modernised forms of metaphysical thinking, much of which was (is) the kind of dogma that the critic Ivor Richards thought was either obsolete or nonsense (Eagleton 2022: 90). He might have been wrong in his view, but maybe not that wrong.

10.   REGULA EST, QUAE REM QUAE EST BREVITER
      ENARRAT. NON EX REGULA IUS SUMATUR,
      SED EX IURE QUOD EST REGULA FIAT. PER
      REGULAM IGITUR BREVIS RERUM NARRATIO
      TRADITUR, ET, UT AIT SABINUS, QUASI CAUSAE
      CONIECTIO EST, QUAE SIMUL CUM IN ALIQUO
      VITIATA EST, PERDIT OFFICIUM SUUM

> *A rule is a brief description of what something is. The law does not arise out of a rule, but is made by the law. By a rule, then, a brief description of things is transmitted and, as Sabinus put it, it is as if it is a succinct explanation of the cause which when it is shown to be faulty loses its function.*

> (Paulus, D.50.17.1)

What, then, of the status of the maxims (*regulae iuris*)? If one returns to the thesis that knowledge of law is knowledge of rules, it would appear from the opinion of the Roman jurist Paul that such a thesis should be treated with care. Paul's statement in itself is easy enough to comprehend: the source of law is not to be found in rules (*regulae*). Yet his view is not as straightforward as it might seem. First, because the notion of a rule (*regula*) was certainly important enough for it to have quite a central place in the writings of the

Roman jurists: the expression 'the rule is...' (*regula est*) is not rare (see e.g., D.22.6.9pr, D.28.2.13.1, D.30.12.2) and, indeed, some jurists wrote books entitled *regulae* (see generally Stein 1966). Secondly, it is quite possible that not all of the jurists shared Paul's view. Thirdly, the increasing use of legislation from the end of the third century onwards – the post-classical period of Roman law – would have involved an epistemological shift from the opinions of the jurists (the *ius honorarium*), which focused for the most part on factual situations and their variation (see maxim 122), to the abstract idea of a written command (*lex*) (see maxim 7), that is to say a *regula legis*. In fact, even in the classical period one can see this association: *In his, quae contra rationem iuris constituta sunt, non possumus sequi regulam iuris* (where something has been established that is contrary to legal rationality, it cannot be followed as a legal rule) (Julianus D.1.3.15). So how is Paul's statement to be understood? Peter Stein (1926–2016), in his examination of the *regulae iuris*, concluded that the Roman jurists "recognised that their decisions should harmonise with each other, but did not conceive of the legal system as founded on a comprehensive framework of broad general principles." But "this does not... mean that they had no rules, or that they failed to abstract the effect of their decisions" (Stein 1966: 102).

Does all of this have any relevance for the English law student? Stein thought so. He thought that an uncodified system like the common law displays many similarities to the Roman attitude regarding a *regula* and he used as an example the notion of the *ratio decidendi*. As we have noted (above maxim 6), the *ratio* is not to be seen as an abstract rule divorced from the facts of the relevant precedent; it has to be understood in the context of the material facts of the precedent. This would suggest that describing the *ratio* of a case as a strict rule not that different from a statutory one would be very misleading. "In some branches of the law," wrote Stein, "a certain formulation may be adopted which provisionally sums up the effect of certain decisions, acts as a useful guide in the decision of similar cases, and is then discarded in favour of another formulation" (1966: 104). The position is different in the civil law where the *regulae iuris* became *principia* (see maxim 2) which in turn became *axiomata* on an analogy with mathematics. In other words, the *regulae iuris* were to achieve an epistemological function that was different from that of the common law (see maxim 124). They were, in the form of codification, to become, in theory, the unique source of law.

11.   OMNIS DEFINITIO IN IURE CIVILI PERICULOSA EST: PARUM EST ENIM, UT NON SUBVERTI POSSET

Any definition in civil law is dangerous: for there are few occasions when it cannot be overturned.

(Javolenus D.50.17.202)

Another *regula iuris* from Roman law is one often associated with Paul's description of a rule as simply a brief summary (maxim 10). This is Javolenus' assertion that definitions are dangerous. Many may find this observation nothing more than common sense, and there are plenty of situations where a definition is unable to account for all factual situations that arise in law. As Lord Wilberforce once said of possession:

> Viscount Jowitt has said of it "the English law has never worked out a completely logical and exhaustive definition of possession" (*United States of America v Dollfus Mieg et Compagnie SA* [1952] AC at p 605). In relation to it we find English law, as so often, working by description rather than by definition. Ideally, a possessor of a thing has complete physical control over it; he has knowledge of its existence, its situation and its qualities; he has received it from a person who intends to confer possession of it and he has himself the intention to possess it exclusively of others. But these elements are seldom all present in situations with which the courts have to deal, and where one or more of them is lacking, or incompletely present, it has to be decided whether the given approximation is such that possession may be held sufficiently established to satisfy the relevant rule of law. As it is put by Pollock and Wright, possession is defined by modes or events in which it commences or ceases, and by the legal incidents attached to it (*Warner v Metropolitan Police Commissioner* [1968] 2 All ER 356, 392).

Academic lawyers, or some of them at least, can be unhappy with such loose thinking. The American jurist Wesley Hohfeld (1879–1918), for example, was concerned that the word 'right' was used by judges in an indiscriminate manner, and he sought to construct a model of jural relations that would confer upon it a certainty of definition. He thought this could be achieved by contrasting the word 'right' with other terms such as 'liberty' and 'power' with the result that the term 'right' would be restricted only to situations where someone owed the potential right-holder a 'duty' (see Hohfeld 1919). There is no doubt that his model has been hugely influential, especially in relation to differentiating a 'right' from a 'liberty'. But the model is not without its problems since there are factual situations that cannot be made to conform to the structure. This does not by any means render it worthless, but the problems would probably not have surprised Javolenus.

CONCLUDING REMARKS

This chapter has attempted to present maxims and principles that show insight into what has been considered to be – and is still considered to be – legal knowledge. Perhaps the most important debate to emerge from these maxims is the one surrounding rules. Is knowledge of law just knowledge of legal rules, or is there more to it than that? The debate has become central today because of research into Artificial Intelligence (AI) and law (see e.g., Deakin & Markou 2020). To put it rather crudely, what needs to be fed into the machine in order that it can think and operate like, or as, a judge? The answer to this question – if there is any convincing answer – is of course highly relevant for law students. What needs to be 'fed' into them to become competent lawyers and, perhaps, jurists?

2. Historical considerations and the development of English law and its institutions

The AI question mentioned in the last chapter raises a further interesting issue regarding legal knowledge. Is such knowledge a-historical (synchronic)? That is to say, is it knowledge that exists as knowledge independent of the historical background that has led up to this modern-day knowledge? Or is such knowledge only to be understood through its historical (diachronic) development? There is no easy answer to this question. For example, one can be a top-class mathematician without knowing anything about the history of mathematics. It would seem, also, that one can be a top-class lawyer without ever having studied legal history (there are plenty of law graduates who have never studied the subject).

This chapter takes Gaius' view that an understanding of the history, if not in great depth, is more than helpful in comprehending why the system is the way it is today. Indeed, the history of Roman law in later Europe (from the 11th century onwards) is equally helpful in understanding contemporary legal knowledge. Accordingly, this chapter will examine, through a range of *regulae*, the historical development of English law.

12. SED QUOD IN OMNIBUS REBUS ANIMADVERTO ID PERFECTUM ESSE, QUOD EX OMNIBUS SUIS PARTIBUS CONSTARET: ET CERTE CUIUSQUE REI POTISSIMA PARS PRINCIPIUM EST

> *But I note that in all things perfection is when all the parts of a thing are set out: and surely the most important part of anything is its beginning.*

> (Gaius, D.1.2.1)

12A. NECESSARIUM ITAQUE NOBIS VIDETUR IPSIUS IURIS ORIGINEM ATQUE PROCESSUM DEMONSTRARE

> *And so it would seem most apposite for us to set out the origin and processes of law itself.*

> (Pomponius, D.1.2.2pr)

The rediscovery of Roman law in the 11th century gave rise to a body of academic doctors in Italy who devoted themselves to commenting upon the Roman texts. These academics, who earned their name Glossators by writing their commentaries as marginal notes ('glosses'), were to lay the foundation for what some have seen as a legal revolution in continental Europe (Berman 1983). The work on Roman law started by the Glossators was within a few centuries to dominate legal thinking on the continent. Yet while "the Glossators mainly busied themselves with the interpretation and systematic exposition of the Roman texts, they knew well enough that much of what they taught had no effective influence outside the doors of the lecture-room" (Jones 1940: 14). The reason for this is that the living law was the feudal and customary law.

In Britain, it was quite a different story in that feudalism provided the context for the development of a customary system that was to resist not just Roman law in substance but also the methodology and mindset that accompanied the historical process of codification. Unlike the civil law, the tradition of the common law is not associated with a book (the *Corpus Iuris Civilis*). It is, instead, associated with a number of institutions that developed out of the historical facts of their time and which did not necessarily conform to any rational 'plan'. The institutions were functional, and they have bequeathed a number of characteristics to modern common law that are not to be found in Roman thinking. Accordingly, in order to understand the common law, one must essentially understand the history of its institutions.

13.   FEUDUM CONSISTIT IN IMMOBILIBUS

A feudal relation concerns land.

(Ioaannis de Anania, *De Alienatione Feudi Disputatio*, Question 1, no 1.)

13A.   FEUDUM EST CONTRACTUS BENEFICIALIS IN QUE HINCINDE ORITUR OBLIGATIO

A feudal relation is a beneficial contract which gives rise to an obligation.

(Baldus, Comment on C.6.46.1 no 2)

The foundations of the common law undoubtedly reach back to before the Norman invasion of 1066. Nevertheless, this event is a good starting point for the history of English law because the Normans created the context in which the main institutions of the common law were to develop and to flourish. Certainly, the Normans retained not only the legal system that they found in their new country but also the existing administrative and feudal structure. Yet in extending feudalism to the whole of the country and in consolidating the means by which Royal power could be asserted, the Normans created the context for new developments.

The importance of the feudal structure was that it furnished a political and social context in which the legal concepts of the common law were to form. Indeed, it must always be remembered that Roman law was not just a body of rules and legal institutions; it was also an ideological vision of government and society, and thus one can talk of a Roman model (Ullmann 1975: 46–47). The feudal model of government and society was quite different. It did not have at its foundation the two great Roman concepts of *imperium* (state power) and *dominium* (private ownership) and thus did not really adhere to a basic separation between the public and the private (see maxim 40). Feudal power was based first on land and then on contract and thus intermixed the ideas of *imperium* and *dominium*. As Maitland (1850–1906) noted, "we may describe 'feudalism' as a state of society in which all or a great part of public rights and duties are inextricably interwoven with the tenure of land, in which the whole governmental system – financial, military, judicial – is part of the law of private property" (Maitland 1908: 23–24).

On conquering England, William I supposedly claimed the whole country as his and then set about granting large domains to his followers who would, in turn, bind themselves to him via the feudal contract. They were the tenants-in-chief. Certainly, from the 12th century onwards, nobody actually considered the king to be the owner of the country as a matter of social and economic reality; but equally, a feudal Lord was not an owner of his domain in the Roman sense (Baker 2019: 249). Each feudal lord would in turn grant parts of his domain to those who swore an oath of allegiance to him and thus governmental power could be said to be based on what was in reality a series of contracts (Ullmann 1975: 147). Even today, land has a special status in English law and so, for example, the word 'goods' does not include real property.

In this feudal model, the administration of justice was, then, associated with feudal lordship and the church. However, it has to be remembered that the king was also a feudal lord — he was indeed the Lord Tenant in Chief — and as such he was not just integrated directly into the justice system but also entitled to have his own court, which could be used to control inferior tribunals, to assure the King's Peace and to protect his own interests. In addition, the king could use his legislative power and his status as the fountain of justice to fashion new remedies, something that Henry II (1133–1189) did to great effect with respect to protecting real rights in land. As we have mentioned, these real rights were not really forms of ownership but "seisin", which was closer to a form of possession (see maxim 80). However, these remedies were to give the emerging common law a very powerful institutional base that would act as one obstacle to the importation of Roman law. The concepts associated with this land law are still at the basis of the modern English law of real property.

14.   REX EST LEGALIS ET POLITICUS

The king is both a legal and a political figure

(Lane's Reports, 27)

William I did not arrive just with his army; he also had his King's Household, consisting of his advisors and administrators, over which he was the head. Gradually, this household transformed itself into his Council or Court, which became known as the *Curia Regis* (in fact both a legal and political body) and in which various specialist bodies, in particular law and finance, developed. Members of this Council would go on circuit around the country, collecting taxes and judging crimes, and gradually these specialists became a body of royal judges.

One section, Exchequer (named after its room in which there was a table covered with a cloth resembling a chessboard pattern), dealt with finance and taxation and thus consisted of a body of accounting experts. However, they found themselves having to judge legal matters arising out of financial issues, and at the end of the 12th century, a tradition had developed that these experts – the Barons of the Exchequer – would have a lawyer at their head. By the 16th century, all the Barons had the status of judges. Yet even in the 12th century, Exchequer had a legal function, and two centuries later, this function had detached itself from the *Curia Regis*.

Another body of specialists was the advisors to the king. They were involved not just with administration and government but equally with petitions from subjects that affected the king's interests, and they would often decide these matters in sessions with the monarch seated on benches beside him. These became known as hearings in *Coram rege* – the king having a personal jurisdiction to decide cases – and over time the advisors distanced themselves more and more from the monarch, deciding cases in a court that became known as the Bench (*in banco residentes*). From as early as 1268, this court had its own Chief Justice, and during the 14th century, the Court of King's Bench became detached from the *Curia Regis*, holding sessions in which the king was no longer permitted to sit. Nevertheless, because of its closeness to the king and to the government, this court had jurisdiction over matters that were primarily 'public' in their orientation; that is to say administrative law (not that this term existed until relatively recently) and criminal jurisdiction. In fact, the boundary between civil and criminal law was not easily perceptible during the 13th and 14th centuries, and as a result, the judges were able to use the action of trespass – an action that in its origin was more criminal than civil – to extend their jurisdiction into private law. With respect to 'administrative' law, this was not a matter of rules as such; the jurisdiction was rooted in a number of 'prerogative' remedies that were used by King's Bench to control the decisions of inferior tribunals, local authorities, and even the other royal courts (see maxim 61).

During the reign of Henry II, it was normal for the judges to follow the king during his voyages to Bordeaux or to the royal forests. This situation evidently created much inconvenience for litigants, and in the early 13th century, the lords managed to impose on the then-reigning king a 'Great Charter' (*Magna Carter 1215*) in which it was declared that 'common pleas' would be heard by a permanent group of judges in London. At first, it was not possible to distinguish between the judges of King's Bench (*Coram rege*) and those hearing Common Pleas (*in banco*); but gradually, two separate groups did emerge out of the *Curia regis,* with the result that from the 13th century onwards, *Coram rege* became the Court of King's Bench while the judges *in banco* became a third court of common law, the Court of Common Pleas. Until the 16th century, Common Pleas was the most important of the common law courts because, as its name suggests, it was dealing with the common litigation between subjects; it became, in other words, the court specialising in 'private' law matters, and it increased its jurisdiction by taking cases away from the local courts. However,

Common Pleas in turn saw its own jurisdiction reduced by King's Bench and Exchequer, which used legal fictions increasingly to draw ordinary litigation between subjects away from the other court.

Consequently, up to the 17th century, common law was a matter of three royal courts competing for litigation. However, during this century, the competition between the judges disappeared, leaving three royal courts with more or less equivalent jurisdiction, although King's Bench retained its supervisory role while Exchequer continued to specialise in financial matters (Sutton 1929: 36). These three royal courts lasted until 1875, and the case law that issued from them over the centuries became the 'common law'.

15.   AD QUÆSTIONEM FACTI NON RESPONDENT JUDICIES; AD QUÆSTIONEM JURIS NON RESPONDENT JURATORES

Judges do not decide questions of fact; juries do not decide questions of law.

(Coke on Littleton, 295b)

While it is perfectly reasonable to refer to these three institutions as courts of justice, they had, in comparison to courts within the civilian (continental) tradition, a number of special procedural characteristics of which two need to be mentioned in detail. The first was the jury, which consisted of a group of ordinary subjects drawn from the local community whose role at first was to familiarise the judge on circuit from London with the facts of a crime. They were, in effect, a group of witnesses in a criminal law trial (see Baker 2019: 79–83). Gradually, however, not only did their role change, but the distinction between criminal and civil law became more marked, and when there was a separation between the two types of trials, the same procedure was transferred from criminal to civil procedure. Thus, the jury became an institutional element in all common law cases. As for their role, the jury gradually evolved from being a group of witnesses to being a central part of the trial process itself. They became the judges of fact while the judge would (later) decide questions of law. This duality was to remain a central characteristic of the common law trial process until the end of the 19th century, and even today the jury has not completely disappeared. It continues to play a central role in serious criminal trials and some civil cases (mainly defamation).

The effects of these late medieval developments were considerable not only because the members of the jury were for the most part illiterate but also because they were ordinary people with their own livings to pursue. Accordingly, cases had to be presented to these non-professionals in a way that they could understand and in a manner that would take days rather than months. Thus, the common law 'trial' was oral and efficient time-wise, the idea of a case being based on a written set of documents (as in the civil law system: see maxim 27) being impossible. In addition, the lawyers had to reduce a case to a series of questions that could be decided by the jury, and there developed a set of rigid procedural rules to control this process. Indeed, Bracton (1210–1268), a famous 13th-century legal writer, observed that litigation was like a game of chess (Baker 2019: 84). The result of all this was that the common law largely consisted of knowledge of procedural formulae and so, in the 14th century, there was no body of 'English law' in the same way as there was a body of 'Roman law' (Milsom 1981: 83). What a lawyer of this period had to know were the appropriate procedures for presenting a case.

Up until the 16th century, then, the central institution was the jury. As for the judge, his role "could be characterized as having as much in common with that of sports referees as with the proactive role of the modern English judiciary" (Baker 2003: 49). In other words, before the beginning of the 16th century, no one looked to litigation as a means of refining the law; indeed, "reasoned final judgments were seldom called for" (Baker 2003: 50) and there was little separation, in terms of the verdict, between law and fact.

However, this situation was to change during the 16th century. There was growing pressure on the judges to decide points of law, but if this was to happen such decisions had to be removed from the realm of the jury. Such removal became possible thanks to a procedure known as *in banc*, whereby judges in London could, after a jury verdict had been given, consider the matter as a question of law before entering the final judgment in the case. At this secondary stage, a defendant could apply for a motion on arrest of judgment, and this would result in the judges considering the case as a question of law rather than fact, and final judgment might be refused on legal grounds. Equally, where there was a verdict for the defendant, judgment would be entered for him unless the plaintiff could show cause as to why such judgment should not be entered. Other motions, such as one for a new trial, subsequently developed with the result that a clear distinction emerged between the role of the jury, as arbiter only of fact, and the role of the judge or judges *in banc*, as arbiters (and declarers) of law. Accordingly, the motion for a new trial put the whole case before the court and resulted in the process whereby a final judicial decision became so important that a majority amongst the judges considering a verdict became the way of achieving it (Baker 2003: 51). Majority decisions are still the means by which cases are decided on appeal (Kirby 2007).

This procedure was still much in evidence in the 19th century. Take, for example, the famous contractual damages case of *Hadley v. Baxendale* ((1854) 156 ER 145). The plaintiff (claimant) was the owner of a broken mill shaft who arranged for it to be sent speedily to the manufacturers by a firm of transporters (Pickfords). Pickfords delayed the delivery in breach of contract, with the result that the mill had to shut down for lack of the shaft. The owners claimed not just ordinary damages (the value of the mill shaft) but compensation for the loss of their profits arising from the closure of the mill. At the trial, the jury awarded damages for the loss of profits, but the defendant transporters successfully applied to the Court of Exchequer for a motion for a new trial. The court held that the loss of profit was not recoverable because it was not in the contemplation of the defendant that the mill would have to close if the shaft was delayed. The judgment delivered by the court – and in this case, it was a single judgment of the court – remains an important declaration of the law concerning remoteness of damage in contract (see maxim 100).

16.   NON POTEST QUIS SINE BREVI AGERE

One cannot bring a legal action without a writ.

(Bracton, vol 4, p 286)

The second procedural characteristic was the system of writs. This was, in its origin, simply an administrative process through which a subject gained access to the royal courts and was necessary because these courts were at first exceptional jurisdictions, with the administration of justice being the primary concern of the local feudal courts. The *Curia Regis*, within which the common law courts formed, was concerned at first only with the protection of royal and governmental interests, but gradually their jurisdiction was extended as they proved more popular than local justice. Thus, the local courts found their jurisdiction being slowly removed in favour of the common law courts (Baker 2019: 25–27). Nevertheless, litigants never formally had the right to go to the royal courts: they needed a kind of 'ticket' to enter their case, and this ticket was the writ, which would be obtained from the Chancery section of the *Curia Regis,* headed by the Lord Chancellor (Baker 2019: 60–77).

The writs were a series of formulae that reflected the interests of the king or more generally the typical disputes of the time (the 'common pleas'). The writ of trespass, for example, was originally fashioned to deal with de-possession of land by force of arms (*vi et armis*) while the writ of debt was the means by which an unpaid supplier of goods or a service would obtain his money. Each writ, with its own formula, was based on a model factual situation and once defined became a sort of administrative and legal precedent (Baker 2019: 63). At the beginning of the 13th century these 'precedents' were to be found in a large book entitled the *Register of Writs,* but as the century progressed there was disquiet with its growth not just by the feudal lords, who saw their jurisdiction diminishing, but by the common law judges themselves (there were only twelve) who feared being overwhelmed by litigation. As a result, the

Register became closed in that no new writs were permitted, the only exception being the possibility of fashioning writs 'on the case', that is to say analogous to the writ of trespass (Milsom 1981: 300–305). The consequences of this closure proved fundamental not just to procedure but to English legal thought itself. Because access to the common law courts depended on an existing writ within which the litigant could categorise the facts of his case, these formulas or 'precedents' came to define the objective law in that they effectively defined a person's 'rights' at law. An absence of a suitable writ meant an absence of a legal remedy (see maxim 116).

This system of writs, or 'forms of action', lasted until the 19th century, and before their abolition in 1852, there were more than seventy. It is, of course easy to criticise them as medieval and rigid, but they undoubtedly shaped the common law mentality. They kept legal thinking tied to categories of factual situations, and this acted as an obstacle to the methods associated with the civilian jurists of the 16th and 17th centuries (on which see Samuel 2022: 121–127). In other words, the system stood in stark contrast to the *mos geometricus* mentality, which saw substantive law in terms of a 'logic of norms'; solutions and legal rights were, according to this mentality, a matter of deduction from a highly coherent model. The common lawyer, instead, used analogy: the facts of a dispute were simply compared to the models of factual situations to be found in the *Register of Writs*.

17.   ÆQUITAS DEFECTUS SUPPLET

Equity makes up for defects.

(Loft Reports, 500)

Despite the popularity of the royal courts, there were a number of serious defects with respect to the whole system. With one exception (order for the repossession of land), the common law courts could only grant monetary remedies, namely debt and damages. With the exception of the prerogative writs (see maxim 61), they could not order a party to do something or not to do something (other than to pay a debt or return land to its rightful possessor). The judges themselves were also very conservative and proved largely unwilling in the early centuries of the common law to adapt the law to new circumstances. In addition, there were serious defects of procedure, especially with respect to the rigidity of the forms of action; if, for example, a claimant chose the wrong writ, he risked seeing his whole case fail on the ground of want of form (for a 19th-century example see *Jacobs v Seward* (1872) LR 5 HL 464). The procedure was equally rigid with respect to documents under seal: the common law judges refused to look beyond the seal to see if there was fraud or duress. And of course, the jury was hardly the best of institutions when it came to litigation based on documentary evidence. In fact, once a jury had given its verdict it was very difficult to appeal against this decision, for there was no proper system of appeal courts over and above the three courts of common law. Added to all this were the problems of delay and corruption.

One possibility open to a disgruntled litigant in the 13th and 14th centuries was to petition the king directly since he remained the source (the 'fountain') of all justice. From the 14th century onwards, the king would pass these petitions to his Lord Chancellor, whose role was to be the 'keeper of the king's conscience', as well as being of course, the head of the judicial section of the *Curia Regis*. In turn, this high-ranking officer would often take advice from the royal judges before responding to a petition. This whole procedure attracted the name 'Equity'. However, at the end of the 15th century, the Lord Chancellor had started to decide these petitions in his own name using as a guide a mixture of his Christian discretion (since before the 16th century most Lord Chancellors were ecclesiastics), canon law and Roman law. Gradually, the Lord Chancellor moved from being an individual taking decisions to a royal court dispensing justice in the name of the king. To the three common law courts was added a fourth court, the Court of Chancery, and the case law issuing from this court became known as Equity.

18.   ÆQUITAS SEQUITUR LEGEM

Equity follows the law.

(Gilbert's Reports 136)

At first, the duality functioned, on the whole, in a cooperative fashion, but in the 17th century, a conflict developed, above all between the Lord Chief Justice Coke and the Lord Chancellor, Lord Ellesmere (Lord Chancellor from 1596 to 1617). This was a serious crisis that was only settled when Lord Ellesmere convinced the king, James I, to intervene in favour of Equity: when rules of common law and equity came into conflict, those of equity would prevail (see now Senior Courts Act 1981 s 49). After the death of Ellesmere, his successors re-established cordial relations with the common law judges. Moreover, from the 17th century onwards, the Lord Chancellors progressively came to regard Equity less as a multitude of decisions founded upon conscience and more as a body of principles (Van Caenegem 1999). Yet these principles were never seen as being in opposition to those of the common law (*æquitas nunquam contravenit leges*). The whole point of the Court of Chancery and its system of principles and remedies was to fill the gaps existing as a result of the defaults of the common law. In particular, of course, there was in the common law courts a lack of non-monetary remedies, together with the rigidity of the forms of action and the jury system.

19.   CURIA CANCELLARIÆ OFFICINA JUSTITIÆ

The Court of Chancery is the manufacturer of justice.

(2 Coke's Institutes 552)

The Court of Chancery accordingly used a quite different procedural model, one perhaps closer to the *ius commune* pattern to be found on the continent (cf Baker 2003: 180–181). There were, then, no writs and no juries, and it tackled the shortcomings of the common law through the development of a range of new remedies, of which the most important was the injunction. This was a negative order made by the court against a party in person (*in personam*) not to do something, and it could be employed to stop a litigant from pursuing his rights at common law if such an act appeared to the Lord Chancellor as being an abuse of power or rights. In addition to the injunction, equity developed other non-monetary remedies such as specific performance of contracts, rescission of transactions, and rectification of documents. In other words, the Court of Chancery developed remedies that could look behind documents and the like to see if there had been fraud, mistake, duress, or undue influence (for a modern example see *Daventry DC v Daventry & District Housing Ltd* [2012] 1 WLR 1333).

In addition to these new remedies, the Court of Chancery was able to fashion some new institutions (often indirectly through the use of injunctions) such as the trust. In the late Middle Ages, it was frequent that an owner of land would transfer it to another to be held 'on trust' for the benefit of a third person. The common law courts would look only at the form of the transfer and thus not recognise the 'trust' obligation attaching to the new owner. The Lord Chancellor took a quite different position on the basis of the King's Conscience and would force the new proprietor (the trustee) to respect his obligations towards the third party (the beneficiary). Gradually, this position changed from being a matter of equitable remedies to one of property rights; the beneficiary acquired under a trust a real right in the trust property, and there thus developed two forms of 'ownership', one at common law and one in equity.

20. LEX MERCATI DIFFERT A COMMUNI LEGE REGNI TRIBUS MODIS IN GENERE[:] PRIMO QUOD CELERIUS DELIBERAT SE IPSAM

Mercantile law differs from the ordinary law of the land in three ways: first it is generally faster in its deliberations.

(13th century treatise on the *lex mercatoria*: Little Red Book of Bristol)

Commercial law – the *lex mercatoria* – has its own history within the civil law tradition and, to some extent, in the medieval common law. As John Baker says, in England the borough courts and pie powder courts provided justice that was far speedier than the royal courts (Baker 2019: 30). This said, the shortcomings of the common law might seem surprising in the context of the importance, today, of commerce to English law. The procedural rigidity and remedial limitations would hardly seem attractive to the merchants of the late Middle Ages. In fact, before the 18th century an important part of mercantile law was not to be found in the royal courts but in the Court of Admiralty.

The Court of Admiralty was partly the result of a jurisdictional limitation that attached to a jury which could not be convened with respect to a case that happened outside of England. This gap was at first filled by the *Curia Regis* and then by several specialised courts, of which Admiralty was the most important. This was a court that formed around the Lord High Admiral, who was the head of the navy and who had jurisdiction over piracy. Later, this jurisdiction was extended to the law of the sea and then to commercial law in general, guided by judges trained in Roman and civil law. There were two reasons why Admiralty was able to capture this work from the old mercantile courts. First, it employed the fiction that any commercial case happened *super altum mare* and thus it simply pretended that the law of the sea and commercial law were one and the same. Secondly, to some extent, these two areas were one and the same since England was a seafaring nation. Even today, many commercial cases involve shipping, and this was particularly true in the 18th and 19th centuries. However, the success was not to last, and from the 17th century, Admiralty found itself gradually being relieved of its jurisdiction by the common law courts.

The common law courts were able to attract this commercial work because of several important developments. First, the law itself had matured at the level of theory; in particular, a remedy based on the notion of trespass had been extended to cover damage caused by a person failing to do what he had promised. This new action of *assumpsit* in effect provided a compensation claim for a party who had been the victim of a breach of contract even though in the

17th century there was no theory of contract in the civilian sense of the term. Secondly, the Lord Chief Justice Coke (1552–1634) had attacked the Court of Admiralty with Writs of Prohibition, which had the effect of suppressing litigation in this court and attracting some of it to the common law courts. Thirdly, in the 18th century, Lord Mansfield (1705–1793), a common law judge, succeeded in adapting the procedures of the common law to the needs of the commercial classes, with the result that commercial law got absorbed into the common law (or vice-versa as some think).

All through the 19th century, the common law courts built upon these developments and succeeded not just in fashioning a general law of contract but in developing specific areas of commercial law such as sale, charterparty, and insurance contracts. This is the reason why common law is regarded by many as a commercial law. In 1875, the Court of Admiralty was absorbed into the Probate, Divorce and Admiralty Division of the High Court, and in 1970, when this Division became the Family Division, Admiralty was absorbed into the Queen's Bench Division (Administration of Justice Act 1970 s 1). Thus Admiralty was finally merged with the common law at both the substantive and the formal levels. However, an Admiralty Court remains as a separate court within the King's Bench Division.

Nevertheless, these 19th- and 20th-century developments did not result in a system that was perfectly suited to the needs of the commercial community. At the end of the 19th century, a commercial court was constituted within the Queen's (now King's) Bench Division of the High Court with the aim of speedily and efficiently dealing with commercial cases (see Lord Hamblem 2020: https://www.supremecourt.uk/docs/speech-201013.pdf). But even this development seems not to have overcome problems of delay and expense with the result that, during the 20th century, arbitration was drawing commercial matters away from the courts (*Report of the Committee on Supreme Court Practice and Procedure*, Cmnd 8878, 1953, para 895). Today, arbitration is not seen in a negative light and indeed has been given legislative support (Arbitration Act 1996). Moreover the commercial court has embraced Alternative Dispute Resolution (ADR) procedures whereby parties are encouraged to resolve their disputes through mediation (see *Halsey v Milton Keynes General NHS Trust* [2004] 1 WLR 3002). As to the point of having a separate (informal) commercial law, Lord Leggatt claims that it has its own moral value (https://www .supremecourt.uk/docs/what-is-the-point-of-commercial-law.pdf) while Lord Hodge says that it generates much economic benefit for the United Kingdom (https://www.supremecourt.uk/docs/the-rule-of-law-the-courts-and-the-brit-ish-economy.pdf). Commercial law, as provided by London, is, in other words, a service like accountancy or banking offered to the world. One might note that in some civil law countries, there are commercial courts that are separate from the ordinary courts, with substantive commercial law rules (or some of them) contained in codes separate from the civil codes. In other words, commercial law is formally regarded as being separate from the ordinary civil law.

21. PRIUSQUAM INCIPIAS, CONSULTO; ET UBI CONSULUERIS MATURI, FACTO OPUS EST

Before you begin, consult; and when such consultation is brought to fruition,
get the work done.

(Sallust, *Bellum Catilinae*, 1; Riley's Latin
Dictionary 343)

The maxim *priusquam incipias, consulto* may seem a curious one in the context of the development of English law – especially as it is not a legal one in its origin. But it does sum up the attitude of the 19th century reformers. There was much consultation in the form of Parliamentary Commissions on the state of the courts and procedure during this period – and there needed to be. For, despite the important adaptations within the common law system, the beginning of the 19th century nevertheless saw England with a set of courts and procedures that were feudal and medieval in origin. In the age of science if all this was to seem somewhat irrational, and from a litigant's point of view, it probably was. Why were there three courts of common law with equivalent jurisdiction? Why were there two systems of legal rules, law and equity? Why was there no proper appeal structure? Why was there so much emphasis on the form rather than the substance of a legal claim? In addition, there were the scandals associated with delays in the Court of Chancery (see Dickens's *Bleak House*).

The 19th century was accordingly to become the age of reform. In 1830, a Court of Exchequer Chamber was established to act as a court of error, that is to say, a kind of appeal court; the new court consisted of judges from the common law courts, other than from the one from which the appeal came. This idea of error was the result of the old writ of error, which had been one means of appeal within the common law system, along with the procedure for a motion for a new trial (neither of which can be properly described as 'appeals'). A jury verdict could be overturned if an error was discovered in the legal record of the case. In fact, the 1830 Court was not the first Exchequer Chamber to have appeared: there had been three others over the centuries, though none had found long-term success (see Baker 2019: 147–148). In 1851, the legislature established a Court of Appeal in Chancery which was set up as a true appeal court – that is to say, to rehear a case – rather than as a court of error (Baker 2019: 151–152).

In addition to these institutional reforms, Parliament set about reform-
ing the law of procedure. The forms of action were effectively abolished by
the Common Law Procedure Act 1852, and some progress was made in fus-
ing law and equity with respect to remedies and the ability of a single court
to have recourse to both systems. In 1846, a system of local County Courts
was established. At first, the jurisdiction of these new courts was restricted,
but their increasing popularity encouraged the progressive extension of this
jurisdiction, with the result that today the County Courts play a major role in
the English civil law system. Another procedural change that was to have an
important long-term effect was the power granted to a judge to dispense with
a jury in civil claims; by the middle of the 20th century, it had virtually disappeared from non-criminal cases, its role having been taken over by the trial
judge (*Ward v James* [1966] 1 QB 273).

To a certain extent, then, the procedural and institutional mentality of the
Court of Chancery was, thanks to these legislative reforms, imposing itself on
the common law. As for the Court of Chancery itself, there had been a number of important reforms since the beginning of the 19th century. The Lord
Chancellor gradually decided fewer and fewer cases at first instance, and in
1851 a Court of Appeal in Chancery was established. This new institution was
a genuine appeal court and not a court of error; as such, it became the model
for the future Court of Appeal (1875). A few years later, statute gave judges
the power to award damages in lieu of an injunction or specific performance
(Chancery Amendment Act 1858; see *Jaggard v Sawyer* [1995] 2 All ER 189).
From then on, it was possible to obtain damages (in equity) without having to
go to another court if refused an equitable remedy.

However, the principal reform of the English legal system came in 1875
with the Judicature Acts 1873–75 (Supreme Court of Judicature Act 1873 and
1875). This statute swept away the old system of central courts and established
a new model called the Supreme Court, which operated at two levels. The
first level was the High Court, which consisted of an amalgamation of the
three old common law courts, the Court of Chancery, the Court of Admiralty,
and the ecclesiastical courts. The High Court was the court of first instance
and had (after 1881) three divisions: the Queen's (now King's) Bench Division
(QBD, now KBD), Chancery Division (ChD) and the Probate, Divorce and
Admiralty Division (PDA), this last consisting of all those old courts that had
largely dispensed Roman and civil law. In 1970, this third division was abolished and replaced by the Family Division (Administration of Justice Act 1970
s 1). Most cases were to be heard by a single judge who would decide (if there
was no jury) both questions of fact and law; however there were also Divisional
Courts, often with two judges, of which the most important were those of the
KBD, deciding questions of law arising from the magistrates courts and deciding questions of administrative law.

The second level of the Supreme Court consisted of the Court of Appeal. This new appeal court took as its model not the old Court of Exchequer Chamber but the Court of Appeal in Chancery; it was therefore a genuine appeal court and not a court of error. Normally a case would come before three judges, and each had the right to issue his (or her) own judgment, although sometimes there would be a joint one issued as the judgment of the court. This Court of Appeal was originally envisaged as being the first and final appeal; thus further appeal to the House of Lords (which had jurisdiction to hear appeals thanks to its old *Curia Regis* status) was to be abolished. However, between 1873 and 1875 there was a change of government, with the result that a decision was made to retain the House of Lords as an appeal court. Consequently, the old three level structure (common law or Chancery court, appeal or error court, and then the House of Lords) was ultimately retained, although statute ensured that the judicial section of House of Lords was turned into a proper appeal body staffed by fully qualified Lords of Appeal (Appellate Jurisdiction Act 1876).

A much more recent development regarding the House of Lords as an appeal body is in respect of its name. It has become the Supreme Court (thus necessitating a change with respect to the 1875 Supreme Court) and is housed in a building independent of the House of Lords itself (Constitutional Reform Act 2005). Mention must also be made of the Privy Council as an appeal court. This became independent of the *Curia Regis* in the 16th century with jurisdiction to decide appeals coming from overseas colonies, and this was formalised by legislation during the 19th century (Judicial Committee Act 1833 and 1844). It also heard appeals from the ecclesiastical courts and from the Court of Admiralty and is staffed by Lords of Appeal (now judges of the new Supreme Court).

22.   QUI PARCIT NOCENTIBUS, INNOCENTES PUNIT

Whoever spares those that do harm, punish the innocent.

(Jenkins' Centuries 126)

When one turns to the development of criminal law, both the institutional and theoretical context prove rather different from that of civil law (using civil here to mean the opposite of criminal). There are several reasons for this difference. The first is that from an historical viewpoint, the emphasis has been as much (if not more) on the notion of punishment as on the formal role of law; this was true of what might be seen as the philosophy or theory underpinning crime (see generally Pradel 1989). One historical aspect of this philosophy, particularly under the influence of the Church and canon law, has been the focus on the nature of the criminal, either as a sinner (canon law) or as someone who is ill and in need of a cure. Another aspect has been the reaction against crime. There have been two broad currents: one on social defence based on neutralisation or treatment (*utilitas publica*, one might say); the other on ideas of intimidation and retribution (Pradel 1989: 122–123). *Pona ad paucos, ad omnes perveniat* (punishment for the few, [generates] fear for everyone), as one maxim puts it (Lofft's Reports 189). In fact, these philosophies have by no means disappeared, as anyone might discover if they listen to, or participate in, any discussion about prisons. One will hear arguments about the need to protect society, to rehabilitate, to deter others, to allocate personal responsibility, to atone for wrongs and so on and so forth. Many of these arguments are either obsolete or nonsense.

23.   NULLA POENA SINE LEGE

No punishment without law.

(relatively modern maxim perhaps derived in part from D.50.16.131.1)

As far as the law is concerned, the most influential writer in Europe on law and crime was Cesare Beccaria (1738–1794). In fact, he was more of a philosopher than a legal technician, but his principal contribution was to insist that criminal law should be based strictly on the law rather than on the arbitrary discretion of the judge. Law for Beccaria was legislation which, in turn, represented the will of the people; as such, the judge should be confined to a strict interpretation of the text and to examining the facts in order to determine whether or not they fell under the relevant penal provision (Pradel 1989: 27). Punishment equally should be determined only by the law. Beccaria's influence was considerable, if not revolutionary, with respect to criminal law; in England, this influence was reflected in particular in the writings of Jeremy Bentham (1748–1832) who took a utilitarian and arithmetical approach in formulating his ideas for a criminal law code. England did not end up with such a criminal code, but by far the greater part of contemporary criminal law is today based on legislation. This said, the substance of criminal law from a practical point of view is rarely on the interpretation of legislative texts, since many factual situations that come before the criminal courts, if proved, clearly fall within a legal provision. The most important practical aspects of criminal cases are evidence and proof.

24.   VOX POPULI VOX DEI

The voice of the people is the voice of God.

(origin unknown)

As for the institutions of criminal law in England, the focus is in many ways on the 'people' rather than the judge, even if the people are not actually to be regarded as the voice of God. The reason for this emphasis is that in serious criminal cases, the primary arbiter is the jury consisting of twelve ordinary citizens, while lesser crimes come before a Justice of the Peace (JP) who, again, is usually not a professional lawyer but a (supposedly) worthy citizen (*R v Horncastle* [2009] UKSC 14, para 17). Such a JP, or magistrate, is unpaid and so much criminal justice might be said, in comparison to the situation on the continent, to be in the hands of amateurs rather than professionals.

This situation is the result of history. After the Norman conquest, members of the *Curia Regis* – later judges – would go on circuit around the country to hear and judge legal disputes. When arriving at a town, they would not know the facts of any alleged crime, and so local people who were aware of the case were assembled to inform the judge of the facts. They were originally, then, witnesses rather than arbiters. Very gradually, the situation evolved until the jurors were finally incorporated into the trial itself and were there to decide whether or not the defendant was guilty of the crime charged.

As for JPs, they, again, originated in the early days of the common law after the Norman invasion. At first, they were loyal knights of the king to whom a responsibility had been given to maintain the peace within the county in which they lived, and their position later became formalised by legislation in the 14th century (Spencer 1998: 9; Wilson 1973: 77). They participated within their county in a court known as Quarter-Sessions which tried, with a jury, cases involving less serious criminal cases (trial on indictment). The serious criminal cases (felonies) were reserved for the Assize courts, which involved a professional judge and jury. Before the establishment of a police force, JPs were also charged with investigating offences and so had a role as a kind of *juge d'instruction* (on which see Lord Phillips in *R v Horncastle* [2009] UKSC 14, paras 59–62); they had other administrative roles as well. Today the JPs – or magistrates – are, of course, no longer loyal knights but, instead, ordinary citizens who take on a role that is really not that different from the one that the knights had all those centuries ago; they hear, in the Magistrates' Courts, less serious offences. The Assize courts and Quarter-Sessions have been abolished and were replaced in 1972 by Crown Courts, which are permanent criminal courts with juries hearing serious criminal cases (The Courts Act 1971). In

Principia Iuris

short, then, minor criminal offences are heard in the Magistrates' Court, while serious offences are tried in the Crown Court with a jury.

25. COMPROMISSUM AD SIMILITUDINEM IUDICIORUM REDIGITUR ET AD FINIENDAS LITES PERTINET

An arbitral compromise [ie arbitration] is to be treated like a judicial process and the object is to put an end to litigation.

(Paul, D.4.8.1)

25A. COMPROMISSUM ISTUD COMPARABIMUS ORDINARIAE ACTIONI

An arbitral compromise is comparable to an ordinary legal action.

(Paul, D.4.8.32.9)

So far, the discussion has been concerned with the ordinary courts of law. However, what today is known as Alternative Dispute Resolution (ADR) has roots going back to Roman law. Arbitration remains, at least in the field of commercial law, the principal form of ADR, but there was another alternative dispute process, in the field of public law, that was in many ways similar or analogous to arbitration. This was the administrative tribunal system. One is talking here in the past tense because this administrative system has in this century undergone a change of status and is, probably, no longer to be regarded as a form of ADR. It is now part of the judicial system.

In addition, then, to the system of ordinary civil process courts (High Court and County Court), the 20th century saw the development of a system of tribunals. These tribunals were created by statute and largely dealt with disputes arising between citizens and various public authorities. Thus, they resembled to some extent the administrative courts found in the civil law tradition. The development of these dispute resolution institutions outside the normal court system was not uncontroversial, but they had a number of advantages such as speed, expertise and less formality. They were also very diverse not just in respect of their subject-matter – taxation, social security, rent, licensing and so on – but also in their procedures. There were around 70 different tribunals. Some of these were like courts with court-like procedures, while others were less formal; there were also differences with respect to the possibility of appeals (see *Report of the Committee on Tribunals and Inquiries*, Cmnd 218,

1957, paras 35–37). One major criticism that attached to this system of tribunals was that they were resourced and staffed by the public authority or department that administered the scheme, and thus the tribunal appeared not to be sufficiently independent and neutral. Accordingly, the system was reformed to some extent in 1958 when the great majority of tribunals were made subject both to an appeal route to the High Court and to control by judicial review proceedings (see maxim 61) (Tribunals and Inquiries Act 1958).

The present century has seen further and major reform. The Tribunals, Courts and Enforcement Act 2007 has created a new unified structure of tribunals which in its structural pattern resembles in outline (or by analogy) the two-tier system of the old Supreme Court established by the Judicature Act 1873. There is a First-tier Tribunal which is divided into various chambers and an Upper Tribunal, also organised into chambers; both of these tiers are staffed by judges as well as by lay members, the Upper Tribunal actually consisting of High Court judges. However, as Lady Hale pointed out, although the "new structure may look neat… the diversity of jurisdictions accommodated means that it is not as neat as it looks" *(R (Cart) v Upper Tribunal* [2012] 1 AC 663, para 23). For example, the Upper Tribunal is certainly an appeal court in the full sense of the term, but it is equally a court of first instance for some matters and it is not too clear why some of these matters should be assigned to this superior tier while others are not (Lady Hale para 23).

It would appear, therefore, that there are now two parallel court systems in the UK rather than one court system and a mode of ADR via tribunals. As a result of the 2007 Act, there exists something of a separate corps of judges under the responsibility of a Senior President (see Lady Hale, para 22) with the consequence that the idea of a unique common law court system covering both private and public law matters might have to be rethought. It could be that there really is now a "system of specialised administrative courts" (Boyron 2010: 126).

Arbitration, as has been noted, has a long history dating back to Roman law, and in England it has now been put on a secure statutory basis (Arbitration Act 1996). This Act is said to represent a new philosophy in that recourse from arbitration decisions to the courts has become difficult, thus making arbitration more independent of the courts system (*Lesotho Highlands Development Authority v Impregilo SpA* [2006] 1 AC 221). As for arbitration itself, it has been defined by the Law Commission in the following way:

> Arbitration is a form of dispute resolution. If two or more parties have a dispute, which they cannot resolve themselves, instead of going to court, they might appoint a third person as an arbitrator to resolve the dispute for them. They might appoint a panel of arbitrators to act as an arbitral tribunal (*Review of the Arbitration Act 1996*, Law Com No 413, 2023, para 1.1)

The advantages can be summarised under the four 'S's, namely saving, secrecy, specialisation and speed; but these aims and objectives are not always achieved. Some disputes can end up, for example, costing as much as litigation. The actual basis for arbitration is the contract, and many commercial and consumer contracts will contain arbitration clauses; the actual validity of these clauses is not, however, dependent upon the validity of the contract itself (Arbitration Act 1996 s 7). In many respects, arbitration is like litigation, and so arbitrators are under a duty to act fairly and impartially and to give reasons for their decisions; the remedies available are similar to those available in the ordinary courts. Nevertheless, despite these processes in some ways mirroring the ordinary court system, the great advantage of arbitration is that arbitrators can be specialists in the area in which the dispute has arisen. Ordinary judges are not likely to be experts in, say, the chocolate trade.

Similar, in some ways, to the old tribunal system are the ombudsmen schemes. These are now well established in both the public and private sector since the creation of the Parliamentary Commissioner in 1967 to investigate claims of governmental maladministration (Parliamentary Commissioner Act 1967). Other ombudsmen have been established to investigate, for example the health service and local government. In the private sector, there are now ombudsmen covering a range of commercial and consumer activities, for example, banking and insurance, pensions, telecommunications and estate agents. There are said to be three essential features that define an ombudsman: he or she is an independent and non-partisan officer who deals with specific complaints from the public and who has the power to investigate, criticise and publicise injustice and maladministration (Verkuil 1975). One important feature that emerges from this definition is that the ombudsman, at least in the public sector, has no power to reverse an unjust decision and her decisions are not binding; the primary weapon is persuasion and publication. This can lead to serious difficulty when the government refuses to act on a report (see generally https://www.citizensadvice.org.uk/consumer/get-more-help/how-to-use-an-ombudsman-in-england/).

26.   CUM LICET FUGERE, NE QUÆRE LITEM

If one can avoid it, do not enter into litigation.

(Taylor's Law Glossary 58)

Other forms of ADR are mediation and negotiation. These alternative forms have become increasingly important since the Woolf Report (see maxim 31), which felt that many disputes could be resolved through mediation (see *Cowl v Plymouth CC* [2002] 1 WLR 803 paras 1–3), but there were important advances taking place before the reforms. Mediation has been developed in the commercial court (Commercial Court Practice Direction [1994] 1 All ER 34) and is seen as being of particular value in family law disputes (Family Law Act 1996 s 8). There is even a mediation scheme attached to the Court of Appeal. One problem is whether this form of ADR should be compulsory; the Court of Appeal once indicated a reluctance to penalise parties who refuse mediation since this could amount to interfering with the right of access to a court (*see Halsey v Milton Keynes General NHS Trust* [2004] 1 WLR 3002), but the decision has attracted criticism and it may be that the attitude of the judges has changed (see, for example, *Northrop Grumman Mission Systems Europe Ltd v BAE Systems Ltd* [2015] 3 All ER 782; *Churchill v Merthyr Tydfil County Borough Council* [2023] EWCA Civ 1416). Whatever the position on costs, it is likely that mediation will become an increasingly important form of ADR (see *Churchill, supra*).

Mediation does have both a long history and a vital comparative dimension. In terms of history, it is associated with particular communities such as those founded on religious beliefs, but more recently it has gained importance in areas such as the professional, employment, landlord and tenant and consumer environments. No doubt these community and interest-based groups can provide a rich source for research. Equally, some countries like China can offer much potential for legal anthropologists and comparatists, given the country's long cultural tradition of mediation as a dispute resolution process (see Roberts & Palmer 2005). There are however problems with processes such as mediation. Is it actually effective in terms of its take-up rate? The research so far is by no means conclusive. Indeed, there is even a powerful argument to be made against forced, or partially forced, settlements which might result from ADR (Fiss 1984). There are other difficulties as well. Such methods often function in the 'shadow of the law,' with the result that there is a permanent threat of 'juridification', especially as mediation operates within an atomised ideology of rights. Yet this juridification is itself weakened by the lack of any precedent system. Furthermore, the process can be manipulated by state power for reasons of economic efficiency, and this may mean that it ends up operating as an adjunct to the ordinary court procedures (justice on the cheap). The historical and comparative possibilities can even have a negative effect in as much as there is a temptation to introduce mediation procedures by way of transplantation from one society to another without proper consideration of cultural context. These are by no means fatal problems, but they do indicate that teaching and research, which perhaps is lacking at the moment in law schools because of the emphasis on positive law, need to take ADR much more seriously.

CONCLUDING REMARKS

The history of the English law courts is one that many may see as not being governed by any rational plan. That, perhaps, is the price to be paid for a historical development that was 'bottom-up' so to speak. This finally led to change in the latter part of the 19th century. Yet, given the history, it might be useful to leave the concluding remarks to the Judicature Commission that reported in 1869:

> This distinction [between law and equity] led to the establishment of two systems of Judicature, organized in different ways, and administering justice on different and sometimes opposite principles, using different methods of procedure, and applying different remedies. Large classes of rights, altogether ignored by the Courts of Common Law, were protected and enforced by the Court of Chancery, and recourse was had to the same Court for the purpose of obtaining a more adequate protection against the violation of Common Law rights than the Courts of Common Law were competent to afford. The Common Law Courts were confined by their system of procedure in most actions – not brought for recovering the possession of land – to giving judgment for debt or damages, a remedy which has been found to be totally insufficient for the adjustment of the complicated disputes of modern society. The procedure at Common Law was founded on the trial by jury, and was framed on the supposition that every issue of fact was capable of being tried in that way; but experience has shown that supposition to be erroneous. A large number of important cases frequently occur in the practice of the Common Law Courts which cannot be conveniently adapted to that mode of trial; and ultimately those cases either find their way into the Court of Chancery, or the Suitors in the Courts of Common Law are obliged to have recourse to private arbitration in order to supply the defects of their inadequate procedure. The evils of this double system of Judicature, and the confusion and conflict of jurisdiction to which it has led, have been long known and acknowledged (Judicature Commission: *The First Report of the Commissioners*, 1869, Cmnd 4130, PP XXV, pp 5–6).

3. Procedure and appeals

Elements of the English procedural tradition have already been indicated in the previous chapter, for a clear separation between legal institutions and the procedural forms that attach to them cannot realistically be made. Nevertheless, much more needs to be said about the history and philosophy of civil procedure if an understanding of the common law is to be gained. Moreover, procedure is an area that lends itself to a comparative approach; consequently, it will perhaps be useful, first, to indicate the outlines of the procedural model that has dominated in the civil law. An appreciation of this continental model will permit one to see how the common law model is different and how these differences are in fact part of the characteristic elements of English civil procedure. However, this is not to suggest that the two models do not share common ideas.

27. QUOD NON EST IN ACTIS NON EST IN MUNDO

> *What is not in the legal file does not exist.*
>
> (Exact origin unknown, but thought to be 14th century; a similar maxim exists in writings of the early 16th century)

"The Romano-canonical procedure is one of the wonders of legal history", claims Professor Van Caenegem; "it was not based on a haphazard accumulation of unrelated remedies, dominated by different rules according to the moment of their creation" (1971: para 19). The main features, as described by Van Caenegem (1971: para 15), of this Romano-Canonical procedure were as follows. There was a single professional judge who investigated the complaint in an active inquisitorial manner. Proceedings were in writing (*quod non est in actis non est in mundo*) and they were opened with a written libel (*libellus*) delivered by plaintiff to judge. The defendant could invoke various *exceptiones* while the witnesses were examined by *interrogatores*. The whole procedure was marked by formal stages (especially the *litis contestatio*: the stage where the parties have agreed the issues to go before a judge) which amounted to a cohesive system in itself; judgments, of course, were always on the written case.

Appeals were possible within the Church and, later, state hierarchy, and such appeals, in theory and often in practice, could end up in the hands of the Pope or the king (see maxim 33). This procedure was 'undemocratic' in the sense that it was entirely bureaucratic and involved only professionals; yet it quickly came to dominate in France, Italy and Spain. In Germany, it followed the reception of Roman law, and only in England did it fail to dominate, although the procedure in the Court of Chancery, so very different from that of the common law, did resemble it. After the Middle Ages, the main characteristics of the Romano-canonical model were preserved by legislation or by the courts themselves (for example, in the *Parlement de Paris*) and thus the model's main features became imprinted on the great codes of procedure in the 19th century (see Van Caenegem 1992: paras 91–92, 132–134). In addition to the Romano-canonical procedure itself, the history of particular aspects of procedure (for example, types of Roman actions, the notion of judgment, role of the judge, proof) and the effect that these have had on substantive rights are of importance in understanding the civilian mentality.

How, then, can this historical procedural model be summed up? Legal procedure in the civil law tradition can be described as follows: "A single judge, a professional with academic training, received the complaints, heard the parties and the witnesses, saw the documents, decided on questions of fact and of law and gave judgment according to his conviction (in a later stage this was altered by the theory of legal proof...)". In addition, these "judgments were liable to appeal along the hierarchical ladder" (Van Caenegem 1971: para 15). This procedural model attracted the name 'Romano-canonical' because, as the term implies, it was based on the structure to be found in the *Corpus Iuris Civilis* (the Roman law texts rediscovered in the 11th century) as modified by the work of the canon lawyers of the late Middle Ages. The edifice was built around the inquisitorial model whereby a judge took control *ex officio* of a case and opened an inquiry on receiving a written *libellus*. This inquiry then became part of a segmental and unfolding process in which judgment was reached only after a long series of separate stages which might literally have lasted a lifetime. Part of the delay problem was caused by the sharp procedural divide between judge and parties. Although the judge might have had a more active role in the investigation, this role became diminished as the emphasis on writing increased. The judge lost control of the proceedings in private law and the conduct of the proceedings itself was exclusively in the hands of the parties (Cappelletti & Garth 1986: para 3). There was an important ideological logic to this development as well: private litigation was considered a private affair and this was the dominant paradigm in continental procedure up until the 19th century.

28. SEULES LES PARTIES INTRODUISENT L'INSTANCE, HORS LES CAS OÙ LA LOI EN DISPOSE AUTREMENT

Except where the law provides otherwise, only the parties can institute proceedings.

(French *Code de Procédure Civile* art 1)

With the coming of the modern era, there was, needless to say, a break with the *ius commune* past. In the French model, to take a central example, the reliance on writing and inquisitorial methods gave way to a greater role for 'orality' (*plaidoiries, débat oral*) and fewer segments with the result that legal cases unfolded more rapidly and were less constrained by formal rules and regulations concerning the taking of evidence, the hearing of arguments and the formulation of decisions (Cappelletti & Garth 1986: para 4). Equally, there was a return to the more active role of the judge. Accordingly, although it is a fundamental principle of continental civil procedure that a judge can never commence legal proceedings on his own motion (*nemo judex sine actore*), once the parties have started an action, the judge has the power to, and may be required to, make enquiries on his own motion (see e.g., *Code de Procédure Civile* art 10). Indeed, "party control over civil proceedings is being reduced by the fact that wider and wider powers of investigation are being given to the examining judge, and even to the trial judges" (Kohl 1982: para 129). Accordingly, one can say that an emphasis on the written file (*dossier*), an unfolding process (*le déroulement du procès*) and on an active role for the judge (*instruction*) remain important characteristics not just of French, but of continental civil procedure (Cappelletti & Garth 1986: paras 3, 5).

29. NEMO SINE ACTIONE EXPERITUR, ET HOC NON SINE BREVI ET LIBELLO CONVENTIONALI

No one attempts to go to court without an action and this means without a writ or written statement of claim.

(Bracton, de Legibus, 112)

If one returns to the English common law and to its history, this tradition developed its own specific form of procedure quite separate from the Romano-canonical model found in the countries that received Roman law. It has already been noted (see maxims 15–16) that from a procedural viewpoint two institutional focal points dominate, namely the form of action (writ) and the jury.

Indeed, in the time of Bracton (circa 1210–1268), the common law was not seen "as a system of substantive rules at all" (Milsom 1981: 43). English law was founded at this time on "a procedural logic" itself involving the art of pleading. And the "logic of medieval pleading was directed to the possible misleading of juries" (*ibid* 79). As a Report from 1851 pointed out:

> Originally pleadings were verbal; the advocates or pleaders appeared in Court, and stated the cause of action or ground of defence in the presence of the Court. Any deviation from the rules was objected to at the time; the defect was at once amended, and the issue in fact or in law was evolved without further expense or delay; indeed, the proceedings, judging from the Year-Books, had more the appearance of a school disputation, than of real business; When, however, the transactions which led to lawsuits increased, and became more complicated, and the carrying on pleadings verbally or *ore tenus* was found impossible, the parties were obliged to put their respective statements into writing, but in a form, still preserved, which supposes that the parties are orally pleading in the presence of each other (*First Report of Her Majesty's Commissioners for Inquiring into the Process, Practice and System of Pleading in the Superior Courts of Common Law*, PP, 1851, xxii 567, p 19)

Moreover:

> A mistake as to the form of action may be of much more serious consequence than the defects in pleading which we have been hitherto discussing, as it is not always cured by pleading over (as errors in form, strictly so called, are), or even after verdict; but the objection may be raised on general demurrer, or, after verdict, by motion in arrest of judgment, or by writ of error, although it may be quite beside the real merits of the case (*ibid* 31).

All this meant that English procedure had distinct characteristics. In particular it was an oral procedure because decisions of fact were made not by judges learned in Roman law and trained in the university faculties; they were made by juries which consisted of ordinary people who were often illiterate. To the Roman and canon lawyers of the late Middle Ages the idea that "the decisive verdict in a law case" might be put "in the power of a dozen illiterate rustics" was considered "as utterly ridiculous and absurd" (Van Caenegem 1987: 119; cf *R v Young* [1995] QB 324). Yet the jury was to dominate the civil procedure of English private and criminal law up until the end of the 19th century and even today, in order to understand the structure of the legal process, it is necessary to imagine, as a jurist once said, *le jury fantôme* in every tort and contract case (Jolowicz). The rigid distinction between the trial and pre-trial process and between questions of fact and questions of law result from the existence of the jury (see maxim 15). Moreover once the jury had issued its verdict, appeal against the decision was in theory almost impossible and in practice difficult. Jury trials are now rare in private law cases in England (*Ward v James* [1966]

1 QB 273). However in the United States they still have a central role and thus present special problems when it comes to appeals (Herzog & Karlen 1977: paras 44–48).

30. VIA ANTIQUA [TRITA], VIA TUTA

The old way is the sure way

(Broom Maxims 134)

In the common law system, because of the illiteracy of the jury, the trial was, and to an important extent remains today, an oral process (although there have been recent and fundamental reforms). Witnesses are heard in court and their evidence is open to examination and cross-examination by the parties' lawyers (*Final Report of the Committee on Supreme Court Practice and Procedure*, Cmnd 8878, 1953, para 365). In such a process it is not for the judge to question the witnesses since his or her role is largely passive; indeed too many interruptions by a judge could give rise to grounds for appeal (*Jones v National Coal Board* [1957] 2 QB 55). However this is subject to qualification. First, this passive role applies only to the hearing of evidence; when it comes to arguments of law the judge will assume a much more active role with regard to the parties' (normally barristers') arguments. Secondly, recent reforms have resulted in the judges having a more active general role (Andrews 2000) and documents are becoming ever more central. One might add a third qualification. In family law cases – especially those involving children – the idea of a completely passive judge silently listening to the evidence from both sides is an unrealistic image. Nevertheless an important characteristic of the common law is the practical skill of dealing with evidence both at the pre-trial and the trial stage and this is something that is primarily in the hands of the parties' lawyers and their cross-examination of witnesses. (One might note the procedure in the Post Office Horizon scandal (2024): barristers questioning the witnesses before a largely passive judge.) Fact handling, to put it another way, helps give the common law its empirical flavour and helps shift the emphasis off the idea that legal knowledge is a matter of highly systematised rules.

Yet an emphasis on facts does not necessarily mean an absence of formality. Proceedings were once dominated by the form of the action and this mentality is still to be found on occasions with respect to pleadings (*Esso v Southport Corporation* [1956] AC 218, 238, 241). French judges would appear to have greater freedom, although since the Woolf reforms of 1998 (see below maxim 31) the position in England has probably changed to a considerable extent (see *McPhilemy v Times Newspapers Ltd* [1999] 3 All ER 775, 792–793). Another characteristic of the common law model is the emphasis on the private interests of the parties rather than on the public interest of the legal process (*Air Canada v Sec of State* [1983] 2 AC 394, 438). However, once again, the recent procedural reforms give the judges much more control and the emphasis is now on "the abstract interests of justice" (see Andrews 2000: 34).

More generally, the procedural position in the common law can be summed up as follows: "There is immediacy in the relationship between the parties, counsel and witnesses, and the adjudicating judge or jury, and there is generally concentration of proceedings into one hearing or a series of hearings held in the shortest possible period of time" (Cappelletti & Garth 1986: para. 7). This contrasts sharply with the Romano-canonical model. However, the reaction against the reliance upon an entirely written procedure over the last century and the adoption of oral proceedings would seemingly bring continental civil procedure closer to that of England. This apparent *rapprochement* becomes even more credible when it is appreciated that the procedure in Chancery, which became the model for the common law courts in 1875, was always closer to the civilian model than to the common law one. One might add that recent reforms in English civil procedure take the common law even closer to the French model (Jolowicz 1996); the pre-trial proceedings will be under the strict control of a judge (Andrews 2000).

Yet the differences of history have shaped mentality. In England, the emphasis on argumentation (before a jury) has endowed the law with a particular flavour. It is knowledge to be discovered, not by the court as such, as is the case in the civil law (*da mihi factum, dabo tibi ius*; *jura novit cura*: the court knows the law), but by a debate between plaintiff counsel, defendant counsel and the judge (the judge is not always passive when it comes to arguments of law). Moreover, there is a tradition, resulting from the role of the jury, that witnesses should be seen and heard by the trial judge (see *Final Report of the Committee on Supreme Court Practice and Procedure*, Cmnd 8878, 1953, para 365). Judgments, accordingly, often reflect this style. In civil law the scientific nature of the whole process has given rise to a different style of judgment which traditionally repressed the open-ended and argumentative nature of legal knowledge (cf. *Final Report*, 1953, *supra*, paras 250–252).

31.   ALIA INITIA E FINE

With the end of something, other beginnings arise.

(Pliny the Elder)

The Judicature Act of 1875 represented the break between the old common law system of courts and the new model. The structure put in place by this legislation is more or less the one that is to be found in England and Wales today, even if there have been some further major reforms. However, what is particularly interesting about these modern reforms is that some of them are aimed at what might be described as the traditional procedural philosophy of the common law trial process.

As mentioned, there have been a number of reforms to the English legal system throughout the 20th century, but major change belongs more to the period that might broadly be described as the turn of the last century, that is to say the period from 1990 onwards. The reforms of this latest period have largely resulted from concerns about a number of procedural and institutional aspects of the English justice system.

Towards the end of the 20th century the government appointed a senior judge, Lord Woolf, to head an enquiry and in 1996 he produced a report entitled *Access to Justice* in which he proposed some radical reforms (Woolf 1996). The judge emphasised a number of defects to be found in civil procedure – excessive delay, high costs, complexity and outdated terminology – but he equally criticised the whole philosophy of the trial system in the English common law. Perhaps this philosophy had been summed up by a comment from a Law lord a quarter of a century ago. "In a contest purely between one litigant and another", said Lord Wilberforce, "the task of the court is to do, and be seen to be doing, justice between the parties", for there "is no higher or additional duty to ascertain some independent truth" (*Air Canada v Secretary of State for Trade* [1983] 2 AC 394, 438). What this comment reflects is the traditional nature of the common law trial system in which the judge presides, even with the disappearance of the jury, over an oral process lasting perhaps just a few days (maybe even shorter but sometimes in fact longer). Even in this role the judge's duty was – and indeed remains – largely passive. It is the parties' barristers who call and question the witnesses. The judge, then, is an arbiter and not a controller; he or she decides the questions of fact only with respect to those facts presented to him or her in the courtroom. It is the same with regard to the law. The English judge does not normally do his or her own legal research but decides questions about the law and its application to the facts from legal argument presented to him or her by the barristers (or now solicitors). It is the barristers who are charged with researching the relevant law and they are under a strict professional duty to the court to do this accurately and in good faith (*Copeland v Smith* [2000] 1 WLR 1371).

What worried Lord Woolf about this philosophy was that it seemed to encourage the parties to litigation not 'to put their cards on the table' so to speak. As a result he proposed in his report that the phase before the trial – the pre-trial proceedings – should be governed by a judge who was a specialist in case management. Traditionally this phase was a matter only for the parties – or more usually their solicitors – and this meant that there was often an interest in creating delays and accumulating costs. Lord Woolf also proposed that there should be a single set of procedural rules covering both the High Court and the County Courts and that there should be several procedural 'tracks' depending on the complexity of the litigation and the amount of the claim. For the simplest cases Lord Woolf proposed the use of the small claims procedure before a District Judge in the County Court, such an action attracting an informal procedure. If the sum demanded was modest, but not small, and the case itself not complex, Lord Woolf proposed a 'fast-track' procedure where time and costs would be rigidly controlled. Other cases would follow the 'multi-track' procedure where the pre-trial proceedings would also be strictly controlled. As regards this last category, Lord Woolf thought that it would be restricted just to certain types of case of public importance or (and) where a question of law needed to be tested; the category would also apply to medical compensation claims and cases where there is a right to a jury (defamation).

These reforms proposed by Lord Woolf were welcomed by the government and put into effect by the Civil Procedure Act 1997. A new code of procedural rules was produced whose philosophy is to ensure that the system of justice will be accessible, efficient and fair. Accordingly the first rule of the new Civil Procedure Rules 1998 (CPR) states that a case should be administered above all in a way that is fair.

32. SI ENIM PECUNIAS AEQUARI NON PLACET; SI INGENIA OMNIUM PARIA ESSE NON POSSENT: JURA CERTE PARIA DEBENT ESSE EORUM INTERSE, QUI SUNT CIVES IN EADEM REPUBLICA

If equal wealth is not to everyone's liking; if equal intelligence amongst everyone is not possible: then at least there should be equality regarding the laws amongst citizens in the same state.

(Cicero, *De Republica, I*, 32)

What Lord Woolf underlined as the general principle was that the new procedure should ensure equality between the parties together with greater certainty as to costs. The aim is to provide a system of procedure that will prevent a powerful party from acting in an oppressive and unreasonable manner. One way of achieving this would appear to be the importation into the English common law of the idea that a judge should have a role beyond that of presiding over the actual trial; the pre-trial proceeding should equally be under the control of the judge, something that happens in many civilian systems. In short, there should be a level playing field and the whole process should, perhaps, not become, as Bracton once thought, like a game of chess. One might note, also, that the

Human Rights Act 1998 reinforces this philosophy in as much as article 6 of the European Convention of Human Rights and Fundamental Freedoms guarantees as a constitutional right proper access to the justice system.

The effects of these new procedural rules were beginning to be felt in the case law at the start of the present century. In *Goode v Martin* ([2002] 1 WLR 1828) the claimant (no longer called 'plaintiff' thanks to the new rules), who was suing for damages for injuries suffered in an accident involving a boat owned by the defendant, wanted to modify her statement of claim (formerly called 'pleadings'). The first instance judge refused this modification on the ground that rule 17 of the CPR 1998 seemed to prohibit any such change except in regard to the "same facts" set out in the statement, the judge concluding that the claimant was actually trying to modify the statement of facts. The Court of Appeal allowed an appeal on the basis both of the first rule in the CPR and of article 3(1) of the Human Rights Act 1998, this latter article encouraging a court to interpret a legislative provision in such a manner that it conforms to the European Convention of Human Rights. According to the appeal court it would be unfair to refuse a modification because such a refusal would entail a new legal action which would obviously increase the costs and delay to the claimant.

What is interesting about this decision is that, when compared to a decision given half a century earlier, it is seemingly indicating a change of attitude. In *Esso Petroleum v Southport Corporation* ([1956] AC 218) the House of Lords had refused to allow a claimant to alter its pleadings and add a new cause of action – even although the facts themselves seemed to indicate liability under the proposed new cause of action – on the basis that conforming to the strict rules of procedure would render better justice than being sympathetic to the claimants' substantive rights. The claimant had failed to assert in its pleadings that the defendants owed them a direct (rather than vicarious) duty of care and it was now too late for the claimant to alter the claim. There was probably no clear formal rule preventing such a modification to the pleadings – for according to the Judicature Acts the claimant was probably under an obligation only to state the facts – and thus the reason why the judges took such a formal approach was to be found in the prevailing philosophy of the time. Despite the abolition of the forms of action a century earlier, the attitude that justice was as much a formal process – a game of 'chess' where the right category or categories of liability had to be set out from the beginning so that a defendant need formally answer only these assertions – was still embedded in the common law mentality. Whether Lord Woolf has fully succeeded in re-orientating, in the long-term, the English common law towards a new procedural philosophy no doubt remains to be seen.

Finally with respect to procedural philosophy, mention should perhaps be made of the tribunal system (see above maxim 25) because the procedural philosophy, even before the reform of 2007, was always different from the one associated with traditional civil procedure. An essential characteristic of a tribunal was the much more informal procedural structure and the active roles of the tribunal judges; in other words the tribunals were much less adversarial and this perhaps was one reason for their success. Now that the tribunals have been seemingly elevated into an alternative two-tier court system – and even perhaps into a separate administrative courts regime – it may be that at the level of procedural philosophy a distinction can be made between public and private law procedure. Such a distinction would no doubt be inapplicable to the regime of judicial review and the Administrative Court (a Divisional Court of the KBD), but in terms of statistics many more disputes are dealt with by tribunals than by the Administrative Court.

33.   APPELLANDI USUS QUAM SIT FREQUENS QUAMQUE NECESSARIUS, NEMO EST QUI NESCIAT, QUIPPE CUM INIQUITATEM IUDICANTIUM VEL IMPERITIAM RECORRIGAT

There is not anybody who does not know how the use of appeals is frequent and necessary, above all when they correct the iniquity or incompetence of judges.

(Ulpian, D.49.1.1pr)

Another fundamental motivation underpinning these procedural reforms is the desire to reduce the burden of work on the judges in the Court of Appeal. The new rules are thus designed to deflect the less important appeal work away from the Court of Appeal. To achieve this, a new structure has been put in place in which appeals depend upon the hierarchy of judges. In the civil process an appeal is from one judge to a judge who is immediately superior in the hierarchy and so in principle a case goes from a Circuit Judge (County Court) to a judge in the High Court, although in multi-track cases it would normally still go to the Court of Appeal irrespective of the status of the trial judge. The possibility of a second appeal from a High Court judge to the Court of Appeal still exists, but it will be rare and restricted to cases which give rise to an important point of law or indicate other compelling reasons (*Tanfern Ltd v Cameron-MacDonald (Practice Note)* [2000] 1 WLR 1102). The important development that needs to be stressed here is that there is no longer an automatic right to go to the Court of Appeal, although there are several exceptions; permission of this court has now to be obtained.

Before 1998 an appeal to the Court of Appeal involved a "rehearing" and while this did not mean that the witnesses were reheard (or a jury reconvened) it did mean that the court could make decisions with respect to both fact and law (*Viscount de L'Isle v Times Newspapers* [1988] 1 WLR 49, 62). In other words it was an 'appeal' and not a 'cassation' in the French sense (decision only on a question of law). The whole case itself was reviewed on the basis of the documents (witness statements and the like). The reforms have seemingly changed the orientation from a rehearing to a "review" where the emphasis is now on the judgment of the trial judge and this raises the question as to whether the process has shifted more towards the continental model of a review (cassation) rather than a rehearing of the whole case. In fact it is not clear whether this is a fundamental change since it would be an exaggeration to think that there was ever a clear line between the two notions. However what one can say is that the Court of Appeal will, in theory at least, allow an appeal only where the judge was in error or where there has been a procedural injustice.

As we have seen, a further appeal to the House of Lords was retained in 1875 – and put onto a statutory basis a year later (Appellate Jurisdiction Act 1876) – and so the possibility exists that a case will not end with a decision in the Court of Appeal. However this third tier was always something of a constitutional anomaly because the Law Lords, as members of the House of Lords, were part of a political institution involved with legislation and this violated the principle of the separation of powers, in turn violating the European Convention on Human Rights article 6. Despite the long history of the House of Lords as a legal institution, the government felt that this position could no longer be maintained and this third tier has now become the Supreme Court (Constitutional Reform Act 2005).

Nevertheless access to this third tier is strictly controlled in that permission to appeal must be obtained either from the Court of Appeal or from the Supreme Court itself. The latter procedure is by way of petition which is considered normally by a team of three Supreme Court judges who will allow or reject the petition without giving reasons. The Supreme Court has inherited the jurisdiction of the old House of Lords which in turn had the same jurisdiction as the Court of Appeal; it thus is a genuine appeal court rather than one which strictly reviews the application of the law by the inferior judges. In practice, however, the case must normally raise a point of law of public importance.

34. JUDEX IUDICARE DEBET SECUNDUM ALLEGATA ET PROBATA

The judge must decide according to the pleadings and evidence.

(Baldus, Comment on D.1.18.6)

The notion of an appeal court raises an interesting question. What is the role of an appeal judge in comparison to a judge of first instance? There are a number of ways in which an appeal judgment is now subtly different from a first instance one. Although an appeal court traditionally hears appeals on both questions of fact and questions of law, such a court is always reluctant to interfere with the findings of fact made by a first instance judge who has heard and seen the witnesses (*Watt v Thomas* [1947] AC 484). Jury verdicts are even more difficult, for juries do not give reasons and a verdict cannot normally be quashed simply on the ground of unreasonableness (*Grobbelaar v News Group Newspapers Ltd* [2002] 1 WLR 3024). Moreover, as we have seen, under the new procedural rules an appeal is no longer by way of "rehearing" but by way of "review"; this suggests that there has been a shift of emphasis from the case itself to the appealed judgment under review. However the Court of Appeal have indicated that in practice not all that much has changed (*Assicurazoni Generali SpA v Arab Insurance Group* [2003] 1 WLR 577).

Another reason for the difference between a first instance and appeal judgement is that appeal judgments have a more central role in the precedent system. Thus, according to Lord Diplock: "In a judgment, particularly one that has not been reduced into writing before delivery, a judge, whether at first instance or upon appeal, has his mind concentrated upon the particular facts of the case before him and the course which the oral argument has taken".

Yet even when a case comes before the Court of Appeal this factual dimension must not be lost from view. Lord Diplock thus continued:

> The primary duty of the Court of Appeal on an appeal in any case is to determine the matter actually in dispute between the parties. Such propositions of law as members of the court find necessary to state and previous authorities to which they find it convenient to refer in order to justify the disposition of the actual proceedings before them will be tailored to the facts of the particular case. Accordingly, propositions of law may well be stated in terms either more general or more specific than would have been used if he who gave the judgment had in mind somewhat different facts, or had heard a legal argument more expansive than had been necessary in order to determine the particular appeal.

And he went on to add:

> Even when making successive revisions of drafts of my own written speeches for delivery upon appeals to this House, which usually involve principles of law of wider application than the particular case under appeal, I often find it necessary to continue to introduce subordinate clauses supplementing, or qualifying, the simpler, and stylistically preferable, wording in which statements of law have been expressed in earlier drafts (*Roberts Petroleum Ltd v Bernard Kenny Ltd* [1983] 2 AC 192, 201).

The role of an appeal judge is not, therefore, to assert general principles of law or even general legal rules. It is to fashion a proposition that fits the material facts of the case in hand.

35   COLLEGIALITY IS A VIRTUE THAT ONE HAS TOWARDS ONE'S COLLEAGUES IN A DELIBERATIVE FORUM

Thomas Bustamente (2015) 78 *Modern Law Review* 372, 377

In the civil law tradition it is the court rather than the individual judges that knows the law and renders judgment (*ius novit curia*). There is, in other words, a strong and binding collegiality. In England, with respect to the appeal judgement itself, the tradition that each judge has the right to issue his or her own opinion continues to be the rule. However in practice the Court of Appeal was at one point tending towards issuing a single judgment of the court itself, a practice that was criticised both by academics (Munday 2002) and by Lord Denning (*The Hannah Blumenthal* [1983] 1 AC 854, 873–874). Such a development suggested, again, a shift towards the continental model: the individualism of the common law judge is giving way to the collegiality of the court. In fact if one examines the law reports there are many cases both in the Court of Appeal and in the House of Lords where there is in effect a single judgment because the other judges simply say in their judgments that they agree with the judge issuing a full judgment. More recently, in the Supreme Court, the habit has developed of two or three judges issuing a joint judgment. However, whatever may be the position with regard to the Court of Appeal and Supreme Court, the tradition of independent judgments continues and so there are many cases in which there are several judgments. Moreover it is unlikely that collegiality in the civilian sense of the term will ever become a characteristic of common law procedure since the institution of the dissenting judgment is firmly entrenched in the common law tradition (Kirby 2007).

Nevertheless it would be wrong to dismiss from English law the whole idea of collegiality because it can exist in some weaker forms. In particular the relation between counsel and judges is a close one not just outside of the courts where judges mix professionally and socially with barristers in the Inns of Court, but within the court process as well. The judges rely on counsel to research and to present to them the law, their arguments being tested during the oral debate. In the appeal courts such presentation and argumentation can sometimes seem like an academic seminar with the result that it is not empirically true to say that it is the judges who make the common law. It is in reality a joint effort between barristers and judges and one could say that there is here a kind of professional collegiality, especially in a system where judges are chosen from these practitioners.

Becoming a High Court (and later an appeal) judge in England is not traditionally a profession one chooses after graduating or qualifying and thus one where collegiality is perhaps something of a formal necessity in order to help preserve the bureaucratic nature of applying the law. It is a profession that one might join after many years of practice within a social group that has its own loose kind of collegiality in and around the Inns of Court (which were once colleges). One must also remember that in the early days of the common law there were not many judges, barely into double figures, and so historically one can certainly say there was a corps or 'college' of judges. Today there are many more, but if one focuses just on the senior courts, not as many as in many other European countries' senior courts. However, as John Bell notes, things are perhaps changing; a career pattern is beginning to emerge and the number of judges is increasing substantially (Bell 2006). It is becoming more and more unrealistic to regard judging as a 'cottage industry' in England (Bell 2006: 346). One might note another development. This was the appointment of an academic lawyer (although one with some practical experience) from the Oxford law faculty directly to the Supreme Court (Lord Burrows).

36.   LA PROCÉDURE EST LA FORME DANS LAQUELLE ON DOIT INTENTER LES DEMANDS EN JUSTICE, Y DÉFENDRE, INTERVENIR, INSTRUIRE, JUGER, SE POUVOIR CONTRE LES JUGEMENTS ET LES EXÉCUTER

Procedure is the form in which one must make legal claims in law, defend them, intervene, judge them, appeal against such judgements and enforce them.

(R-J Pothier, *Traité de la procédure civile*, article préliminaire)

Pothier's definition of legal procedure is not that far removed from English law definitions (see Jolowicz 1963: 361). Nevertheless care must be taken because terms such as *procès*, trial, appeal, *renvoi* and *cassation* have their own particular meanings. Accordingly, if one had to choose one single difference between civilian and common law procedure it is, perhaps, to be found in the absence of any idea on the continent of a trial. By 'trial' is meant the notion of a 'day in court' (or series of days) where all the evidence is presented, originally to a jury, witnesses are cross-examined, and the legal arguments are made to the judge, the judge and jury (if there is one) reaching their decisions at the end of these presentations. In other words a trial is a condensed event developed because jurymen had only a limited time period in which they could be away from their normal employment and judges, on circuit from London, had to deal with many cases in each location. The civilian 'process', by contrast, is a much more drawn out event divided up into various stages. In many ways it is more of an inquiry in which the claims and evidence are reduced to a dossier and judgment is given on the contents of this dossier (this is an exaggeration but not much of one). Another important difference, arising out of the distinction between trial and process, is the role of the judge. In continental procedure the judge has a more active role extending over all stages of the process; in English procedure, until 1998 at least, the role of the judge was limited to the trial stage and even here his or her role remained passive as compared to the role of a judge on the continent (although there are exceptions). It is these differences which have given rise to the labels 'inquisitorial' and 'accusatorial' (or adversarial) being applied to civilian and common law procedure respectively (Stein 1984: 36–38)

Judgment rendered in proceedings at first instance may not mark the end of litigation since in all Western legal systems there is the possibility, if not the right, of appeal (see maxim 33). In addition there may be some further possibility of review, if not appeal, from a decision given by the appeal court. Such possibilities assume the existence of a judicial hierarchy – or perhaps pyramid would be a more appropriate metaphor (Cadiet *et al* 2013: 446) – in which there are many courts of first instance forming the base of the pyramid. Above these first instance courts there are courts of appeal which, in the French model in particular, are regionalised. At this level the pyramid is narrower because there are fewer such appeal courts in comparison with first instance ones. Finally there is a single court at the top of the pyramid whose sole function is to review the judgments coming from the appeal courts.

In France, both appeal and review come under the single expression *les voies de recours*. An appeal is where a party asks a tribunal higher up in the pyramid (*une Cour d'appel*) to judge the case a second time and is justified by the idea that judges can be fallible. It assumes, of course, that the judges in the higher court are more competent and experienced. One particular point that needs to be made about an 'appeal' is that it is virtually a second 'process' in that the court can adjudicate on both fact and law (CPC art 561). However such an appeal will in general be governed by the principles *tantum devolutum quantum appellatum* and *tantum devolutum quantum judicatum*: only the litigation judged at first instance can be transported before an appeal court and thus new facts and new points of law cannot in theory be raised (CPC art 561). In practice this rule is subject to certain exceptions (see e.g., CPC art 563).

In England there is only one Court of Appeal in London with a further appeal to the Supreme Court, also in London. In civil law systems, in contrast, the administration of justice tends to be decentralised, even with respect to appeal courts. Thus in France there is not a single *Cour d'appel* situated in the capital; there are regional appeal courts situated in various major towns. In Germany each *Land* has its own appeal structure; there are regional courts which hear some appeals and now higher regional courts acting as final courts of appeal in many cases.

There may also be a reference to a constitutional court if, in any case, a constitutional question emerges from the litigation. Until recently such a reference was impossible in France. However in 2008 the French constitution was changed and thus "when, during the course of a case before a court, it is argued that a legislative provision invades the rights and liberties that the Constitution guarantees, the matter can be submitted to the *Conseil constitutionnel* by way of a reference (*renvoi*) from the *Conseil d'État* or from the *Cour de cassation* which will decide within a fixed time limit" (art 61–1 of the Constitution). Such a reference will not, it must be stressed, decide the actual litigation in issue; that is a question for the civil court. The constitutional court will give a ruling only with regard to the constitutional rights issue.

There is no separate constitutional court in the United Kingdom and so any issues of constitutional law will be decided by the ordinary courts. However with respect to European Union law there was a reference procedure from the English courts to the European Court of Justice (Treaty on the Functioning of the European Union art 267). This was a reference (*renvoi*) and not an appeal because the European Court cannot decide the case itself; it can only give a ruling on the interpretation of European Community law. The role of the European Court is to ensure the uniform interpretation throughout the European Union of community law. Despite Brexit, which has taken the UK out of the EU legal system, the actual idea of a reference procedure is now becoming more established internally in the UK and thus although the UK does not have a constitutional court independent from a supreme court the latter can be described as having a constitutional function.

This role of the European Court is in some ways similar to that of the French *Cour de cassation* whose role is to ensure the uniform interpretation and application of legislation in France. Accordingly the appeal courts in France – and in Germany – are not at the peak of the pyramid. In Germany there is the possibility of a further 'appeal' to a third (federal) level in the hierarchy. However these are not appeals as such, but revision in that the court is not re-judging the case but reviewing the judgments of the appeal court. Consequently if one had to choose one institution that perhaps typifies, if in rather an extreme way, this third level of jurisdiction, it would be the French *Cour de cassation* which has served as something of a model in the civilian world. It was established (largely on the ruins of the old *Parlement de Paris*?) after the Revolution to ensure the uniform application of the *Code civil* in France. Thus its role is *not* that of an appeal court; its role is to review the way a lower court has applied the code and thus the object of its attention is not the litigation as such but the judgment of the *Cour d'appel*.

There is only one *Cour de cassation*, situated in Paris, and its scope of action is procedurally limited: it can in principle do only one of two things. It can reject a *pourvoi en cassation*, thus allowing the judgment of the *Cour d'appel* to stand, or it can quash (*casser*) a decision. If it does the latter it cannot, in principle, substitute its own decision; it has to send the case back to a different *Cour d'appel* from the one from which the case emanated. However, what if the *Cour d'appel* to which the case is sent arrives at the same (quashed) decision as the original appeal court? In this situation a second *pourvoi en cassation* comes before a plenary session (*Assemblée plénière*) of the court and if it quashes the decision it will be sent to yet another *Cour d'appel* which will be bound by the *Cour de cassation*'s interpretation of the law. The court is now divided into six chambers; and there is also a new procedure whereby the court can give an advisory opinion and in certain cases make its own decisions.

One can see therefore that, despite the three-tied court structure in England and in France, the Supreme Court and the *Cour de cassation* are rather different institutions. Indeed some even argue that the *Cour de cassation* is not actually a 'court' but an institution that oversees the interpretation and application of legislation. In other words, it is a legislative body rather than a court. However many of the judges in this institution would probably not agree with this assessment. Whatever the situation, the United Kingdom Supreme Court is not a review court as such but an appeal court which can render its own decisions. It can therefore decide issues that would formerly have been decided by a jury (see e.g., *Bolton* v *Stone* [1951] AC 850). However, this said, the Supreme Court hears only around eighty or ninety cases a year (maybe fewer) whereas the *Cour de cassation* deals with over twenty five thousand cases every year. Another difference is to be found in the style and structure of the judgments issuing from the two systems. In the case of all English courts the judgments are usually individualised and very discursive. In contrast, the *Cour de cassation* renders only one short and terse judgment set out in the form of a syllogism (although it is now slightly more expansive than it was). In order to appreciate the substantive reasons as to why the French court has decided the way it has the researcher will need to examine the reports of both the *juge rapporteur* and Advocate-General plus the academic commentary in the law journals (Lasser 2004).

37. IUS GENTIUM EST, QUO GENTES HUMANAE UTUNTUR

> *The* ius gentium *is what all peoples everywhere use.*
>
> (Ulpian, D.1.1.4)

One characteristic that has emerged from the comparisons so far is that the Romano-canonical model is said to be inquisitorial while the common law adheres to an accusatorial or adversarial procedure. The accusatorial procedure is normally characterised as being public, oral and contradictory (which means that the accused is free to rebut during the trial the arguments raised against him by the accuser); whereas the inquisitorial is secret, written and non-contradictory (which means that the accused will be able to defend himself only at a certain moment in the process) (Stein 1984: 36–8). In fact the labels are misleading since the civilian process now has an accusatorial dimension and there are aspects of English law that seem more inquisitorial than adversary (family law cases involving children for example). As for secrecy, English judges and politicians are probably in no position any longer to lecture other nations. This said, both in the French and the German models there are certain general principles to be found in the codes of procedure which act as foundational starting points for the modern process. In Germany civil procedure is regulated by the *Zivilproßordnung* (ZPO) and in France by the *Code de Procédure civile* (CPC). Are these principles really any different from those that underpin the procedural philosophy of the common law? Are there some basic procedural rules in Western law that come together to form a transnational (*ius gentium*) set of principles? There are certainly a number of what appear to be such common principles.

The first principle is a requirement, on the part of the parties, of a legitimate interest in the proceedings. It is probably true to say that it is a general principle throughout the civil law that only those persons who have a legitimate interest in a case can be a party to proceedings (see maxim 121: *pas d'intérêt, pas d'action*). This rule is quite specific in French law where only those with such an interest can bring or defend an action (CPC art 31). In English law there is such a requirement in respect of a judicial review action, but there does not seem to be a specific procedural rule requiring such an interest in private law claims. However the reason for this absence is that the substantive law which lies behind most common law remedies will itself preclude those without a sufficient interest from bringing a claim. Thus an action in negligence requires a duty of care to exist between the parties and in most tort and contract claims there is a requirement that the victim suffers damage (see recently *George v Cannell* [2024] UKSC 19). For example in a claim for public nuisance or breach of statutory duty the claimant must be able to show special damage over and above the damage suffered by the public in general. This interest, or standing, question has become particularly acute when "more and more frequently the complexity of modern societies generates situations in which a single human action can be beneficial or prejudicial to large numbers of people, thus making entirely inadequate the traditional scheme of litigation as merely a two-party affair" (Cappelletti 1989: 271). A commercial organisation pollutes the environment: who has standing to sue? A seller hugely profits by committing a fraud on his customers but each individual customer suffers only a minute loss: does this mean no one can sue for lack of a sufficient interest? These are important access to justice questions which affect both the civil and the common law.

A second overriding principle to be found in civilian procedure is that civil proceedings are subject to party control (see maxim 34: *Judex secundum allegata et probata partium judicare debet*). Thus the French procedural code states in its first article that except where the law provides otherwise, only the parties can institute proceedings (*l'instance*). And they are free to put an end to the proceedings before they are extinguished by the effect of judgment or by law. A similar principle is to be found in German law. It should be noted, however, that once a case is before a judge, the latter is usually required to make a decision independently of any initiative taken by the parties (see e.g., CPC arts 7, 12). What the judge must not do is to make a decision *ultra petita* (see e.g., CPC art 7). This emphasis on the parties principle is undoubtedly true of English law as well since it is an essential characteristic of the accusatorial model.

Thirdly, there is now a principle of orality in the civil law and so despite the fundamental importance of the dossier in Romano-canonical, and in modern, continental civil procedure, the right to an oral hearing has become a basic procedural principle. Parties must have the right to present facts, evidence and legal arguments orally in court. However in practice this right does not seem to be that important, partly because there is not a legal tradition of cross-examination of witnesses in public in front of a jury. Indeed in France hearings before the full court are brief and it is not common for lawyers to present their arguments of law orally. The *dossier* remains the basis of French procedure and in Germany written presentation and written documentation is the norm. In English law the principle of orality has receded to some extent, especially with respect to appeal proceedings (Zander 2007: 682–685). Since 1983 there has been a requirement that counsel should provide to the Court of Appeal a written document briefly setting out the arguments that they intended to use (Practice Direction [1983] 2 All ER 34) and this requirement followed a similar development with regard to the House of Lords. Today these skeleton arguments are now an important part of the civil process, but, this said, the judges still see oral argument as a central feature of the litigation process (*Khader v Aziz* [2010] 1 WLR 2673, paras 37, 52).

Fourthly, proceedings are subject to the principle of contradiction. This principle is basically a translation into a procedural rule of the maxim *audi alteram partem* (hear the other side) and so for example the French procedural code specifically states that judgment shall not be given against a party who has not been summoned (CPC art 14) and that the "parties must inform each other within a reasonable time of the grounds of fact on which they base their claims or defences, the evidence that they adduce and the legal grounds they invoke, so that each can be in a position to organise his claims and defences"

(CPC art 15). If the judge bases his decision on legal grounds that he has raised *ex officio*, he can only do this "if he has first invited the parties to give their observations" (art 16). A similar principle is found in German civil procedure and the maxim *audi alteram partem* has central importance not just in English procedural law but equally in English substantive administrative law. Judges are normally very reluctant to rule on any matter that has not been properly argued before them.

Finally, there is the principle of publicity: as a general rule all hearings are in public although there are exceptions. The French procedural code accordingly states that the "hearings are in public, except in cases where the law requires or permits that they take place in camera" (art 22). Once again there is no doubt that this maxim applies equally to the English common law (CPR r 39.2(1)), but as the French rule indicates it is often rather meaningless in its scope in that the second half of the rules goes far in negating the first half. The law is able to require that proceedings take place in secret (CPR r 39.2(3)). Moreover there is now a true 'secret court' – or more precisely a 'secret tribunal' – in which cases are heard involving the security services. This is the Investigatory Powers Tribunal established under Section 65 of the Regulation of Investigatory Powers Act 2000. In fact the situation turns out to be complex in English law because although there are now situations where proceedings are indeed held in camera there are also a range of intermediary situations. Thus there are powers for the courts to restrict the reporting of cases (see Contempt of Court Act 1981 s 11), even if under the Convention of Human Rights (art 10) this restriction must be balanced against the right of freedom of expression.

38. ADVOCATORUM OFFICIUM NECESSARIUM EST IN IUDICIIS

> *In litigation, advocates are necessary.*
>
> (Tancred, *Ordo iudiciarius* 1.5pr, 111)

As the 13th-century maxim reveals, the legal profession has a history going back to medieval times (see Brundage 2008). And so, in addition to legal procedure itself, mention needs to be made of what might be called legal services in general, for very, very few legal issues and disputes ever reach the courts. The questions is this. What lies between a legal dispute and access to the courts? The answer is a range of legal, quasi-legal and non-legal services. These services are provided by people and institutions which, in recent years, have become much more diverse as a result of quite fundamental changes in the structure of the legal professions and the funding of litigation.

The starting point is the legal profession or, more precisely in England, the legal professions. In England and Wales this group of legal professionals has been divided into two each of which enjoyed monopolies during the 20th century. Barristers as a legal profession have a long history associated with the Inns of Court which date back to the end of the 13th century. A century later there were four such Inns – Gray's Inn, Lincoln's Inn, Inner Temple and Middle Temple – and during the 17th century only members of these Inns could practice in the common law courts. These practitioners were professional advocates who not only acted as the intermediaries between litigants and judges but became the specialists of procedure and substantive law with the result that the tradition developed of appointing judges only from these advocates. During the 19th century the rule emerged that barristers could not be hired directly by a litigant but had to be appointed by a solicitor.

This second group of professionals grew out of the rather diverse history of English practitioners in as much as there existed by the 17th century various classes of professionals, one of which was the class of 'solicitors' who solicited clients by helping them through the procedural complexities of the law. At first there was no clear distinction between barristers and solicitors but gradually a division of functions led to a separation with the solicitors becoming a fully professional body with the establishment of the Law Society, in the 19th century. This professional body was subsequently confirmed by statute (Supreme Court of Judicature Act 1873 s 87).

The monopolies enjoyed in England by the profession during the last century were court representation for barristers (advocacy) and conveyancing (sale and transfer of title in land) for solicitors. These two areas of work still define the essence of being a barrister and a solicitor, although the scope of work for solicitors has always been very much wider than just dealing with the transfer of real property. Generally speaking solicitors were the professionals in control of the pre-trial proceedings while barristers handled the trial stage. Solicitors also offered general legal advice and service – they are sometimes compared with the General Practitioner (GPs) in the medical profession – and, with the growth of the large city practices, this advice became more and more specialised. It is the solicitors firms that are now the experts on large areas of commercial and international commercial law. Barristers, as well as being advocates, were equally often specialists in particular areas of law and thus were often hired by solicitors to provide counsel's opinion on a point of law for a client. If one continues the medical analogy, barristers were and are sometimes regarded as the specialist consultants. This pattern of work has not changed that much, although the growth of large city firms of solicitors has rendered the medical analogy a little obsolete. However the laws that enshrined the pattern as monopolies have changed with the result that the 21st century may turn out to look rather different from a legal services point of view than the previous century.

The Conservative government that came to power in 1979 was largely in favour of economic liberalism and thus had a distrust of all monopolies which they regarded as anti-competitive. Both the court representation and the conveyancing monopolies were progressively loosened (Courts and Legal Services Act 1990; Access to Justice Act 1999) and the regulation of each profession has also been subject to quite dramatic change. The professions are now supervised by an independent board (Legal Services Act 2007). In addition the traditional business structures have been subject to reform. Barristers cannot form partnerships and so operate as individual contractors working in groups known as chambers traditionally within an Inn of Court. Solicitors can form partnerships – even limited liability ones – but now there is the opportunity to create licensed alternative business structures in which other non-law firms can invest (Legal Services Act 2007). There is the possibility that household banking and supermarket institutions might open law centres within their own premises and this new development has attracted the name 'Tesco law' (after the large supermarket called Tesco). Developments are at an early stage and these new structures are not without their critics. Is the provision of legal services to be regarded as no different to the provision of baked beans? Even if law services are different from the provision of other services, there is no doubt that many regard the service provided by English professionals as governed by market forces. The large city firms of solicitors now have a major international presence and can be seen as, amongst other things, selling English law as a commodity. As for 'Tesco law', this still has not really materialised. There are law centres and university law clinics providing advice for those who cannot afford solicitors (who are on the whole extremely expensive), but widespread legal centres in shopping centres do not seem to be prevalent.

39.   SI NON HABEBUNT ADVOCARTUM, ERGO DABO

> *If they do not have an advocate, I will provide one.*

> (Ulpian, describing the Praetor's Edict, D.3.1.1.4)

Accordingly, these Alternative Business Structures will no doubt provide a high-quality service to the commercial community. But what about the other classes? What about the ordinary people of limited, sometimes very limited, financial means? What if they cannot afford to consult or employ a lawyer? (In Roman law, it would appear that the state magistrate, the Praetor, would provide one thus suggesting an early form of legal aid.) Here the situation in English law is more complex. Various models of funding are possible. At one extreme of course there is the neo-liberal model in which financing is left entirely to the market and if this results in exclusion of a large class of persons so be it. Law is simply no different than a luxury hotel: it is open to all who can afford it. However this model attracts two serious criticisms. The first is that law is not like a luxury hotel; it is a fundamental social institution founded upon the idea that all are equal before the law and thus nobody should be excluded from its services on the ground of economic circumstances. A second, and linked, criticism is that equal access is seemingly guaranteed as a human right under article 6 of the European Convention of Human Rights and Fundamental Freedoms. It is arguable that the state is obliged to ensure such access.

How can such access be achieved? If one moves from the neo-liberal model to the other extreme, the state could provide legal aid to all those who cannot afford access themselves. At this extreme the cost would be demand led; that is to say legal aid would be available to fund any litigant without means who wanted to pursue a reasonable case. England went far in establishing such a scheme with the Legal Aid and Advice Act 1949. However, as Lord Bingham in a brief but informative survey indicated this model encountered problems in respect both of its huge cost and of the classes that it excluded. It served the poorest well, but not those of modest means (*Callery v Gray* [2001] 1 WLR 2112, para 1). This led to a change of model; a scheme was introduced that shifted the focus off funding litigation to funding service providers by way of contract between a Legal Aid Board and firms of solicitors. When this also proved unsatisfactory in respect of personal injury claims the government moved to a model whereby the cost was placed on the service providers themselves, including insurance companies (Access to Justice Act 1999). This was achieved through the conditional fee agreement and insurance whereby the solicitor firm of the successful party can claim not just its costs but an uplift fee (Lord Bingham in *Callery v Gray*, paras 2–6; see also Lord Hope paras 47–54). The government has now restricted to an absolute minimum state provided legal aid (Legal Aid, Sentencing and Punishment of Offenders Act 2012); the model will thus be one where access to justice is to be facilitated only through schemes provided by the legal service providers and litigants themselves. In other words the move is towards a neo-liberal model.

The provision of financial legal aid to poor litigants is not the only method through which legal services can be financed. Reducing the costs of legal services and litigation is another method and so the recent legal aid reforms have to be viewed in the context of the reform of civil procedure and of business structures. In addition the legal service providers, and other institutions, can offer schemes such as free advice and low cost aid to the less well off. In addition one must not forget that litigants themselves are not legally obliged to employ solicitors and barristers; they can act as litigants in person (LIPs) often with the aid of a friend (*McKenzie v McKenzie* [1970] 3 All ER 1034). In the small claims court this probably works well enough, at least with respect to debt claims. In the higher courts a LIP can put the judge in an awkward position because such a LIP can often require court assistance in presenting a case.

CONCLUDING REMARKS

One can easily conclude that the history of English law is largely a history of procedure. Such a conclusion is in many ways a fair one, and certainly accurate with regard to the reforms of English law in the 19th century. As Henry Maine said, "substantive law has at first the look of being gradually secreted in the interstices of procedure" (1890: 389); and this is true not just of the period of the forms of action but in many ways the 19th century as well. For, with the abolition of the forms of action and a new procedural structure, English law was forced to rethink aspects of its substantive law. Procedure cannot, of course, be seen as something separate from remedies and so one will be returning to the relationship between actions and substantive law in a later chapter. More immediately, if one had to emphasise one contemporary problem, it is the cost of litigation; and this is a problem that Lord Woolf tried to tackle in his report at the end of the last century. What is to be regretted is the failure of this objective, as Lord Neuberger explained. It might be appropriate, therefore, to end this chapter with his observation:

> One of the main, and laudable, aims of the proposals made by Lord Woolf in his report *Access to Justice* (1996), which led to the enactment of the Civil Procedure Act 1997, and the introduction of the Civil Procedure Rules the following year, was to try and achieve a better relationship between the costs and benefits of litigation. As the figures in this case show, and as is reflected in many other cases, that target has not merely proved elusive, but it is often missed by a very wide margin indeed. It is, of course, easy to criticise, and, having been Master of the Rolls until 2013, I am as aware as anyone how hard it is to ensure that a case, particularly one that does not involve a very large sum of money but is potentially complex in terms of fact, law and expertise, such as the present case, is both properly and proportionately litigated. It is also right to acknowledge that the reforms proposed by Sir Rupert Jackson in 2010, which do not apply to this case, have been largely introduced and are being absorbed. Nonetheless, even without the effect of Part II of the 1999 Act, to which I must shortly turn, it would be wrong for this Court not to express its grave concern about the base costs in this case, and express the hope that those responsible for civil justice in England and Wales are considering what further steps can be taken to ensure better access to justice. It is only fair to emphasise that this concern relates to the current system and that it is not intended to imply any criticism of the lawyers in this case (*Coventry v Lawrence (No 2)* [2014] UKSC 46, para 36).

4. Legal taxonomy and legal theory

Having looked at the courts and procedure, something must now be said about substantive law. As will be seen in a later chapter, the division between substantive law and procedure is not always an easy one to determine, given the important role of legal remedies in the common law tradition. But what is vital before looking in depth at the substantive material of the law is to have an overall vision or 'map' of the various areas. How is law divided up? Or, to put it another way, what are the various categories and sub-categories of law?

40. HUIUS STUDII DUAE SUNT POSITIONES, PUBLICUM ET PRIVATUM. PUBLICUM IUS EST QUOD AD STATUM REI ROMANAE SPECTAT, PRIVATUM QUOD AD SINGULORUM UTILITATEM

> *In this study [of law] there are two categories, public and private. Public is what concerns the Roman state, private what concerns the interests of individuals.*

> (Ulpian D.1.1.1.2)

One of the defining features of civil law is the distinction between public and private law. As we shall see (maxim 41 below), the spirit and internal structure of private law were given textual permanence first by the *Institutiones* of Justinian (and of course Gaius) and, secondly, by the civil codes of Europe, but there was no general code to be found in the Roman sources covering the whole of public law. And although the category of *ius publicum* stands at the forefront of the *Digest,* the Romans did not give it much substance as a system. Public law as a domain is therefore a relatively modern creation in terms of its substance yet very old in terms of its form. By this is meant that the category itself is to be found in the Roman sources, and many of its building blocks have equally been extracted from these sources (see Chapter 5). However, the spirit and structure of public law, as it exists in the civilian tradition today, is not that old. It is a spirit that has developed very slowly over the last millennium and very generally might be said to be about the gradual control of naked political power by the law. As one Roman law specialist once noted, "it is on this one text [of Ulpian], probably of no importance to Roman lawyers themselves, that a great modern edifice has been built" (Jolowicz 1957: 53). Nevertheless, the very general definition provided by Ulpian remains of much relevance: the emphasis on the distinction between the two classes of interests – those of the state and those of individuals – is a dichotomy that underpins modern legal, political and economic thinking.

41.   OMNE IUS QUO UTIMUR VEL AD PERSONAS PERTINET VEL AD RES VEL AD ACTIONES

All law that we use consists of persons, of things or of actions.

(Gaius, *Institutes*, 1.8; D.1.5.1)

When one turns to private law, Gaius' institutional plan is of immense importance in the history of legal thought (see Stein 1984: 125–129; 1999: 18–20). It underpins Western legal thinking, and common lawyers cannot escape from its influence. In fact, what Gaius, a second-century jurist, produced was not so much a plan of the whole of law but a plan of private law. A legal system sub-divides into three main categories: the law of persons, the law of things and the law of actions. Each of these three sub-divisions further divides into sub-subcategories, and so the process continues downwards. One should note, however, that the great *summa divisio* between public and private law (above maxim 40) is not really treated by Gaius in his *Institutes*. Gaius' plan was adopted by Justinian in his *Institutes* published centuries later, and it was this book that brought the plan into later Europe.

By modern standards, the scheme itself remained somewhat incomplete, and it was subsequent European civil lawyers who refined the structure and its contents. Nevertheless, the basic scheme of thought was created by the Roman jurists, and although at first sight it might seem somewhat bland, the scheme remains possibly the most important conceptual development ever to be made in legal thought. The late Professor Birks (1941–2004) described it as the 'software' programme for all law.

There is a range of reasons why the scheme is fundamental. First, it was a comprehensive classification of rules. The scheme succeeded in encompassing all private law norms, and thus one can take almost any private law rule from any system – including English law – and it can, more or less, be made to fit into this Gaian scheme. Indeed, the 18th-century English jurist Sir William Blackstone (1723–1780) did just this: his *Commentaries on the Laws of England* is an institutional work.

Secondly, it made a distinction between patrimonial and non-patrimonial rights. Now the point must be made at once that although the Romans did not think in terms of 'rights' as we presently understand the term, the distinction between persons and things represents a difference between laws dealing with 'rights' (*iura*) which attach to people and are inalienable (cannot in theory be sold) and 'rights' attaching to things which are alienable. The distinction thus represents the difference between constitutional and social rights on the one hand and commercial law on the other. An argument today about whether one can sell one's body parts is simply an argument about whether they are patrimonial (things) or non-patrimonial (persons). Moreover, certain aspects of the law of persons such as status have been attractive categories for English jurists (see e.g., Graveson 1953). In fact there is even an official recognition of the category; status is "the condition of belonging to a class in society to which the law ascribes peculiar rights and duties, capacities and incapacities" (*The Ampthill Peerage* case [1977] AC 547, 577).

Thirdly, the Gaian scheme was centred on institutions. That is to say, the 'person', 'thing' and 'action' are focal points for legal rules in that each exists at one and the same time in the world of fact and the world of law. Thus, persons and things are the object of attention by both sociologists and lawyers, and consequently they act as the means of moving from the world of fact and reality (for example, drivers, cars and victims) to the world of law (legal personality and property). Actions can be seen as having a social reality in courts and enforcement procedures (dispute resolution and remedies). Gaius' scheme, therefore, represents a bridge between factual reality and law. It is the means by which law attaches itself to social reality and social reality expresses itself in law. However, it is more than just a set of institutions with a real and conceptual existence.

A fourth reason, then, why the Gaian scheme is fundamental to Europe is that it was, and remains, a system. Just as the system of mathematics can create minus numbers, the notion of a thing (*res*) can be extended from a physical thing (*res corporalis*) to an intangible thing (*res incorporalis*). The same is true for a person (*persona*): this can be extended from a physical person to a legal person (corporation), which of course has no physical existence (see maxims 66–67). Actions also have their role here. For example, the moment one says that a town can sue in its own right (that is that the town can bring an action), the scheme has effectively turned the town into a 'person', a point seemingly recognised by Gaius himself (D.50.16.16). These developments enabled the construction of a public and a commercial law in later Europe; and they are at the heart of what it is to reason like a lawyer (see maxim 66).

A fifth reason why the scheme is important is that it amounted to an exercise of what today we would call scientific reductionism. Gaius himself insists on the importance of generic and specific categories and the need not to confuse them; and the use of this scheme allows him to build a conceptually complete ('scientific') structure of law from the basic subdivision of law into three parts down to the lowest and most detailed category. His scheme is not just internally *coherent* but, via the categories of persons, things and actions, all aspects of law are brought together under the single concept of law (*ius*). The later civil lawyers did not have a complete copy of Gaius, and thus many of his ideas came into modern Europe through the *Institutes of Justinian* and through extracts preserved in the *Digest* (on which see Stein 1999: 32–36). The key work was therefore Justinian's rather than Gaius' *Institutes*. However, an almost complete copy of Gaius was discovered in 1816, and there remain in print today translations in several European languages.

The scheme did not quite survive unaltered. In the 16th century, the jurist Hugues Doneau (1527–1591) was very critical of the way the Romans had failed to distinguish properly the law of actions from substantive law; they had put the means of obtaining a judgment, that is to say, the method by which we obtain our right, before teaching us what our right was (*Ergo iudicium, iuris nostri obtinendi rationem, informant prius, quam, quid esset iuris nostri, quod in iudicum deducere possemus, nos docuissent*) (*Commentarii de Jure Civili*, Book I, Chapter 1, para 2). Doneau thus removed actions from the three-fold plan and replaced them with the law of obligations. In fact, the two categories – obligations and actions – were actually combined in the Digest (D.44.7) and thus provided the jurist with some authority for his change. Today, then, modern civilians, in their civil codes, divide private law into persons, property and obligations, the latter category having been part of the law of things in Gaius and Justinian.

42.   YOUR LORDSHIPS' TASK IN THIS HOUSE IS
        TO DECIDE PARTICULAR CASES BETWEEN
        LITIGANTS AND YOUR LORDSHIPS ARE NOT
        CALLED UPON TO RATIONALISE THE LAW OF
        ENGLAND. THAT ATTRACTIVE IF PERILOUS
        FIELD MAY WELL BE LEFT TO OTHER HANDS
        TO CULTIVATE.

(Lord Macmillan in *Read v J Lyons & Co* [1947] AC 156, 175)

The interesting question, of course, is the extent to which the Ulpian and Gaian plans apply to the common law. The judges seem indifferent, if Lord Macmillan is to be believed. However, Professor Birks thought that it did, since he considered that the system transcended Rome to become a scientific structure applicable as a universal 'truth' (or at least until someone came up with a better plan). There is no doubt that some aspects of English law appear to conform to the categories in the Roman scheme. Thus, for example constitutional and administrative law make up one of the foundational subjects of the Common Professional Examination, namely Public Law; and three other categories, Property, Obligations I (contract) and Obligations II (tort), seem Roman. In the Roman scheme, these three latter categories were part of the law of things, but property and obligations formed the two major sub-categories within things and this was reinforced by the principal sub-division in the law of actions between an *actio in rem* and an *actio in personam*. The first action was used to enforce a claim to an item of property based upon ownership (or some other property right such as a servitude) and was a remedy aimed at the thing itself. The second was a personal action aimed at another person and based on the existence of a binding obligation described by Justinian as a *vinculum iuris* (legal chain) (see maxim 83). The paradigm binding obligation was a contract (see maxims 85–86).

At a certain level, then, the common law seems to use Roman categories and sub-categories. Yet on closer examination, there are problems. The boundaries between the various categories – for example, between persons and things and between property and obligations – are by no means watertight. Indeed, in English law, the law of property as a subject area is confined to land law, and the distinction between real and movable (personal) property was not of fundamental importance in the Roman scheme (see maxim 76). Moreover, in English law, many of the remedies for protecting both real and personal property rights are to be found in the law of tort, which, of course, is part of the law of obligations. In fact, English law has no *actio in rem* as such, all 'real' actions having fallen into disuse in the 14th century. The same is true for some 'law of persons' rights; there is often nothing to distinguish a non-patrimonial right from a patrimonial right since most claims sound in the law of tort. For example, the remedies for harassment are part of the law of tort, and there are even cases that seem to intermix status, contract, property and tort (see, e.g., *Stevenson* v *Beverley Bentinck Ltd* [1976] 1 WLR 483).

In addition to this lack of 'scientific' precision, there is the well-entrenched division between Law and Equity, the latter forming one of the Common Professional Examination categories (maxim 17). Equity is a legal category completely unknown to the civil law systems. This is not to say that civilians have no understanding of the Aristotelian notion of 'equity'; what they do not understand is the rationality of formally distinguishing between two systems of law, namely Common Law and Equity. Thus, the idea that a single item of property can be owned at one and the same time by two different people – an owner at common law and an owner in equity (for example, the trust) – makes no sense to someone brought up in the Roman tradition because ownership is seen as indivisible (see maxim 79). The distinction between common law remedies and equitable remedies must seem strange as well (see maxim 118). Another oddity is the idea that one can be the 'owner' of money in another's patrimony (that is to say in another's bank account). It is a fundamental principle of the civil law that money is a consumable item, like bread, and so when handed over to another by way, for example, of a loan this latter person becomes the owner of it. The borrower's liability is simply one sounding in the law of obligations (debt) and not in the law of property. However, the Court of Chancery was prepared to see trust money fraudulently transferred to a third party as being 'owned' by the trust and thus capable of being 'traced' by the owner (see maxim 118).

Nevertheless, these difficulties do not seem to deter academic lawyers from attempting to apply, from time to time, the Roman institutional scheme to the common law. What was important about the renewed attempt by Birks to impose the plan of Justinian's *Institutes* on the common law is that it indicates that, at a certain level, legal theory is still flirting with Roman legal science. This flirtation is not universally accepted. Jeffrey Hackney has shown how meaningless it is to impose the Roman institutional structure on the old forms of action thinking (Hackney 1997: 136–138) and Stephen Waddams (1942–2023) observed that the "variety of maps produced since Blackstone's time shows that precision in legal map making has been elusive" (Waddams 2003: 21). More importantly, Waddams' own research into the categories and concepts used by courts since Blackstone's time led him to conclude that "it has not been possible to explain Anglo-American private law in terms of any single concept, nor has any map, scheme, or diagram proved satisfactory in which the concepts are separated from each other, as on a two-dimensional plane". Thus a single-minded search for precision in law is likely to be self-defeating (Waddams 2003: 226, 231).

Yet, as we have said, some academics and indeed even some UK judges continue to flirt with Roman legal science on the basis that the common law lacks taxonomical coherence (see for example Descheemaeker 2009). Reform of the law means reform of the law books. Whatever the merits of this kind of thinking – much of it, arguably, is epistemologically suspect (Samuel 2000, 2004) – structure and taxonomy have been topics that bring together legal thought in the civil and the common law. It is an area of legal thought that was once central to 'jurisprudence' but has now been relegated from legal theory to, largely, private law. Legal theory as a subject may have moved well beyond the debates of the 19th century and might reasonably be described, or some of it at least, as quite forward-looking. Debate amongst private lawyers is, in contrast, more backward-looking and, as such, is continually drawing on (consciously or unconsciously) the history of the civil law.

43.   ÆQUITAS PARS LEGIS ANGLIÆ

Equity is part of English law.

(Lofts' Reports 497)

It has already been seen how the distinction between Law and Equity is funda-mental to English law as a result of the development of the Court of Chancery (see maxims 17–18). At the level of procedure, the two regimes are now inte-grated in the sense that any court can dispense both law and equity, although there remains something of an institutional difference within the High Court. Common law problems are usually heard in the King's Bench Division while litigation involving areas of law that have been fashioned by the Court of Chancery are heard in the Chancery Division, which, of course, consists of judges who are specialists in equity law. Thus, legal problems involving trusts or, say, intellectual property will go before this latter division because these areas of law were developed in the old Court of Chancery.

The distinction between Law and Equity probably makes little sense as a *summa divisio* to those raised within the civil (Roman) law tradition, and it seems to make little sense as well to some brought up in the common law envi-ronment. If one were designing a legal system from scratch it would, it must be said, be unlikely that one would adopt this divide as a starting point. Its existence, as we have seen, is a result of the vagaries of history. And, as jurists like to think that their subject is rational and internally coherent, a distinction that appears not to be based on a rational foundation is unlikely to be viewed favourably. But is equity as a legal category devoid of all rationality?

The late Bernard Rudden (1933–2015) thought not. He wrote that the com-mon lawyers might well have preserved equity as a separate entity in order to have an 'alibi effect' (Rudden 1992). Perhaps this point can be illustrated by cases in which equity has been able to come to the aid of parties in private law where a common law rule seems to have created a logical impasse. In *Sinclair v Brougham* ([1914] AC 398), a bank carried on a business which turned out to be ultra vires, which meant that all the contracts between the bank and credi-tors were void. When the depositors argued that they should be able to obtain repayment via a debt claim in quasi-contract (an action for money had and received) (see maxim 112), they were met with the argument that such claims were based on an implied contract, and such contracts were equally void. The House of Lords, however, was able to get around this logical impasse by hav-ing recourse to equity. There was, it must be said, considerable variation in the way the Law Lords in *Sinclair* dealt with the problem in equity, with two judges holding that there was a resulting trust while another thought that there was a broad equity of restitution (see *Westdeutsche Landesbank Girozentrale*

v *Islington LBC* [1996] AC 669, at 686–689). Yet here was an almost perfect example of equity as alibi. When a debt claim at common law finds itself
blocked, there is always the possibility of an account claim in equity (*Att-Gen
v Blake* [2001] 1 AC 268). Or, indeed, through the enforcement of the common law debt – unenforceable at common law because, say, of the privity of
contract rule – by means of the equitable remedy of specific performance of a
contract (*Beswick* v *Beswick* [1968] AC 58). In another case, unknown to the
sellers of a piece of land to a property company, after an exchange of contracts
but before conveyance, the property company successfully sought planning
permission using the name of the sellers. This resulted in the land becoming
far more valuable than the contractual sale price. Only after the conveyance
did the sellers discover what had happened, and they brought a claim both in
damages (common law) and an account of profits (equity). They were unable
to succeed at common law because silence is not a misrepresentation; equity,
however, came to their rescue in that the account of profits claim succeeded
(*English* v *Dedham Vale Properties Ltd* [1978] 1 WLR 93). What equity provided in all of these cases was a taxonomical alibi.

Some might still regard this dichotomy between law and equity as indefensi-
ble. Does it not make.the law uncertain by having two sets of rules, often, some
would say, contradicting each other? Does it not make the law too complex?
Yet one equity specialist has written recently that were the two categories of
law to be merged, "we would lose many vital mechanisms in the law, especially the trust", and so while more cooperation between the two areas might
be desirable, "this should not extend to total assimilation" (Virgo in Barnard,
O'Sullivan & Virgo 2021: 148). One wonders, also, whether complete assimilation would actually be possible. The legal device of a trust is based on the
idea of two separate forms of ownership, one at common law (trustee) and one
in equity (beneficiary).

As a member of the House of Lords commented in an 1873 debate: "are
you going to abolish trusts?" These distinctions, he said, cannot be abolished (see Tiley 1968: 8). John Tiley also warned that one should not confuse a conflict between rules with a difference between rules. Conflicts do
occasionally occur, he said, but often there are just differences (1968: 20–21).

44.   PRIVATUM IUS TRIPERTITUM EST: COLLECTUM ETENIM EST EX NATURALIBUS PRAECEPTIS AUT GENTIUM AUT CIVILIBUS

Private law is threefold: it is derived from rules from natural law, from the law of peoples and from the civil law.

(Ulpian D.1.1.1.2)

What of law itself? Can bodies of law be divided up into different kinds? The Romans certainly thought so, and their categorisation was adopted and continued for many centuries after the rediscovery of Justinian's compilation in the 11th century. According to Ulpian, the *ius naturale* is the law that has been taught by nature to all animals and so is not confined to humans; it includes, for example, the union of male and female for the purposes of procuration (D.1.1.1.3). The *ius gentium* is the law used by all societies of people and is to be distinguished from natural law in that it is restricted to humans and their mutual relations (D.1.1.1.4). The civil law is law that is not fully independent of the *ius naturale* and the *ius gentium* but, equally, is not subordinate to these laws. Ulpian then goes on to say that when we make additions or deductions from these 'common laws' (*iuri communi*) we establish our own law (*ius proprium*), that is to say, the civil law (D.1.1.6). It is worth noting at once that Ulpian, in the language he used, was suggesting, perhaps unconsciously, two other legal categories that were to have their own histories in the subsequent history of Roman law in Europe. These were the categories of the *ius commune* and the *ius proprium*.

The expressions *ius commune* (*communi omnium hominum iure*) and *ius proprium* are also to be found in Gaius (G.1.1), although he does not mention the *ius naturale* as an independent category. One can see in these Roman texts a very rich vocabulary which was to act as the foundation for a range of legal theories in the history of legal thought in Europe.

45.   IUS GENTIUM POTEST VOCARI IUS NATURALE,
        SECUNDUM VERUM SIGNIFICATUM. (NAM CUM
        VERBUM NATURALE REFERTUR AD RATIONEM,
        INTELLIGITUR DE IURE GENTIUM. NAM NON
        EST COMMUNE ANIMALIBUS CARENTIBUS
        RATIONE)

The ius gentium can be called the ius naturale, according to true meaning.
For when the word natural refers to reason it is to be understood in terms of
the ius gentium. *This is because it is not common to animals that lack reason.*

(Bartolus, Comment on D.1.1.9)

With the rediscovery of the Roman texts in the 11th century, the jurists, who
were all part of the *Societas Christiana*, found Ulpian's definition of the *ius
naturale* difficult because law was based upon reason (*ratio*) which, as Bartolus
notes, animals lacked. Gaius had said that the *ius gentium* was founded upon
the natural reason (*naturalis ratio*) of mankind (D.1.1.9), and so the *ius gentium*
became absorbed, so to speak, by the *ius naturale* (or one could equally say the
ius naturale absorbed the *ius gentium*) (Jones 1940: 106–107). Natural reason
was the foundation of natural law. One can see this development as early as
the 14th century with the Post-Glossators (Commentators). In the centuries
that followed, this *ratio naturalis* gradually became ever more 'scientific' and
in the 17th and 18th centuries was associated with mathematical reasoning
(*mos mathematicus*); just as two plus two equals four in any human society
anywhere in the world, so the precepts of natural law were seen as being fundamental in any human society. Indeed, these precepts for some were the fundamental *principia* as given expression in the *regulae iuris* which from the
16th century were also being described as *axiomata*. Some of the basic legal
notions such as property, contract, marriage, constitutions and so on became
justified on the basis that they were axioms created by the *ius naturale*.

There is, evidently, an ideological dimension to this thinking which was
intensified by the ambiguous term *ius,* which by the 16th century had come to
mean a 'right' as well as law. Thus, the *ius naturale* could be interpreted not
only as natural law but also as a natural right. This, in turn, meant that notions
such as private property and contract, together with aspects of public law,
could be regarded as 'natural rights'. As Walter Jones noted, it "soon became
a commonplace that private property was an institution of the law of Nature
and, as such, could not be meddled with by the law of the State, except for a
just cause" (1940: 109). One can, of course, see this as nothing but ideology,
but it also represented a 'philosophy' or 'theory' of law. This is not to suggest
that jurists before the 17th century had no theory or philosophy; much of the

writings of the Post-Glossators can certainly be seen as political and social theory operating through legal concepts and reasoning. But natural law thinking became a philosophy in the writings of authors such as Hobbes (1588–1679), Locke (1632–1704) and Rousseau (1712–1778) who were not jurists as such. One could, in other words, see the beginnings of a clear dichotomy emerging between 'law' and 'philosophy of law', a process that in retrospect had its roots in the writings of Thomas Aquinas (1225–1274). Indeed, one writer has asserted that natural law has suffered an excess of philosophy, with the result that both 'nature' and 'law' have many different meanings, in turn leading to 255 different meanings of 'natural law' (Sériaux 2003: 508). Whatever the situation, the theory of a natural law, as a theory in itself, has persisted right up to contemporary times, though of course in various different forms (see e.g., Finnis 1980).

This said, the theory became eclipsed, as will be seen (maxim 46 below), during the 19th century. One reason for this, as Jones explained, was the problem of dualism. "The fundamental assumption on which the idea of a law of Nature rested", wrote this author, "was that there was a dualism in the realm of law". And as he went on to say, such "a dualism could not for a moment be admitted by any philosophy of law" (1940: 205). Law, according to the positivist philosophy of the 19th century thinkers, had to be "consistently monistic" because a "rule either is or is not law; it cannot at the same time be both" (1940: 206). Yet despite this eclipse, the ideas of *ius naturale* thinking were never to be expunged from legal thought. It lives on in ideas about equity, human rights, international law, legal science and so on. Indeed, legal principles – the *regulae juris* – are by no means dead; judges and jurists remain willing to cite principles such as 'no one should be enriched at another's expense' (maxim 112) and 'no one should take advantage of his own wrong' (maxim 113) as valid legal expressions. The *ius naturale*, one might say, is always with us, even if it is hiding in plain sight.

46.   IUS HUMANUM APPELLATUR IUS POSITIVUM

> *Human law is called the* ius positivum.
>
> (Panormitanus, I, 262)

The expression *ius positivum* (or *ius positum*) is not Roman. It first appears with the canon lawyers in the 11th century and, as the Panormitanus maxim states, it was a term to describe what the Romans would have called the *ius civile* (see Kuttner 1936). The expression was used to contrast human law with natural law: *Omne enim ius aut naturale aut positivum*, wrote a 12th century decretalist (Kuttner 1936: 731). The expression was, however, to attract a very different meaning during the 19th century in that 'positivism' became a theory of law that rejected what had in previous centuries been the theory of natural law. There was no such thing as natural law, only the law posited by each jurisdiction. Moreover, the "law must be free from contradictions and complete in itself"; and "that law proceeds only from law" so that to "speak of the law of Nature is to ignore the bounds which the law itself has placed upon its own creative power" (Jones, 1940, 206). Accordingly, in Germany, Carl von Savigny (1779–1861) and his successors were forging a pure science of law (*Rechtswissenschaft*) that was entirely conceptual; it was an abstract model of law that was completely independent of social, historical, political and moral realities and from which solutions to legal problems were a matter only of syllogistic logic. The model was, then, systematic and coherent in which there could be no gaps. These jurists – the Pandectists – "did not believe that, as jurists, their task was to understand the law through means of higher principles rooted in human nature." They thought "it was to find the law in texts invested with legal authority" (Gordley 2013: 212). The expression *ius positivum* – positivism – now had a completely different meaning from the one it had in earlier times.

This theory was imported into England by John Austin (1790–1859). He had been a law professor in one of the first faculties of common law in England (although he gave up because of the lack of interest in legal education), but he also spent time in Germany and was much influenced by the Pandectists (on which see further Stein 1999: 119–123). According to Austin, law was a series of "commands" from political superiors to political inferiors backed up by sanctions. These commands (law) are quite independent of moral rules, and to this extent, as Jones has noted, "Austin was therefore aiming at a 'pure' science of law long before the appearance of the school which later adopted the term 'pure' as a specific designation for its own teaching" (Jones 1940: 96). Austin accepted of course that in common law systems judges made law, but this was because the sovereign had delegated the power to them to do this.

In 1961, one of the most influential books on English legal theory was published in the United Kingdom. Herbert Hart's *The Concept of Law* (Hart, 1961) replaced Austin's *The Province of Jurisprudence Determined* (1832) as the foundational text in legal theory, and it did this in part by providing a powerful critique of Austin's command thesis. This thesis might, to some extent reflect criminal law, but it could not account for whole areas of private law and legal procedure (for example, wills) where the command-sanction simply did not accord with reality. Hart consequently distinguished between two categories of rules – primary (direct obligation-imposing) and secondary (power-conferring) – and defined law as a union of these two types of rules. However, from the position of case law, what is perhaps one of the most important aspects of Hart's thesis is his acceptance of the open texture of law: "there is a limit, inherent in the nature of language, to the guidance which general language can provide" (1961: 123). Faced with such ambiguity in a rule, a judge has *discretion* in respect of the interpretation and application of the rule. The judge's "conclusion, even though it may not be arbitrary or irrational, is in effect a choice". And he continued: "the criteria of relevance and closeness of resemblance [between a line of cases] depend on many complex factors" and to "characterize these would be to characterize whatever is specific or peculiar in legal reasoning" (1961: 124). Hart does not, then, provide a theory of legal discretion or legal reasoning as such.

Positivism was and remains a hugely influential – one might say dominant – theory both in the common law and in the civil law traditions. It is at the foundation of the rule model, that is to say, an epistemology (theory of knowledge) which sees legal knowledge as simply a body of positivistic rules emanating from official (sovereign) sources. This knowledge is independent of other disciplines, and so for the committed positivist, interdisciplinary approaches to law are irrelevant (see Priel 2019). Knowledge of law involves uniquely knowledge of rules together with an ability to analyse in a positivistic fashion legal concepts. Of course, not all jurists take this purist view (see Cownie 2004), but its influence should not be underestimated.

47. THE LIFE OF THE LAW HAS NOT BEEN LOGIC: IT HAS BEEN EXPERIENCE

(OW Holmes, *The Common Law*, 1881, 1)

Hart, as has been mentioned, did not provide an explanation of legal reasoning other than his view that in some situations where language was ambiguous, the judge had discretion. This 'failure' of positivism to provide an account of legal reasoning beyond that of choice and discretion left a gap or weakness which has been exploited by other schools and/or individual theorists. The first of such schools that was to make a major inroad into positivist and conceptual thinking in United States law faculties was the school of American Realism, which flourished in the 1930s but whose influence is still very much felt today in the common law world ('Realism is dead; we are all realists now', became a popular saying). The central epistemological theme of Realism is that knowledge of law is not to be found in rules, concepts, and so-called logical coherence, but in what the actors in law (policemen, court officials, lawyers, judges and so on) actually do. "What... officials do about disputes is," said Karl Llewellyn, "the law itself" (1951: 12). It was stimulated by the attitude summed up in the words of Oliver Wendell Holmes (an American judge). In asking what constitutes law, he said that you "will find some text writers telling you that it is... a system of reason, that it is a deduction from principles of ethics or admitted axioms or what not." However, "if we take the view of our friend the bad man we shall find that he does not care two straws for the axioms or deductions, but what he does want to know [is] what the... courts are likely to do in fact" (Holmes 1897).

Nevertheless, great care must be taken since the realist school was so wide and diverse that its ideas cannot be reduced to a few propositions. What the realists were doing, in their diverse ways, was reacting against legal formalism and thus they brought into legal knowledge what might generally be termed sociological and psychological dimensions. Predicting how judges would decide a case was not simply a matter of looking at rules and the facts, since rules were hopelessly unreliable guides (rule scepticism) and facts utterly elusive and selectively constructed (fact scepticism). It was equally a matter of looking at the social background of the judge and the psychological dimensions of his conduct. Now, one important aspect of American Realism is that it was essentially a law school phenomenon; it was a reaction against the 19th-century positivist and conceptualist approach to legal education, and one of its most important effects was to shift the emphasis in US law teaching onto case-law and casebooks. This in turn stimulated important reflection and scholarship on the nature of facts in law and upon what motivates judges when it comes to choice and discretion. Another important effect was to destroy the myth that legal rules are certain and that legal solutions and case-law are the result of deductive methodology. There is a body of common lawyers, thanks to realism, who now regard such formalist and logical thinking as vaguely ridiculous.

Realism was to evolve throughout the 20th century, giving rise to other, more politically or socially radical movements such as Critical Legal Studies and Feminist Jurisprudence. Critical Legal Studies (CLS) has challenged the idea of law's neutrality, and its theorists, unlike the earlier liberal Realists, were more to the left of the political spectrum. Indeed, the CLS movement was a reaction against both legal formalism and liberalism, and it has undoubtedly left its mark on legal education; yet the extent of its influence in United Kingdom faculties is a matter of debate (Cownie 2004: 53). Feminist Jurisprudence has proven very challenging as well. However, this movement has not operated just at the theory level; it has engaged with central areas of law such as tort and property (Cownie 2004: 53). Indeed there has been an important contribution to legal reasoning (precedent and statutory interpretation) by Professor Rosemary Hunter, who has published a collaborative work that takes some leading English judgments and rewrites them from a feminist perspective (Hunter, McGlynn & Rackley 2010).

48.   [T]HE CRITERION FOR JUDGING WHETHER
        ACTS AND INSTITUTIONS ARE JUST OR GOOD
        IS WHETHER THEY MAXIMIZE THE WEALTH OF
        SOCIETY

(R Posner, *The Economics of Justice*, 1983, 115)

Another aspect of realism is the law and economics school, which sees law as a reflection of economic interests; and, that being the case, the role of judges and legislators is to produce legal solutions that encourage economic efficiency. This movement has certainly left its mark on legal education, but, in addition, it has also made an impact on legal reasoning. Judges sometimes make specific references to economic outcomes, and they may well withhold a remedy such as an injunction or specific performance if the granting of such an order would lead to obvious economic inefficiency (see, e.g., *Co-operative Insurance Society Ltd v Argyll Stores Ltd* [1998] AC 1). However, as Stephen Waddams points out, it is often not easy to distinguish between reasoning based on principle and reasoning based on (economic) policy. The dichotomy suggests that an area of law like contract – a favourite with the law and economics theorists – can be divided clinically into an 'internal' legal view of the subject based on coherent principle and an 'external' view consisting of economic considerations. Such a dichotomy is, in practice very difficult to apply because, when viewed historically, many 'external' considerations have been 'internalised' and incorporated into legal contract knowledge as a matter of principle (Waddams 2011: 222–223). "The application of pure principles without any attention to their practical consequences", observed Waddams, "would bear little resemblance to contract law as it has been" (2011: 223).

The law and economics school is also important in the way the latter discipline appears to provide an empirical 'object' against which law can be measured using a causal analysis. A strictly internal view of law as a body of coherent rules and principles is amenable only to structural and interpretative (hermeneutical) techniques (see below maxims 129–130); the system itself can be examined for its coherence, and the words of the normative propositions can be analysed for their meaning. Economics permits a different technique. Law can be examined in relation to its economic function and (or) it can be assessed in terms of a causal relationship between, for example, the outcome of cases and the economic environment and efficiency. Indeed, this relationship is not confined to micro analysis. Whole legal systems can be tested in terms of their economic efficiency and so, for example, "the trust concept has proved to be a very cost-efficient device for certain types of financial transactions, and civilian systems have been under pressure, at the very least, to recognise the existence of the concept" (Ogus 2007: 162). It has even been suggested that countries adopting legal institutions from the common law tradition experience faster growth than those countries influenced by the civil law, although perhaps one ought to be more than a little sceptical about this kind of causal analysis (see Glanert, Mercescu & Samuel 2021: 250–275). Whatever the situation, an economic analysis of law has a very powerful presence within the common law world.

49.   INTERPRETATIO FACIT IUS

Interpretation makes law.

(Paulus de Castro, Comment on D.1.3.9)

Nevertheless, it would be quite wrong to think that idealism in the common law world has been completely destroyed by realism. In particular, the work of Ronald Dworkin (1931–2013), who succeeded Herbert Hart to the Chair of Jurisprudence at Oxford, is of particular importance because it offers a striking alternative not just to realism but equally to Hart's vision of law as a system of positive rules in which there are gaps. Just as Hart established his own thesis on the destruction of Austin, so Dworkin built his theories on the dismissal of Hart's vision. Dworkin's contribution to the theory of legal method and reasoning is so striking that it will need to be dealt with in some detail.

Ronald Dworkin's work is of major importance in the common law world not just because of its own inherent qualities but also because of the reaction it has provoked from his critics. This has given rise to a debate of extraordinary diversity, quality and indeed complexity in the Anglo-American legal and philosophical literature. In terms of philosophy, Dworkin's theories can certainly be regarded as a resurgence of idealism. But in terms of methodology, they are hermeneutical in that Dworkin not only sees the role of the judge as being one of interpretation but regards law itself as nothing less than interpretation (see generally Dworkin 1986). From an epistemological standpoint, Dworkin's model gains its 'truth' value from the coherence of its structure. Thus, while a realist might put the emphasis on the sociological and psychological aspects of judging, Dworkin offers a philosophical theory of this 'doing' based on interpretation by reference to a coherent (rather than correspondence with practice) model of argumentation. It is idealistic rather than empirical in that Dworkin is not claiming (unlike Hart) that his theories are based on an empirical foundation (save perhaps in respect of his analogy with the methods used in literature). He does not, on the whole, claim that he is describing what judges *actually* do (in the sense that his theories are founded on detailed empirical research); he is asserting how they *ought* to decide cases. One might note, also by way of introduction, that Dworkin's theories, unlike Hart's, are rooted not in a system of positive rules, but in adjudication, and he escapes positivism by asserting that judges are interpreting and applying not just rules, but equally principles (Dworkin 1977). These principles may well have sources beyond those formally recognised by the positivists (for example, morality). He is, in other words, recalling the views of the natural lawyers.

In one sense, Dworkin's work reflects a central idea of the realists: that law is to be found essentially in the cases. Or, put another way, he incorporates the judge into his theory of law. However, modern realists, now for the most part classified under the Critical Legal Studies, Postmodernist and (or) law and economics headings, do not regard Dworkin's theories as providing a satisfactory response to the discretion gap; his theories are too idealistic and (or) ideological (American liberalism). Indeed, he has to resort to a fictional superhuman judge (Hercules) in order to promote his legal reasoning thesis. Yet perhaps one of Dworkin's strengths (or weaknesses?) is the relative diversity of his ideas. With respect to adjudication, he does not offer a single thesis; rather, he has propounded a number of different ideas, not all of which easily co-exist one with another (this is debatable), although they do share the same idealism towards judging and they are all readily accessible given Dworkin's skills of presentation.

One of Dworkin's most notable ideas was his striking use of a law and literature perspective as a means of advancing his interpretative theses. In order to illustrate legal reasoning, he drew an analogy with the writing of a chain novel. "In this enterprise", said Dworkin, "a group of novelists writes a novel *seriatim*; each novelist in the chain interprets the chapters he has been given in order to write a new chapter, which is then added to what the next novelist receives, and so on." In addition, each writer "has the job of writing his chapter so as to make the novel being constructed the best it can be, and the complexity of this task models the complexity of deciding a hard case under law" (Dworkin 1986: 229). What Dworkin was pursuing here was, of course, the idea of legal reasoning as an interpretative exercise. It is important to note, however, the requirement both of integrity (the requirement to write a novel the best it can be) and of a model of rights and duties themselves founded upon "the best constructive interpretation of the political structure and legal doctrine of their community" (1986: 255). Thus Dworkin is locating his model very much within a political morality rather than, say, within a model in which the interpreter pursues an economic utility.

One might equally note that the hermeneutical scheme of intelligibility that underpins this literary view of legal reason stands in contrast to the kind of conceptual structuralist model of law fashioned by some positivists in several ways. First, it is not top-down in the sense of a pyramid of downward-flowing norms; it is, instead, a more bottom-up approach which takes as its starting point the judge as author and not the 'rule of recognition' (Hart) or *Grundnorm* (Kelsen) as a 'top-of-the-pyramid' (or top-down) validator. Secondly, in focussing on the judge, Dworkin is really asking a different question than the positivist. Positivists were principally motivated by the question of how a legal norm or rule might be differentiated from other social norms such as those arising out of a moral code. Dworkin, in contrast, was motivated by this question: do judges have discretion? Of course, the positivists, either expressly or implicitly, provide their own answer to this question as we have seen with Herbert Hart. Dworkin set out to challenge the view that, in the hard case, there is such discretion.

Thirdly, Dworkin's hermeneutical theory, while bottom-up in its approach, does nevertheless have something of a structuralist dimension. Dworkin has written that the judge "must construct a scheme of abstract and concrete principles that provides a coherent justification for all common law precedents and, so far as these are to be justified on principle, constitutional and statutory provisions as well" (Dworkin 1977: 116–117). What is striking about this last schematic structure is that it is rather similar to the kind of approach advocated by some of the 17th-century natural lawyers. Indeed, it even recalls an earlier tradition rooted in the 14th and 15th centuries of a *ius commune* which, like Dworkin's principles, filled the gaps in the *iura propria*. There is, then, a certain paradox to be found in Dworkin's work. In focussing on the judge as author of the law, he is undoubtedly a product of the common law case law tradition; but in advocating a structure of principles where legal and moral norms meet and coalesce, he is re-introducing into the common law a theory (or set of theories) that was (were) fashioned by civilians.

50.   HARD CASES MAKE BAD LAW

Original source unknown but cited by OW Holmes in *Northern Securities Co v United States*, 193 US 197, 400 (1904)

Dworkin reminds his readers that one important distinction made by Anglo-American legal philosophy is between hard and easy cases. "The term 'clear case'", writes Bengoetxea, "refers to a situation of isomorphy in which the applicability of a legal rule or a set of legal rules to certain facts is clear and unproblematic." And in "these cases of isomorphy, where the facts of the case clearly fit into the operative facts of the legal rule, which attaches a legal consequence to those facts, judicial action can be accounted for by pointing to the fact that a rule is being almost unreflectively applied" (Bengoetxea 1993: 184, 186). A hard case is where no valid rule seems to govern the case or there is a choice between two seemingly equally valid rules. Hard cases can also include those cases where a rule appears to govern but leads to undesirable consequences. The rule needs to be interpreted, but it is clear that this will take the interpreter into "the domain of axiology, morality, or politics and yet legal justification is not expected to question the very system of law nor the ideology of adjudication embodied therein, i.e., the postulate that legal decisions have to be grounded on legally relevant sources, a postulate that embodies the rule of law ideal..." (Bengoetxea 1993: 146). To the positivist, the hard case is peripheral and results from the open texture of law; law defines itself by reference to the easy case. In contrast, the hard case for Dworkin is central to the understanding of law because it raises difficult questions such as those of judicial discretion and of reasoning models.

Dworkin's response to the discretion question is that judges do not have free choice because there is always a right answer to all litigation problems (see Dworkin 1977). He bases this thesis on the idea that legal method is one of interpretation and argumentation and that the law itself is a seamless web not just of rules but equally of principles. These principles ensure that there are no gaps in the model; judges are thus always constrained in their act of judging, if not by the immediate rule, then by the web of principles that exists behind the rules (*principia iuris*, as the old jurists would have said). The existence of this seamless web does not of itself give rise to a right answer but acts as a general theory within which legal argumentation can take place. Dworkin draws an analogy with an argument about artists. If one asks whether Picasso is a better artist than Racine, Dworkin would reply that it is a bad question because one cannot compare two artists from very different artistic traditions. But to say this requires a general theory of art which holds that art is a response to particular traditions and that it is meaningless to try to compare, in terms of quality, two artists from two quite different traditions. His non-response is thus supported by the model. However, law is different because its general theory, as envisaged by Dworkin, provides no basis for a non-response of the Picasso and Racine kind. In a hard case, it may seem at first sight that two (or more) opposing arguments have equal validity, but one argument will always be superior to another because to deny this is to make a theoretical claim that cannot be supported within the general theory of law itself (as it can in the artist analogy). For, in every case that one studies, there is, according to the legal model as envisaged by Dworkin, one argument that turns out to be superior to the others (Dworkin 1995: 233).

CONCLUDING REMARKS

Having noted that the Gaian scheme of legal taxonomy does not transfer itself with ease into English law, it nevertheless remains a useful generic plan for setting out the substantive areas of English law. Peter Birks was right to see that the scheme has value, but it would be misleading to try to subvert the whole of the common law into any 'scientific' taxonomical model based on Roman law. In fact, the Romans themselves used the model only for educational purposes – to provide a simplified overview for students. The practitioner materials contained in the *Digest* and the *Code* had no 'rational' plan, as Doneau complained in the 16th century. Materials that today would be classed under a single category – contract or tort, for example – are scattered around the *Digest* and substantive law is intermixed with legal actions (remedies). As for different types of law – natural law, positive law, equity, international law, and the like – they, or some of them, have acted as the basis for modern legal theories, but these categories upon which theories are based are far removed from what the categories meant in the Ancient – or indeed medieval – worlds. Nevertheless, much of the language of Roman law itself has survived into the modern world, some of which is relevant for common lawyers, as will be seen.

5. Public law

In the civil law tradition, the *summa divisio* is, as was seen in the previous chapter, the one between public and private law. The category of public law goes back to Roman law, but the Romans did not fill the category with much substance. That was left to later European jurists. What the Romans did bequeath was a number of potentially creative statements that became fundamental public law maxims. The creativity was not essentially in the maxims themselves – since some were taken out of their original contexts – but in the subsequent interpretation of these sayings.

51. ECCLESIA VIVIT LEGE ROMANA

The Church lives through Roman law.

(Lex Ribuaria 61.1)

It may seem odd to commence a discussion of public law by referencing the Catholic Church. However, modern constitutional law – one of the sub-divisions of public law – is the result of ideas first developed, if not in Roman law itself, certainly within the Church of the later medieval period and beyond (see Tierney 1982). As will be seen, there were vigorous debates by medieval jurists regarding certain Roman texts, and in these debates one can see Roman law being employed in terms not just of law but also of political theory. However, as Walter Ullmann pointed out, medieval law "was, one might well say, applied political doctrine, and in fact, for large stretches of the medieval period, the law was the only means which allows the historian to recognize pure political doctrine, because it was enshrined in, and applied by, the law" (1975: 15).

One must note also that there were two governmental structures in medieval Europe. One was secular – the rule of lords, dukes and kings – the other was theocratic, the papacy. And it was within the papal governmental and administrative structures that many ideas that we now see as political were developed (see Ullmann 1975; Tierney 1982). Roman law was fundamental in this development because from the 12th century "the overwhelming majority of popes were jurists who had either been professors of law at Bologna (or some other university) or had in some other ways distinguished themselves in law" (Ullmann 1975: 119).

In addition to Roman law, there had developed over the centuries another body of law, namely canon law, and with the establishment of the medieval law faculties this canon law produced a corps of specialist canonist lawyers. But these canonists saw themselves as lawyers rather than theologians, thus bringing into the debates about governmental power a distinctly legal flavour. It was only later that a distinction between law and political science emerged. In fact, in France today, the two disciplines are often to be found in the same faculty; to be a public lawyer in France is also to be a political scientist.

52.   OMNIA PRINCIPIS ESSE INTELLIGANTUR (EVERYTHING IS UNDERSTOOD TO FLOW FROM THE EMPEROR) (C.7.37.3).

Everything is understood to flow from the emperor.

(C.7.37.3)

The historian of the papacy and of medieval public law, Walter Ullmann (1910–1983), used the image of a pyramid to explain the sources of political power. There were two models. There is the ascending thesis whose "main feature is that original power is located in the people, or in the community itself." Thus, the duke or king "had no power other than that which the electing assembly had given him." In terms of the metaphor of the pyramid, "power ascended from the broad base of a pyramid to its apex, the king or duke" (Ullmann 1975: 12). In contrast to this ascending thesis, there "was the descending thesis of government" where "original power was located in a supreme being" (1975: 13). In the *societas christiana* of medieval Europe, then, "power descended from God." In terms of the metaphor, one "can here also see a metaphorical pyramid but it was at its apex that the sum-total of power was located" (1975: 13). The reference to Christianity is important because this was the religious and political context in place when the Roman laws were rediscovered in 11th-century Italy. This corpus of law was, like the Bible, endowed with an unquestionable authority since it was sanctified by Justinian, God's representative on earth. It was, in essence, divinely inspired. The *omnia principis* maxim thus had enormous legal, political and ideological power and was one of the foundations upon which a descending thesis could be based.

In modern constitutional thinking, the descending thesis does not base itself – usually – on a *ius divinum* itself linked directly to God. In terms of political theory, it is much more secular, although there are, of course. exceptions.

Yet one only has to look at countries such as China to appreciate that the descending thesis and the *omnia principis* principle still have a major presence in political thinking. China regards its constitutional structure as the alternative to the Western model. Even in the West, there are constitutional structures that seem to effect something of a compromise between the ascending and the descending model. One way of describing these models is as a form of elective dictatorship, that is to say, a descending model operates but needs to be renewed periodically by elections. Just how free such elections are in practice is a delicate matter.

53. QUOD PRINCIPI PLACUIT, LEGIS HABET VIGOREM: UTPOTE CUM LEGE REGIA, QUAE DE IMPERIO EIUS LATA EST, POPULUS EI ET IN EUM OMNE SUUM IMPERIUM ET POTESTATEM CONFERAT

What pleases the prince has force of law: for with the royal law (Lex Regia), *which was passed about his imperium, the people transfer to him and confer upon him all their sovereignty* (imperium) *and power* (potestas).

(Ulpian, D.1.4.1pr)

This idea of a compromise between the two models is older than it might seem. The maxim dictating what pleases the prince has the force of law echoes the *omnia principis* thesis; all law flows downward from the top of the pyramid. Yet the second part of the maxim proves more intriguing. The reason why the prince has this absolute sovereignty (*imperium*) and power is because the *populus* transferred its inherent sovereignty and power to the emperor via a law entitled the *Lex Regia*. This expresses the idea that the ultimate source of political power was the *populus* and not some supreme deity. The *populus* became a fundamental focal point in late medieval Italy when the question arose as to whether city-states could themselves legislate or if the only legitimate legislator was the Holy Roman Emperor. The medieval jurist Bartolus (1313–1357) ingeniously interpreted this Roman text as saying that the *populus* is itself the prince: *civitas sibi princeps est* (Comment on D.4.4.3 and on D.49.1.1) and thus that the *populus* can act as the prince in a city-state: *populus est princeps in hac civitate* (Comment on D.43.6.2). What this jurist achieved, then, on the basis of this Roman text was a reversal of the descending thesis.

The descending thesis was, of course, re-established (at least in part) at the level of theory in the 17th century by Thomas Hobbes (1588–1679), who thought that only a strong ruler (monarch) could save humans from chaos and civil wars. He did not actually see the transfer of power from the *populus* to the prince or king as a legislative act (*lex*) but as a contract (*pactum*) which could not be revoked, although other political philosophers argued that it could be if the king was in serious breach of the contract (this revocation debate was also of importance among the medieval jurists). The king had absolute legislative authority, which led Hobbes to make two of his most well-known statements – indeed, they are regarded as the foundation of legal positivism (see maxim 46). 'Law is a command' (*lex imperatum est*) and *Auctoritas non veritas facit legem* (authority not truth makes law) (the Latin expressions are in Hobbes's Latin version of *Leviathan*, chapter 26). Not long after his death, with the defeat of the monarchists in the civil war, England finally underwent its Glorious Revolution of 1688, which set the country on a path back to an ascending thesis of government with the establishment of the supremacy of Parliament. Nevertheless, the late Brian Tierney's warning must never be forgotten. Even if there was an evolution towards an ascending thesis, this evolution must never be seen as a matter of inevitable 'progress'. For "the whole historical tradition of Western constitutional thought – both its origin and persistence – can be explained only as the result of a random play of contingent circumstances" (Tierney 1982: 108).

54.   QUOD OMNES TANGIT AB OMNIBUS APPROBETUR

What touches all must be approved by all.

(C.5.59.5; *Liber Sextus* regula 29)

If the *omnia principis* maxim offers a solid foundation for the descending thesis, the *quod omnes tangit* rule seems to do the same for the ascending thesis. It even has the same respectability in that it comes from Roman sources. The problem, however, is that while these words are found in the Code of Justinian, they are in a provision that has nothing to do with public law. The words are found in a text dealing with co-tutorship, a subject far removed from constitutional law (although the notion of tutorship itself has been used on occasions as an analogy for the relationship between ruler and ruled). As Brian Tierney explained, the phrase was first employed by the canonists in the context of corporate bodies (see below maxim 55), which became the form for envisaging the Church and its sub-structures, and then got taken up by secular authorities with the result that the "maxim was accepted as a normative principle of constitutional law in other countries during the second half of the thirteenth century" (1982: 25). And even in England, it got adopted by Edward I and thus became a constitutional principle on this side of the Channel. Again, to quote Tierney, the history of expressions such as the *quod omnes tangit* maxim "provides a good example of the interplay between secular and ecclesiastical ideas on government that characterized medieval thought and practice" (*ibid*). As for the maxim itself, it not only survived the end of the medieval era but remains today a fundamental principle of constitutional thought in liberal democracies. Why, for example, are students represented on university committees? *Quod omnes tangit.*

55. OMNIS NUMEROUS EORUM, QUI LOCO UNIUS SUBSTITUUNTUR, PRO SINGULARI PERSONA HABENDUS EST

All people in a collection who are treated as one must be treated as a single person.

(Baldus, Comment on C.6.26.2)

In addition to the maxims and phrases, Roman law equally supplied a number of concepts or institutions that were to become fundamental to public law and constitutional thought. The most important of these, taken from the law of persons, was the corporation (*universitas*) (see maxims 66–67). This concept of the *universitas* was adopted by the Post-Glossators as the framework for understanding the city-state (*civitas*) and various ecclesiastical bodies, including the Church itself. These bodies were a *persona* – that is to say, a fictional person (*persona ficta*), sometimes itself seen as an intangible 'thing' (*res incorporales*: see Paulus de Castro, Comment on D.3.4.7 no 5). The *populus* of a city-state thus became a corporation itself regarded as a single *persona*. This was a fundamental constitutional development. "The major significance of Baldus' conception of the city-*populus* as a corporation composed of political men", writes Joseph Canning, "lies in its implications for the development of the idea of the state" (1987: 206). This idea of the *civitas* as a single person – *civitas* now meaning something more than a city-state – was taken up by Hobbes. *Civitas persona una est* (Chapter 17, *Leviathan*, Latin version). Hobbes, of course, was a political philosopher rather than a lawyer, but his political thesis is built almost entirely upon the concepts of Roman law as interpreted and developed by the Post-Glossators.

56.   REX NUNQUAM MORITUR

The king never dies.

1 Blackstone, *Commentaries*, 249 (probably
stimulated by *ecclesia nunquam moritur*, the Church
never dies, which was a medieval maxim: see e.g.,
Baldus, Comment on D.3.4.9 no 4)

Yet, as influential as Hobbes' ideas were, it remains difficult to envisage the
United Kingdom today (or ever) as a corporation (other than a very loose one).
Certainly, in the civil law countries, the concept of the state is largely seen as
a corporation. But the problem with English constitutional law is that there is
no overriding notion of the state; there is the Crown and a range of public and
semi-public institutions, each with its individual *persona*. If one is searching
for a concept that comes closest to the idea of the state as a 'thing', then the
overriding icon is the Crown. As Lord Diplock put it:

> My Lords ... it is not private law but public law that governs the relationships
> between Her Majesty acting in her political capacity, the government departments
> among which the work of Her Majesty's Government is distributed, the Ministers
> of the Crown in charge of the various departments and civil servants of all grades
> who are employed in those departments. These relationships have in the course of
> centuries been transformed with the continuous evolution of the constitution of
> this country from that of personal rule by a feudal land-owning monarch to the
> constitutional monarchy of to-day; but the vocabulary used by lawyers in the field
> of public law has not kept pace with this evolution and remains more apt to the con-
> stitutional realities of the Tudor or even the Norman monarchy than to the constitu-
> tional realities of the twentieth century. To use as a metaphor the symbol of royalty,
> "the Crown", was no doubt a convenient way of denoting and distinguishing the
> monarch when doing acts of government in his political capacity from the monarch
> when doing private acts in his personal capacity, at a period when legislative and
> executive powers were exercised by him in accordance with his own will (*Town
> Investments Ltd v Department of the Environment* [1978] AC 359, 380).

And he went on to argue:

> ...I believe that some of the more Athanasian-like features of the debate in your
> Lordships House could have been eliminated if instead of speaking of "the Crown"
> we were to speak of "the Government" — a term appropriate to embrace both
> collectively and individually all of the Ministers of the Crown and Parliamentary
> Secretaries under whose direction the administrative work of government is car-
> ried on by the civil servants employed in the various government departments. It is
> through them that the executive powers of Her Majesty's Government in the United
> Kingdom are exercised, sometimes in the more important administrative matters in
> Her Majesty's name, but most often under their own official designation. Executive

acts of government that are done by any of them are acts done by "the Crown" in the fictional sense in which that expression is now used in English public law (*ibid* 381).

In the same case, Lord Simon also observed:

> Nor can the first two questions be answered without also bearing in mind that your Lordships are concerned with symbolic language which cannot be understood without regard to constitutional history. The crown as an object is a piece of jewelled headgear under guard at the Tower of London. But it symbolizes the powers of government which were formerly wielded by the wearer of the crown ; so that by the 13th century crimes were committed not only against the king's peace but also against "his crown and dignity" (Pollock and Maitland, *History of English Law,* 2nd ed 1911, vol. 1, p. 525). The term "the Crown" is therefore used in constitutional law to denote the collection of such of those powers as remain extant (the royal prerogative), together with such other powers as have been expressly conferred by statute on "the Crown" (*ibid* 397).

He then went on to point out:

> However, for centuries thereafter the King's secretary remained within the royal household. Unlike the officials holding offices of ancient origin, the King's secretary was therefore "free to enter into every new branch of royal administration as it developed". So it was that with the increase in the powers of the Crown in the 16th century the Secretary rose to the first rank among the King's servants. But under the Restoration the Secretaries (for their office was now duplicated) too became heads of Departments of State, charged like the holders of the ancient offices with executing the royal will. (For the foregoing historical development, see DL Keir *The Constitutional History of Modern Britain* (3rd ed 1947, pp 16, 17, 113, 245–6, whence also came the quotations). With the development of modern government fresh departments were formed to be headed by Ministers or by Secretaries of State. Just as all were originally appointed to carry out departmentally the royal will, so today all Ministers are appointed to exercise the powers of the Crown, together with such other powers as have been statutorily conferred upon them directly (*ibid* 398).

Lord Simon concluded his historical account with a final observation about the Crown:

> My Lords, it will, I hope, be apparent from the foregoing that "the Crown" and "Her Majesty" are terms of art in constitutional law. They correspond, though not exactly, with terms of political science like "the Executive" or "the Administration" or "the Government", barely known to the law, which has retained the historical terminology (*ibid* 398).

This idea that the Crown represents the executive, the government, or the administration, or indeed the state, is interesting when compared to the *universitas* as *persona ficta*. As has been seen, some of the medieval jurists saw such a *persona ficta* as a *res incorporalis*, that is to say, as an intangible thing.

The Crown, however, is a tangible thing (as Lord Simon observed) sitting in the Tower of London; it is a *res corporalis* that can be viewed by any visitor. One can, in other words, actually 'see' the British 'state' in terms of a physical object.

57.   PRINCEPS LEGIBUS SOLUTUS EST

The emperor is not bound by laws.

(Ulpian, D.1.3.31)

What was the status of the ruler vis-à-vis the law? Roman law seemed to provide a clear answer: he was not bound by the law. This notion was, not surprisingly, extended to kings after the rediscovery of Roman law in the 11th century. There is also a certain logic to the maxim if one regards the emperor, prince, or king as the source of all law (see maxims 52–53), for he always has the legal power to free himself from any such law. Moreover, a king cannot issue commands to himself. Nevertheless, even in the Roman sources, the maxim seems to be qualified by another statement found in the Code of Justinian: *Digna vox maiestate regnantis legibus alligatum se principem profiteri: adeo de auctoritate iuris nostra pendet auctoritas* (it is a worthy confession of the majesty of a prince for him to profess himself bound by the laws: for our authority is based on the law) (C.1.14.4). The sources are thus nuanced, and this nuance was perceived by later jurists. The prince may be free from the positive laws of the land (*ius positivum*) but not from the *ius naturale* and *ius divinum*. With the abolition of the monarchy in France, following the Revolution, the powers of the king passed to the legislative assembly but the state was also, seemingly, freed from the civil law. The law of 16–24 August 1790 dealing with the organisation of civil justice forbade the judges from "interfering" with the exercise of legislative power and "disturbing the administrators in the exercise of their functions". The 1791 Constitution repeated this provision: "The courts can neither interfere in the exercise of the legislative power or suspend the operation of the laws, nor become involved with administrative functions, or order to come before them the administrators for reasons to do with their functions" (title III, chap V, art 3). However, this did not in the end result in the institutions of the state being free of the law, for there developed a separate system of administrative courts which dealt with disputes involving public bodies. Interestingly, the United States Supreme Court has in effect re-established the principle of *legibus solutus* with respect to American presidents: they are in effect above the law, at least with respect to their public acts (*Trump v United States* (2024) case no 23–939). Such a decision has surprised many jurists within the Western legal tradition, although it has no doubt been welcomed by some political heads of state around the world. Whatever the situation, the US case shows that the maxim is by no means one that belongs to the past.

58.   REX NON DEBET ESSE SUB HOMINE, SED SUB DEO ET SUB LEGE, QUIA LEX FACIT REGEM

> *The king ought not to be under any man, but under God and the law, because the law makes the king.*

> (Bracton, Lib 1, fo 5)

The position in England was different because the common law developed within a feudal model of government largely free from Roman law. Even Bracton, who knew Roman law, seemed to think that the king was subject to the common law (*sub lege*). A feudal model of government was essentially based on land and contract, and thus it was difficult to exclude the king from the whole legal network. Yet, whatever the situation, the Bracton maxim was confirmed by the judges at the beginning of the 17th century (*Case of Prohibitions* (1607) 12 Co Rep 64). And even the exercise of the Crown's royal prerogative power – that is, the Crown's own inherent legal powers recognised by the common law – is subject to review by the law (*Council of Civil Service Unions v Minister for the Civil Service* [1985] AC 374).

59.   ROY N'EST LIE PAR ASCUN STATUTE SI IL NE SOIT EXPRESSEMENT NOSME

> *The king is bound by no statute if he be not expressly named.*

> (Jenkins' Reports 307)

Yet even if the monarch – now the Crown – is *sub lege*, this does not mean that it lacks certain privileges attached to its status. The modern British government, as has been noted, has inherited all powers, privileges, and immunities that once attached to the monarch. In particular, the Crown may be able to avoid certain legal liabilities under a doctrine known as 'Crown immunity'. Regarding the question of whether the Crown is bound by a statute (which has been described recently by a Supreme Court judge as not actually being an immunity from liability), Lord du Parcq said:

> The general principle to be applied in considering whether or not the Crown is bound by general words in a statute is not in doubt. The maxim of the law in early times was that no statute bound the Crown unless the Crown was expressly named therein, 'Roy n'est lie par ascun statute si il ne soit expressement nosme.' But the

rule so laid down is subject to at least one exception. The Crown may be bound, as has often been said, 'by necessary implication.' If, that is to say, it is manifest from the very terms of the statute, that it was the intention of the legislature that the Crown should be bound, then the result is the same as if the Crown had been expressly named. It must then be inferred that the Crown, by assenting to the law, agreed to be bound by its provisions (*Province of Bombay v Municipal Corporation of the City of Bombay* [1947] AC 58, 61).

The immunity from statute has not, however, been immune from criticism. As Lady Hale observed in 2017:

> Mr Havers points out that the rule has been subject to criticism from distinguished commentators, ranging from Glanville Williams, who called it "a gap made in the 'rule of law'" (in *Crown Proceedings*, London, Stevens, 1948, at p 49); and *Bennion on Statutory Interpretation*, which describes insistence on necessary implication as "typical of the unrealistic attitude displayed by some judges in resisting implied meaning in statutes" (London, LexisNexis, 6th ed, Oliver Jones (ed), 2013, at p 181), to Paul Craig, who describes the present law as unsatisfactory, unclear and the product of a misinterpretation of earlier authority (in *Administrative Law*, London, Sweet & Maxwell, 8th ed (2016), at para 29.003). In his view, careful thought is not always given to whether the Crown should be bound, which may be overlooked or receive scant attention when legislation is drafted (*R (Black) v Secretary of State for Justice* [2017] UKSC 81, para 33).

Despite these criticisms, Lady Hale, delivering the judgment of the Supreme Court in the *Black* case, went on to hold that a general smoking ban imposed by statute did not apply to prisons because, in effect, of the maxim that the king (Crown) is not bound by statute.

This might seem a rather extraordinary decision given the clear public benefit objective of the statutory ban. Indeed, it means that a prison sentence now involves not just the deprivation of liberty but also a legalised exposure to a known health hazard. The case thus raises some interesting questions about the state of the United Kingdom constitution, not to mention the health of all those working in Crown institutions. As one academic has commented:

> Privileges of the king were an exception putting him in a preferred or exempted status but extending them to the Crown understood as officers, servants and, eventually, departments themselves clearly contradicted the outcome of the constitutional struggles of the 17th century and the resulting sovereignty of Parliament. It also flew in the face of the rule of law as Dicey understood it, particularly when viewed from the equality before the law component of the Diceyan understanding of the principle. To Dicey, the notion "that the government, and every servant of the government, possesses, as representatives of the nation, a whole body of special rights, privileges, or prerogatives as against citizens" is "alien to the conceptions of modern Englishmen" (Fontin 2021: 319–320).

That the British constitution is still centred, to some extent at least, around a medieval view of kingship might well be of concern to some people today. One wonders whether a specialist constitutional court, consisting of constitutional law experts, might be of benefit to the UK. In many civil law countries, such as France and Germany, there are constitutional courts that are separate from the other courts; these courts adjudicate only on constitutional points of law. These constitutional courts are normally associated with written constitutions, which of course Britain does not have. Failing that, a bold government might legislate to the effect that the Crown is to be regarded 'as if' it was an ordinary legal person when it comes to the applicability of statutes. The maxim that the king is not bound by statute has surely had its feudal day (although perhaps not in the United States)?

60.   REX NON POTEST PECCARE

The king is not able to sin.

(2 Rolle's Reports 304)

Associated with the maxim about the monarch's immunity from statute law is another one which traditionally granted immunity from liability to legal actions. The king can do no wrong and thus, for example, cannot be liable in the law of tort. This maxim shifts the focus from statute and from strict public law to private law in that liability to pay damages is, in English law, a matter of the law of obligations, principally contract and tort. Until 1947 it was not impossible to bring a claim against the Crown, but there was a range of procedural obstacles, the most serious of which was the Crown's immunity to actions in the law of tort. Most of these immunities were removed by the Crown Proceedings Act 1947 (see in particular section 2(1)) which treats the Crown 'as if' it was a private person with regard to most tort claims. One should note, however, that local authorities were and are not part of the Crown and have always been able to be sued for damages. This said, in tort claims in negligence against public bodies, the courts in substance often distinguish public bodies from private in terms of the existence or non-existence of a duty of care (see, e.g., *Michael v Chief Constable of South Wales Police* [2015] UKSC 2).

61.   NON EST MAJOR DEFECTUS QUAM DEFECTUS POTESTATIS

There is no greater default than a default of power.

(Origin unknown, but quoted by J-L Mestre,
*Introduction historique au droit administratif
français*, PUF, 1985, p 260 and by other civilian
writers)

The discussion of Crown liability in tort is of course constitutional, yet it equally forms part of another sub-division of public law. This other division is administrative law. It differs from constitutional law in that while constitutional law is concerned with the actual powers of the state, administrative law concerns the *exercise* of these powers. With the state and all state institutions now being regarded as *sub lege*, it follows that the exercise of any state power must conform to the law. In theory, the focus is on decisions since state officials exercise their powers through decision-making. If a decision does not conform to the law in some way, it can be challenged in the courts. Such a challenge was originally seen as an appeal against a decision (see maxim 33 on appeals), but gradually this developed into a challenge through which an administrative decision might be quashed for a defect or abuse regarding the exercise of power.

In France, such challenges cannot be made in the ordinary private law courts. They have to be brought in an administrative court, which will contain judges who are specialists in public law. Broadly speaking, there are two different kinds of claim. There is the *recours en annulation*, aimed at quashing an administrative decision, and a claim for damages that is similar to an action in private law for compensation and is thus a question of administrative liability (*responsabilité administrative*). This latter liability is in theory based on a decision made by a public body or public official; the decision is the refusal to pay compensation. However, just as in the private law regime, the actual substance of the claim is founded on fault or some principle of strict liability.

In England, there were several forms of action known as the prerogative writs, which survived the abolition of the forms of action in 1852 and 1875. The position in outline was explained by Laws LJ:

> The means by which the King's Bench kept other courts "within the bounds of their authority" (and also required them to exercise that authority) were the prerogative writs, of which of course *certiorari* was one. The others were *habeas corpus*, prohibition and *mandamus*. (For present purposes we may disregard *habeas corpus*, notwithstanding its magisterial place in the common law.) Prohibition was the oldest. The writs had different origins and were used in different ways (see the account

given by Wrottesley LJ in *R v Chancellor of St Edmundsbury and Ipswich Diocese ex parte White* [1948] 1 KB 195, 208–9). Although at various times some of the writs were issued out of the Court of Common Pleas and the Chancery, they were pre-eminently issued out of the King's Bench exercising its supervisory jurisdiction (*R (Cart) v Upper Tribunal* [2010] 2 WLR 1012, para 50)

And he continued:

> The King's Bench, then, was a common law court of unlimited jurisdiction which had developed a general power by means of the prerogative writs to supervise other courts – courts of limited jurisdiction – to ensure that the limitations were respected. These powers devolved to the High Court upon the coming into effect of the Judicature Act 1873 (which also abolished proceedings in error from decisions of the High Court and created the Court of Appeal). They have in practice been exercised since then by the Queen's Bench Division, and in recent years more particularly by the nominated judges of the Crown Office List, now the Administrative Court (*ibid*, para 51).

However, these prerogative writ remedies had their limitations. As Lord Denning once explained:

> In modern times we have come to recognise two separate fields of law: one of private law, the other of public law. Private law regulates the affairs of subjects as between themselves. Public law regulates the affairs of subjects vis-à-vis public authorities. For centuries there were special remedies available in public law. They were the prerogative writs of certiorari, mandamus and prohibition. As I have shown, they were taken in the name of the sovereign against a public authority which had failed to perform its duty to the public at large or had performed it wrongly. Any subject could complain to the sovereign: and then the King's courts, at their discretion, would give him leave to issue such one of the prerogative writs as was appropriate to meet his case. But these writs, as their names show, only gave the remedies of quashing, commanding or prohibiting. They did not enable a subject to recover damages against a public authority, nor a declaration, nor an injunction (*O'Reilly v Mackman* [1983] 2 AC 237, 255).

And he added:

> This was such a defect in public law that the courts drew upon the remedies available in private law – so as to see that the subject secured justice. It was held that, if a public authority failed to do its duty and, in consequence, a member of the public suffered particular damage therefrom, he could sue for damages by an ordinary action in the courts of common law (*ibid*).

In 1977 these prerogative remedies were all amalgamated into a single action of judicial review. Lord Diplock explained the background:

Another handicap under which an applicant for a prerogative order under Order 53 formerly laboured (...) was that a claim for damages for breach of a right in private law of the applicant resulting from an invalid decision of a public authority could not be made in an application under Order 53. Damages could only be claimed in a separate action begun by writ; whereas in an action so begun they could be claimed as additional relief as well as a declaration of nullity of the decision from which the damage claimed had flowed. Rule 7 of the new Order 53 permits the applicant for judicial review to include in the statement in support of his application for leave a claim for damages and empowers the court to award damages on the hearing of the application if satisfied that such damages could have been awarded to him in an action begun by him by writ at the time of the making of the application (*O'Reilly* v *Mackman* [1983] 2 AC 237, 283).

One problem with the old system, then, was that the prerogative remedies were non-monetary actions aimed at enforcing a public body, for example, to perform its duty (mandamus) or to quash a decision of such a body (certiorari). If the claimant had suffered damage as a result of the public body's decision, they had to bring a separate claim in 'private' law – that is to say, a claim in contract or tort. Even after the reform, a judicial review action cannot in itself award compensation; the claimant must still show that there has been a breach of a 'private' law right. However, procedurally, a separate action does not now have to be pursued. More generally, one can see in play here the broad distinction recognised in France between a non-monetary action to quash a decision and a monetary claim for damages based upon contract or tort.

62. RATIO EST DUX INTELLECTUS

Reason is the guide to understanding.

(Baldus, Comment on D.1.3.31 no 101)

What, therefore, are the principles upon which a judicial review action is based? If one had to choose one particular focal point, it is probably the notion of *ratio*, taken in the sense not just of rational reasoning but also reasonableness. As Lord Woolf put it:

Rationality, as it has developed in modern public law, has two faces: one is the barely known decision which simply defies comprehension; the other is a decision which can be seen to have proceeded by flawed logic (though this can often be equally well allocated to the intrusion of an irrelevant factor) (*R v North and East Devon Health Authority, ex p Coughlan* [2001] QB 213, para 65).

Lord Woolf went on to add that one "approach is to ask not whether the decision is ultra vires in the restricted *Wednesbury* sense but whether, for example

through unfairness or arbitrariness, it amounts to an abuse of power" (para 67).
And he continued:

> Abuses of power may take many forms. One, not considered in the *Wednesbury
> case* [1948] 1 KB 223 (even though it was arguably what the case was about), was
> the use of a power for a collateral purpose. Another, as cases like *Ex p Preston*
> [1985] AC 835 now make clear, is reneging without adequate justification, by an
> otherwise lawful decision, on a lawful promise or practice adopted towards a lim-
> ited number of individuals. There is no suggestion in *Ex p Preston* or elsewhere that
> the final arbiter of justification, rationality apart, is the decision-maker rather than
> the court (para 69).

Here, then, is the key secondary or associated concept regarding the rationality
of administrative law judicial review. Has there been an abuse of power by the
decision-maker?

The main sub-elements of this notion were set out by Lord Roskill. His
words are worth setting out in some detail as they provide something of an
overview of judicial review since the middle of the last century. He observed:

> Today it is perhaps commonplace to observe that as a result of a series of judicial
> decisions since about 1950 both in this House and in the Court of Appeal there has
> been a dramatic and indeed a radical change in the scope of judicial review. That
> change has been described – by no means critically – as an upsurge of judicial
> activism (*Council of Civil Service v Minister for the Civil Service* [1985] AC 374,
> 414).

And he continued:

> Historically the use of the old prerogative writs of certiorari, prohibition and man-
> damus was designed to establish control by the Court of King's Bench over inferior
> courts or tribunals. But the use of those writs, and of their successors the corre-
> sponding prerogative orders, has become far more extensive. They have come to be
> used for the purpose of controlling what would otherwise be unfettered executive
> action whether of central or local government. Your Lordships are not concerned
> in this case with that branch of judicial review which is concerned with the control
> of inferior courts or tribunals. But your Lordships are vitally concerned with that
> branch of judicial review which is concerned with the control of executive action.
> This branch of public or administrative law has evolved, as with much of our law,
> on a case by case basis and no doubt hereafter that process will continue (*ibid*).

He then set out the grounds for judicial review:

> Thus far this evolution has established that executive action will be the subject of
> judicial review on three separate grounds. The first is where the authority con-
> cerned has been guilty of an error of law in its action as for example purporting to
> exercise a power which in law it does not possess. The second is where it exercises
> a power in so unreasonable a manner that the exercise becomes open to review

upon what are called, in lawyers' shorthand, *Wednesbury* principles *(Associated Provincial Picture Houses Ltd v Wednesbury Corporation* [1948] 1 KB 223). The third is where it has acted contrary to what are often called "principles of natural justice." As to this last, the use of this phrase is no doubt hallowed by time and much judicial repetition, but it is a phrase often widely misunderstood and therefore as often misused. That phrase perhaps might now be allowed to find a permanent resting-place and be better replaced by speaking of a duty to act fairly *(ibid)*.

Yet he warned:

But that latter phrase must not in its turn be misunderstood or misused. It is not for the courts to determine whether a particular policy or particular decisions taken in fulfilment of that policy are fair. They are only concerned with the manner in which those decisions have been taken and the extent of the duty to act fairly will vary greatly from case to case as indeed the decided cases since 1950 consistently show. Many features will come into play including the nature of the decision and the relationship of those involved on either side before the decision was taken *(ibid 414–415)*

Lord Diplock, in the same case, noted:

Judicial review has I think developed to a stage today when without reiterating any analysis of the steps by which the development has come about, one can conveniently classify under three heads the grounds upon which administrative action is subject to control by judicial review. The first ground I would call "illegality," the second "irrationality" and the third "procedural impropriety" *(ibid 410)*

There is, it might be said, still something of a remedies flavour to judicial review (see maxim 119). This is not surprising since it was the prerogative writs that acted as the vehicle for reviewing administrative and executive decisions, and these writs survived the abolition of the forms of action right up to 1977. Substantive ideas were gradually developed by ricochet, so to speak, and, as Lord Roskill noted, from about the middle of the last century a substantial body of citizen legitimate interests was established by the courts. What is also to be noted is that this substantive law is not founded upon statute but upon case law. It is one of the few areas – along with contract, tort, and restitution – where the basic source of law is a matter of precedent. This case law is not always seen as a blessing by certain politicians, and it has attracted criticism, even from some jurists, of displaying a too interventionist attitude on the part of the judiciary. As the rule of law comes under increasing pressure in the UK – some politicians have in the recent past called upon the government to ignore court rulings – administrative law is likely to find itself under ever more attacks. Indeed, one newspaper suggested that the judges are the 'enemies of the people'. *Ratio* can no longer always be regarded as the means to 'understanding'.

CONCLUDING REMARKS

The category of public law in the UK has grown increasingly conscious of itself over the past century and now often stands in contrast to private law. This may be a valuable development in many ways, but it is also a dangerous one because much 'public' law is still to be found in 'private' law. Whole areas of property and tort, for example, involve constitutional issues – for instance, damages are often obtained from the police through the torts of trespass and malicious prosecution. The tort of defamation has fundamental importance for the right of free speech. The Human Rights Act 1998 is, of course, a constitutional statute, but it is equally important in private law. Sometimes some simple constitutional questions cannot seemingly be answered by the courts. Do people have the right to go onto beaches in England? The Supreme Court does not seem to know (*R (Newhaven Port & Properties Ltd) v East Sussex CC* [2015] UKSC 7). Writing on the history of English constitutional law, the great Frederick Maitland (1850–1906) concluded in saying "our whole constitutional law seems at times to be but an appendix to the law of real property" (1908: 538). As for the category of public law itself, it is usually subdivided into constitutional law and administrative law. But, if one defines public law based on the relationship between the individual and the state, there are other candidates for inclusion, such as criminal law and tax law (see further Jolowicz 1963: 320–327). More factual-based categories such as immigration law are also candidates, and often these categories form specific parts of administrative law.

6. Law of persons

Turning from public to private law, one finds much more of a ready-made internal structure thanks to the Roman jurists (see maxim 41). This is not to say that the common law has adopted, or conforms fully to, this structure, but it has been heavily influenced by it, especially since the abolition of the forms of action. In this chapter, maxims concerning the law of persons will be considered.

63. PATET ERGO QUOD HOC NOMEN, 'PERSONA' QUANDOQUE PONITUR PRO SINGULARI QUANDOQUE PRO UNIVERSALI

It is clear, therefore, that this name 'person' is used sometimes for a single person and sometimes for a group of persons.

(Baldus, Comment on C.6.26.2)

In Roman law itself, the law of persons (*ius personarum*) was largely concerned with status, that is, the position of an individual in society as objectively determined by the law – for example, one is either a slave or a free person, or one is either an adult or a minor. But there are two other aspects to the law of persons which form sub-divisions alongside status; one is legal personality, and the other is personality rights. Legal personality is concerned with the question of who is a 'person', and the primary sub-division here is between natural and legal persons. Personality rights are rights that attach to the person as a human being. These rights are distinguished from property and obligation rights in that they are usually non-patrimonial; that is to say, they are not rights that (supposedly) have a monetary value. The law of persons, technically speaking, also includes family law, and the reason for this inclusion is that marriage is a form of status as well as a contractual relation.

64   QUI IN UTERO EST, PERINDE AC SI IN REBUS
HUMANIS ESSET CUSTODITUR, QUOTIENS
DE COMMODIS IPSIUS PARTUS QUAERITUR:
QUAMQUAM ALII ANTEQUAM NASCATUR
NEQUAQUAM PROSIT.

*One who is in the womb is treated as if he was in existence every time his
interests are in question, although before it is born others cannot profit.*

(Paul, D.1.5.7)

The idea that an unborn child is not treated as a *persona* goes back to Roman
law and remains, today, a maxim of almost universal application, although it
is under threat in some jurisdictions. If an unborn child were to be treated as
a person, this would mean that abortion would be murder and an accidental
killing possibly manslaughter. A child becomes a *persona* – that is to say, a full
legal subject – only when it is born, although its interests, while the baby is in
the womb, are not ignored (see, e.g., Congenital Disabilities (Civil Liability)
Act 1976).

65.   MORS OMNIA SOLVIT

Death dissolves everything.

(Baldus, Index; Decius, 239)

Just as legal personality begins with birth, so it ends with death. However,
at what point does a person die? This is by no means an easy question when
unconscious – perhaps permanently unconscious – people can be artificially be
kept alive thanks to technology, or when a person disappears without a trace.
Several practical legal problems arise in this situation. The first, of course, is
that determining the time of death can be important both for public and private
law and so, to give a very simple example, a person who stabs or shoots a body
thinking that the person is still alive will not be guilty of murder if death had
in fact occurred before the act. With regard to a person who has disappeared,
the relatives will sooner or later want a death certificate so that the presumed
dead person's property can be distributed.

    Secondly, a doctor or a hospital might well want to know, if faced with a per-
manently unconscious patient, whether or not they are under a duty to keep the
body alive by technological means or whatever. In this situation, the English
courts have developed the test of the 'best interests' of the patient (*Airedale
NHS Trust v Bland* [1993] AC 789). If the court determines that it is in the best

interests of the person not to be kept alive artificially, it will issue a declaration to the effect that it would not be unlawful to terminate the feeding or to switch off the life support machine. Once the declaration is issued, the medical personnel cannot be prosecuted for murder or sued in the tort of trespass.

All legal systems are faced with serious problems when people disappear, and many systems presume death after a certain period of time (often seven years) although a death certificate may be obtained much earlier if there is evidence, for example, that the person missing was involved in some tragedy such as a disappeared aircraft or ship. But what if, after many years, a presumed dead person reappears? Can he reclaim his distributed property? This was an issue that fascinated medieval Roman lawyers, who discussed the situation regarding Lazarus: could he get his property and wife back upon being raised from the dead by Jesus?

66. SI QUID UNIVERSITATI DEBETUR, SINGULIS NON DEBETUR: NEC QUOD DEBET UNIVERSITAS SINGULI DEBENT

If a debt is owed to the corporation it is not owed to the individuals: and neither is what is owed by the corporation is owed by the individuals.

(Ulpian D.3.4.7.1)

It is not only human beings who are legal persons. The group as a corporation (*universitas*) is a legal person separate from the individuals that make up the group. Legal personality has long been extended beyond the human individual to groups of humans. Thus colleges and towns were on occasions treated 'as if' they were people, and in medieval canon law the Church was regarded as a *persona ficta*. In civil law it was primarily the medieval jurists of the 14th and 15th centuries who developed out of the Roman materials what became known as corporation theory (see e.g., Canning 1987), this in turn becoming the structural basis for modern public law and modern company law. The expressions used were 'intellectual' (*corpus intellectuale*) or 'moral' person, giving rise to the contemporary French expression of *une personne morale* to mean a corporate legal subject.

Some legal systems use legal personality quite widely, and even small clubs and associations can register themselves as legal persons capable of having their own patrimony, that is to say, a fund of assets and liabilities. In England, the existence of the trust has meant that the need for legal personality has not been so strong. The trust device permits the establishment of an independent patrimony without formally having to create a legal person. As Maitland said, "the device of building a wall of trustees enabled us to construct bodies which were not technically corporations and which yet would be sufficiently protected from the assault of individualistic theory" (that is the theory that only individual humans and not corporations exist as realities) (Maitland 1936: 235). However early English lawyers developed the idea of a corporation sole, which was a device to ensure the continuity of an office, one of the most important of which is the Crown (Crown Proceedings Act 1947). The basic idea of a corporation sole is that the office is deemed separate from the human being holding the office.

These corporations sole are to be distinguished from corporations aggregate, which are collections of individuals organised into a unit that has legal personality and is thus a separate 'person' from the individuals making up the unit. Such a corporation can be established by Royal charter or by statute. The Companies Acts have, since the 19th century, provided a means by which anyone can create a company through a process of registration; and, once created, the company can, metaphorically, be 'likened to the human body' (*HL Bolton (Engineering) Co Ltd v TJ Graham & Sons Ltd* [1957] 1 QB 159, 172). However, according to English judicial theory, this corporate existence is based on a fiction (*Tesco Supermarkets v Nattrass* [1972] AC 153, 170). The English legal person is thus a *persona ficta*. Nevertheless, this has not prevented the judiciary from concluding that such a fictional person can have a real reputation and can thus sue in defamation (*Jameel (Mohammed) v Wall Street Journal* [2007] 1 AC 359).

This idea of an individualised reputation is not the only problem associated with the *persona ficta*. What if an employee of a company causes injury or damage to another person: is it the employee or the company that is directly liable? Companies can find themselves in a direct relationship with another person and so, for example if one purchases goods that turn out to be defective from a corporate vendor, it is the corporation that will be liable in contract to the buyer. However, when a human employee personally causes damage (for example, by dangerous driving while out delivering company goods), liability is normally attributed to the company through a doctrine known as vicarious liability (see maxim 106). An employer will be liable for torts committed by an employee acting in the course of his employment. This is a doctrine that does not actually arise out of the law of persons (personality) but out of the law of tort, with the result that difficult problems used to arise with the course of employment test when an employee deliberately caused injury to another. The company often became isolated from liability. However, in recent years, the courts have alleviated this difficulty by widening the notion of course of employment, and so any act that is connected with the employment will often now be sufficient (*Lister v Hesley Hall Ltd* [2002] 1 AC 215).

67.   PERSONAE LICET MUTENTUR, TAMEN COLLEGIUM NON

The people may change, but the college does not.

(Baldus, Comment on D.3.4.9)

One of the great advantages of corporate personality is that the corporation does not die, at least from natural causes. It lives on as the same person even when all of its original members have died and have been replaced by other humans, a process that continues through the decades (see D.5.1.76). This, of course, is one reason why the notion of a corporation was to prove so useful in public law (see maxim 55) and commercial law.

This personality's ability to escape from the mortality of humans and to exist independently of the comings and goings of the humans that make up the substance of the corporation at any one time has raised a question as to whether the corporation is just a fiction (*persona ficta*). Does it not have its own empirical interests which are separate from the interests of the human individuals? If so, do not these interests in turn suggest that the corporation is, after all, an empirical reality? The problem here is that one is defining the 'existence' of the corporation by reference to a collective interest which logically suggests that where there exists a collective interest, the collective itself should be deemed a corporation. This becomes more pressing if the collective interest is then expressed as a legal 'right'; if there is a collective right, then the collective must be a legal subject right-holder. English law certainly does not accept either thesis. One way of escaping the conundrum is to see the corporation as the creation, not of a fiction, but of the law as a positive system capable of creating its own elements. The corporation thus becomes a 'scientific' construction, with the positivistic legal thesis excluding any intrusions of sociological or philosophical theories (Paynot-Rouvillois 2003: 1156–1157). One can see here that legal theory can have its uses. However, one response to this theory of positivism is to assert that all legal concepts – including the system in which they operate – are fictions (Samuel 2018: 229–257).

68.   SOCIETAS TOTA VIM UNIUS PERSONAE HABET

The whole partnership has the power of a single person.

(Baldus, Comment on C.4.58.4 no 19)

What, then, of collective interests in situations where there is no corporate legal subject? Incorporated groups have, as we have just seen, legal personality and can sue and be sued as if they are people. But what is the position of groups that do not have legal personality? Logically, such bodies are not, of course, 'persons' and so, in theory, the law of persons endows them with no rights of personality. Nevertheless, the law does recognise certain collectivities even if they do not have legal personality. One such collectivity that has its origin in Roman law is the partnership (*societas*). In Roman law itself, this collectivity was uniquely a contractual matter, and so the partnership as a body of individuals had no corporate identity in law; the legal relations between the partners were purely relations to be found in the law of obligations. The position is essentially the same in English law: a partnership does not have a separate legal identity from the partners and so relations must be governed by contract. This said, a partnership can be sued as a firm, but liability attaches to all the partners rather than to the firm itself; whether this means that the whole partnership is to be regarded, in terms of its power, as a single person is open to some doubt. However, one can now establish a limited liability partnership where the liabilities of the partners are limited (Limited Liability Partnerships Act 2000). In addition to partnerships, the law of actions (remedies and procedure) may well permit certain other groups to bring claims or be sued. Trade Unions are one such group that does not have legal personality, but they are legal subjects thanks to legislation (Trade Union and Labour Relations (Consolidation) Act 1992 s 10 and see also s 127). Departments of government and local authorities are also legal subjects and can thus sue and be sued in their own name, but clubs and the like usually have to have recourse to representative actions (CPR r 19.6(1)).

69. THERE'S NO SUCH THING AS SOCIETY. THERE ARE INDIVIDUAL MEN AND WOMEN AND THERE ARE FAMILIES

(Margaret Thatcher, *Women's Own*, 31 October 1987)

One particular group that can raise special problems is the family. One can talk of the family interest. Margaret Thatcher was reported as saying that there may be "no such thing as society", but there "are individual men and women and there are families". If families have a similar real existence as individual humans, should the law not take account of this? One difficult and divisive problem is actually defining a family (*Fitzpatrick v Sterling Housing Association Ltd* [2000] 1 AC 27). What are its limits? Does it embrace only a couple and their children, or does it extend further? Is it founded (and perhaps confined) to a married couple of opposite sexes, or can it consist of a couple of the same sex (cf *Fitzpatrick*, above)?

The family is certainly an important institution in legal systems and has been in Europe since Roman law (see Jolowicz 1957: 141–160). Indeed, as we have mentioned, marriage is not just a contractual relationship but a status and, of course, there are important property issues attached to the family, such as the 'family home'. French law lays down a regime of community property which comes into play upon marriage (CC art 1400 etc) and there are private law duties owed by the spouses to each other. However, in England, the starting point of the law is that there are just two individuals subject to the ordinary law of property (*Van den Boogaard v Laumen* [1997] 3 WLR 284, 292–293). That said, there are statutory rights of occupation with regard to the family home (Family Law Act 1996) and the courts have wide statutory powers to adjust property rights between the parties on divorce. The courts have also used the law of remedies to protect, in particular, wives and children. More generally, the law of actions may indirectly take account of the existence of the family (see, e.g., *Beswick v Beswick* [1966] Ch 538 (CA); [1968] AC 58; *Jackson v Horizon Holidays Ltd* [1975] 1 WLR 1468; *White v Jones* [1995] 2 AC 207).

70. THE REALISTIC ALTERNATIVE TO A CLASS ACTION IS NOT 17M INDIVIDUAL SUITS, BUT ZERO INDIVIDUAL SUITS, AS ONLY A LUNATIC OR A FANATIC SUES FOR $30

(Judge Posner in *Carnegie v Household International Inc* (2004) 376 F 3d 656, 661)

Unincorporated associations might not be legal subjects, but they are often identifiable units, such as a sports club or residents' association. However, there may be a class of people who all have a similar interest in some matter, such as damage suffered by a polluting event or inconvenience resulting from some activity or act of discrimination. How can their common interest be protected or asserted in a legal action? This is by no means an easy question because the traditional approach of the law is to think in terms of individual persons with individual rights and interests. Group actions are simply not the norm, especially when the interest in question might be too general to be reduced to expression via an individual right.

Nevertheless, there are some possibilities. An action may be launched by a particular office holder or public body who has the power to issue proceedings on behalf of a class of persons in order to protect certain interests. For example, a local government can bring actions to protect the interests of local inhabitants (Local Government Act 1972 s 222) and Consumer Rights Act 2015 allows a range of regulators – which includes the Consumers' Association – to bring proceedings in respect of unfair terms in contracts (Schedule 3). Other statutes recognise class interests even if they do not recognise these class groups as being legal subjects. For example, the Communications Act 2003 section 17(4) stipulates a range of different interests of relevance. The Electricity Act 1989 talks of the "interests of consumers" (s 11C(4)(c)). Moreover, the office of the Attorney-General can be used in a relator action to claim, say, an injunction to restrain a public nuisance which affects the interests of a class of inhabitants rather than an individual neighbour (*Att-Gen* v *PYA Quarries Ltd* [1957] 2 QB 169).

Another possibility is a representative action where more than one person has the same interest in a claim (CPR r 19.6(1)). In fact, a recent development has actually introduced a class action, as Lord Sales and Lord Leggatt note:

> A new class action regime was introduced in the United Kingdom in 2015 as part of a wider set of reforms of private actions for breaches of competition law. The central rationale for any class action regime is that it enables claimants to benefit from the same economies of scale as are already naturally enjoyed by the defendant as a single litigant. It does so by allowing numerous individual claims to be combined into a single claim brought on behalf of a class of persons. Such a procedural device is especially valuable where a defendant's wrongful conduct has caused harm to many people but each individual claim is too small to justify the expense of a separate lawsuit. Without such a device what may in aggregate be very substantial harm is likely to go unredressed (*Mastercard v Merricks* [2020] UKSC 51, para 84).

As the two judges go on to point out:

> Group actions which enable a (potentially large) number of claimants to litigate common issues together, allowing them to share costs and obtain one judgment which is binding in relation to all their claims, have long been possible in England and Wales. Collective proceedings brought under section 47B of the [Competition] Act [1998], however, have two notable potential advantages for claimants compared to such group actions. They allow the legal rights of a class of people to be determined without the express consent of the members of the class; and they enable liability to be established and damages recovered without the need to prove that individual members of the class have suffered loss – it being sufficient to show that loss has been suffered by the class viewed as a whole (para 91).

These are the nearest that English law gets to the idea of a class action, in which a group sharing a common interest can bring a claim. (Indeed, as just mentioned, the Competition Act 1998 appears to have introduced an actual class action.) However, the representative action falls short of a class action in that the requirement of "the same interest" has been construed quite restrictively

(*Emerald Supplies Ltd v British Airways plc* [2011] 2 WLR 203). In addition to the representative action, there is also the group litigation order (CPR r 19.10–11) which is often used to amalgamate claims arising out of a single event such as a serious train accident or illness caused by a dangerous and/or defective product (*Bates v Post Office* [2019] EWHC 606). This, again, is not a class action as such; it is the amalgamation of claims where there are common or related questions of fact or law.

The general point to be made here is that with regard to collective or fragmented interests, the law of persons is often in itself unable to produce a conceptual legal subject capable of vindicating or protecting such interests. Sometimes the legislator will create an office or body to protect a collective interest, and when it does this one can certainly see it as a matter of legal personality in as much as a statutory legal subject is being created. However, in the absence of such a statutory legal person, one has to turn instead to the law of actions and to rules of procedure. The emphasis is, therefore, on the remedy more than the legal subject, and perhaps the more important concept to stress is that of an 'interest'. All legal persons have rights, duties and interests; but there are some public and (or) collective interests which cannot be matched to a single legal subject because such a person does not suffer any special or identifiable damage – or the monetary value of the damage is so small that only a 'lunatic' or 'fanatic' would sue. A good contemporary example of such a collective interest is that of having a healthy and unpolluted environment. The question is one of how such a collective or public interest can be vindicated, especially when the class of persons sharing this interest includes those who have not even been conceived (future generations).

71.　　STATUS EST CONDITIO PERSONAE CUIUSQUE

Status is the condition of each person.

(Doneau, *Commentarii*, Book 2, Chapter 9, § 2)

Another aspect of the law of persons is status. This, as we have mentioned, is an aspect of law that deals with a person's legal position in society. It differs from personality in that status is concerned not with defining who is a person; it is about classifying persons into different status groups such as citizen and alien, minor and adult, and married and unmarried. One might note here the inclusion of marriage. This at first sight might seem surprising given that marriage is normally regarded as a form of contracting, but it is a form of 'non-patrimonial' contracting which leads to the creation of the family group. The consequence is that family law is part of the law of persons even if there are fundamental property issues associated with the matrimonial regime.

Status does appear to be a category recognised in English law (Graveson 1953). This is obviously unsurprising given that distinctions between aliens and citizens and minors and adults are embedded aspects of the law. In fact, there is a range of other status groups created by statute that are noteworthy, such as the one between prisoners and non-prisoners, the former traditionally not having the right to vote in Parliamentary elections. Even within the law of things, it is important to recognise certain groups such as 'occupier' and 'visitor' which may be regarded as status groups for some purposes. Thus, a 'trespasser' injured on the land of another will not be owed the statutory common duty of care since this duty is owed only to 'visitors' (Occupiers' Liability Act 1957 s 2(1)). In fact, one difficulty with respect to such groups is distinguishing status from capacity. Take the following example. A person who buys a motor car can, in certain circumstances, acquire good title to the vehicle even from a seller who turns out to be a non-owner holding it under a hire-purchase contract. However, this statutory exception will not apply to a 'trade or finance purchaser'. What if a trade or finance purchaser purchases, in his private capacity, a car from a non-owning hirer purchaser? Will he obtain a good title? The answer depended on whether or not the category of a trade or finance purchaser is a status or a capacity category. The Court of Appeal decided that it was a status category and that therefore the statutory exception did not apply; the buyer had the status of a trade or finance purchaser and thus the fact that he bought the car for his private enjoyment (capacity) was irrelevant (*Stevenson* v *Beverley Bentinck Ltd* [1976] 1 WLR 483).

Status has in the past, and to some extent still today, been used as a means of legal discrimination against certain classes of humans, such as people of a certain skin colour or people belonging to a particular religious group. Notorious examples are Germany under the Nazi regime (1933–1945) and South Africa before the constitutional revolution (1993–1994). Jewish people in Germany were deprived of all rights, including the right to life, and in South Africa, people of colour had fewer constitutional rights than white people. Many European countries might pride themselves on no longer using status as a means of discrimination, and this is underpinned – as will be seen – by human (personality) rights law. But some care must be taken. The Illegal Migration Act 2023 creates in the UK a status with the title of "P" (section 8), and these persons deemed "Ps" (a title denominating in effect migrants deemed illegal) have few, if any, rights in the UK.

72.   PRIMUM, CUM DE IURE, ET STATU PERSONAE QUAERITUR, CONSTAT IN PERSONA IPSA PLERAQUE ESSE CUIUSQUE; CUIUSMODI SUNT VITA, CORPORIS INCOLUMITAS, LIBERTAS, EXISTIMATIO

First, when the question is posed about the legal rights and the status of a person, most are attached to the person himself; such of these are life, physical integrity, liberty and reputation.

(Doneau, *Commentarii*, Book 1, Chapter 1, § 3)

Another, more modern, aspect of the law of persons is the question of rights that attach to the person as a person. Civil law systems tend to distinguish between patrimonial and non-patrimonial rights, the first belonging to the law of things (property and obligations) and the second belonging to the law of persons. The actual distinction can be traced back to the French jurist Hugues Doneau (1527–1591) who identified a group of rights as *jura sua in persona ipso*, that is to say, rights which attach to the person himself and consist of the right to life, bodily integrity, liberty and honour. The significance of the distinction is that non-patrimonial rights are not regarded as commercial assets. Accordingly, in addition to those just mentioned, privacy and dignity are not viewed as forms of property but as what might be termed strictly human rights. In French law, these two personality rights are, accordingly, found in the law of persons section of the *Code civil* rather than the law of things (CC arts 9, 16).

English law certainly recognises a range of rights that the civilian would regard as personality rights. However, until recently, it did not classify these within a separate law of persons category. It tended to treat all infringements of such rights either as torts or as invasions of a property right, which in the civilian scheme would be part of the law of things. Thus, for example, harassment is a statutory tort (Protection from Harassment Act 1997) and invasions of reputation give rise to the tort of defamation. An illegal recording of a Rolling Stones live concert – an invasion of a personality right in France – was considered to be an invasion of a property right in England (*Ex parte Island Records* [1978] Ch 122).

The situation has changed with the Human Rights Act 1998. Those rights classified as human rights can now be considered as belonging to a category separate from the law of torts and protected by a regime of remedies set out in the 1998 legislation. This does not mean that an invasion of a human right might not also be a tort; but what the legislation has done is to set up a category that could be regarded as essentially one of non-patrimonial rights or rights of personality. Traditionally, then, common lawyers do not normally distinguish between patrimonial and non-patrimonial rights; they tend to treat all invasions of protected interests as if they were valuable assets and thus most torts require proof of damage. There are exceptions — for example, in the past, defamation did not require proof of damage (but see now Defamation Act 2013 s 1) – and perhaps these exceptional torts might be seen in terms of being more concerned with personality than property. Yet, whatever the situation in the eyes of the common law, the legislator has now created a separate category of human rights and damages awarded under the legislation are not tort damages (*R (Greenfield) v Secretary of State for the Home Department* [2005] 1 WLR 673, para 19).

CONCLUDING REMARKS

The law of persons may seem a somewhat thin category in substance when compared to the law of things (next chapters). But in practice it is not because, technically speaking, it embraces company law, family law, human rights, immigration status, and so on. These are not subjects that lack substance. In general, one can say that the law of persons is about law that attaches to a person as a person, including of course the legal definition of a person. Yet property law does intrude everywhere: privacy might seem a non-patrimonial right, yet many sell their rights to privacy to the press; and much family law concerns itself with property disputes. Company law, it hardly needs to be said, is a central part of commercial law. Perhaps, with the development of the notion of a 'consumer', one is seeing a merging of the person with a thing: the person is conceived in law only as the consumer of things. Even privacy – and dignity given some types of 'reality' television programmes – is traded for money.

7. Law of things

Having dealt with the law of persons, the next generic category in the Gaius scheme is the law of things. It is tempting to treat this category under its modern title of the law of property, but we shall see that in Roman law itself the law of things was a much wider category.

73. IAM VERO, CUM EIUS, QUOD NOSTRUM EST, PARS SIT ID, QUOD NOBIS DEBETUR, IN QUO VERSANTUR OBLIGATIONES

> *But now since what belongs to us includes what is owed to us, which brings into play obligations.*

(Doneau, *Commentarii*, Book 1, Chapter 1, § 8)

Turning from the law of persons to the law of things, this latter category comprises broadly two types of things. There are things that we own and (or) possess, and there are things that are owed to us. This latter category of things owed to us, while certainly part of the law of things if 'things' are defined widely, is not generally regarded as being part of the law of property. They are regarded as forming the basis of the law of obligations (see maxims 83–84). The foundation of this distinction is to be found in Roman law, but it is not so clearly set out in the Roman sources. Both the law of property (*quod nostrum est*: what is ours) and the law of obligations (*quod nobis debetur*: what is owed to us) are, as just mentioned, to be found in Gaius under the law of things, and Gaius does not make a big issue about separating them. It is the French jurist Hugues Doneau who first makes the distinction very clear and basically establishes the law of property and the law of obligations as two separate generic categories.

74. QUAEDAM PRAETEREA RES CORPORALES SUNT, QUAEDAM INCORPORALES

Furthermore some things are corporeal and some incorporeal.

(Gaius, *Institutes*, 2.13; D.1.8.1.1)

Nevertheless, as Gaius makes clear, when viewed from the position of classifying types of things, the proprietary nature of an obligation – the classic obligation being a debt owed to us – does indicate how what is owed to us is an asset. One only has to think of money in a bank account. We see this as 'our' money, but actually all we have is a debt owed to us by the bank. There is no actual money in the bank's assets that we can point to and say that it is 'ours'.

Such thinking parallels to some extent the thinking associated with the law of persons. Just as one starts with the physical person (then moves to the 'legal' person), so one starts with the physical thing. And thus, as the Roman jurist Gaius explained, tangible things (*res corporales*) are things that can be touched (*quae tangi possunt*) such as land, a man, clothes, gold and the like (G.2.13). Gaius then goes on to point out that 'things' (*res*) also encompass intangible things (*res incorporales*) which exist only in law (*quae iure consistunt*) such as a right of way over someone else's land (servitude) or the right to a debt (obligation) (G.2.14). Just as one extended the notion of 'person' to include 'intangible' or 'intellectual' people (*personne morale*) so the *res* could be extended to embrace property created uniquely by the system of law itself ('intellectual' property). Here it is, in effect, the Institutional system itself that is creating the *res*.

These intangible forms of property are absolutely fundamental to the modern economic system (Lawson & Rudden 2002: 29). For example, two of the most common forms of assets are, first, debts and, secondly, copyrights, patents and trademarks (intellectual property). Thus, if one had the copyright to all the Beatles' records or one was owed several million pounds by a bank, one would be a very wealthy person – as wealthy as someone who owned a house, expensive cars, and the like. Yet debts and copyrights are not physical at all; they are 'intellectual' in the sense that they are forms of property that are created by the mind rather than by nature, so to speak. Indeed, copyrights, patents and trademarks are actually called in law 'intellectual property' (Lawson & Rudden 2002: 38–43). These forms of property find expression through the legal concept of a 'right'; and so, just as one can say that a person has a 'right' to her car or her plot of land, one can equally say that one has a right to a debt or in a work of creation such as a piece of music. In the case of intangible things, the 'right' becomes the thing itself. Intellectual property is a matter of intellectual property *rights*. Consequently, as we have seen, one can even say that a live performance by a musical group is a form of property provided one puts the emphasis on the 'right' rather than the 'thing' itself (*Ex parte Island Records* [1978] Ch 122). This provokes an important legal question: what amounts to 'property' in the eyes of the law? At a general level, the answer seems to be things capable of being *appropriated* (Lawson & Rudden 2002: 20). So there were things that, in Roman law, could not be appropriated. For example, a person was not the owner of his or her own limbs (D.9.2.13pr) – although they were quite happy to assert that one person could own another person (slavery) – and public property was deemed incapable of being appropriated by individuals (see D.1.8.1).

Another important aspect of things is their constructed form, again something recognised by the Romans. When is a thing a thing and when is a thing simply a collection of other things? Is a heap of sand a thing? Is a box of nails a thing? Is a flock of sheep a thing in itself? According to the Roman jurists, there are three kinds of things. There is a thing which is unitary in itself ("having a unitary spirit") such as a stone or a wooden beam; there is a thing tightly constructed (cohering) of other things such as a house or a ship; and there are things consisting of other things but given a single name such as a flock of sheep or an army legion (D.41.3.30). The distinctions remain important in relation to the concepts (see below) of ownership and possession. One can obviously own and possess the first category of things and indeed things in the second category; but the third category presents difficulties and the Roman jurists thought that one did not possess, for example a flock in itself (although there are contradictory texts); one possessed only each individual animal. These categories are equally important for the common lawyer. B buys S's house: what is included in the 'thing' (house) sold? Does the sale include, for example, the light bulbs in the light sockets and the fancy coat hooks screwed into the wall?

75.   HAE AUTEM RES, QUAE HUMANI IURIS SUNT, AUT PUBLICAE AUT PRIVATAE

Such things that are under human law are either public or private.

(Gaius, *Institutes*, 2.10; D.1.8.1pr)

We have seen that the Romans made a distinction between things that can be appropriated and things that cannot. This distinction also reflects the general distinction between public and private law (see maxim 40), for public law property cannot be privately owned but is seen as belonging to the community as a corporate body (*universitas*) whereas private law property belongs to individuals (*Quae publicae sunt nullius in bonis esse creduntur, ipsius enim*

universitatis esse creduntur: privatae autem sunt, quae singulorum sunt)
(G.2.11). This division was certainly true of Roman law in a broad sense, but
on closer examination, the position seems more complex. The Jurist Marcian
(early third century AD) says that "[s]ome things in natural law (*naturali iure*)
are common to all men; some things belong to towns (*universitates*); some
things to no one (*nullius*); but most things belong to individuals acquired on
various different grounds" (D.1.8.2pr). He then refers to natural law in saying,
"so by natural law things in common are: air, flowing water, and the sea together
with the seashores" (D.1.8.2.1). Accordingly, "[n]o one therefore is prohibited
from access to the beach for the purposes of fishing, providing that he abstains
from intruding upon villas, buildings and monuments because, unlike the sea,
they are not part of the law of the people (*ius gentium*) (D.1.8.4pr). (One might
note that in an early project for the French Civil Code, Marcian's rule seems
to have been influential: see Cambacérès, *Projet de Code civil*, 1796, art 402.)

This was the position in Roman law and probably remains the general situation in modern civil law (see e.g., CC art 538). Yet what is the position in English
law? Much public property is owned by public bodies such as local authorities, but some land can still raise legal issues. What is the position regarding
beaches in England? Does one have a right to go onto a beach? According to
two UK Supreme Court judges, the "state of the law relating to public rights
over the foreshore of England and Wales is more controversial than one might
have expected" (Lord Neuberger and Lord Hodge in *R (Newhaven Port &
Properties Ltd) v East Sussex CC* [2015] UKSC 7, para 28). The reason is to be
found in the difference between the Roman and feudal models. In Roman law,
the 'right' to go onto beaches and the like is, as Marcian suggests, rooted either
in natural law or in the *ius gentium*, whereas in England, after 1066, the monarch 'owns' all of the country except for those lands that are either privately
owned or owned by public bodies. Those areas of land that do not fall into
either of these ownership categories are, presumably, owned by the Crown,
and people can enter upon beaches because there is an implied licence to do so
(this would appear to be the opinion of Lords Neuberger and Hodge: para 29).
Yet such a theory means that the Crown can, for example, sell such land to private individuals or indeed just revoke the implied licence, thus preventing people from entering a beach. Is this possible in civil law countries? Well, beaches
cannot be owned according to the general rule, but it would appear from the
jurist Jean Domat (1625–1696) that "it is the king who regulates their usage"
(*Les loix civiles* Preliminary Book, Title III, Section I § 2) which suggests that
in public law, the state may be able to close or even sell certain beaches. And
one might add that the medieval jurist Baldus (1327–1400) blandly stated that
the "prince is able to donate property that is public" (Comment on D.1.8.9).
Beaches seem to be problematic in all of Europe.

76. TOUS LES BIENS SONT MEUBLES OU IMMEUBLES

All property is either movable or immovable.

(*Code civil* art 516)

This distinction between things that can be appropriated and things that cannot indicate that the approach of the lawyer towards property is more one of classification than definition. Some things, like public property, were regarded by the Romans as *res extra commercium*; that is to say, outside commercial activity, while others were not. This, of course, was not the only fundamental distinction. The difference between tangible and intangible property, as we have seen, was (and remains) another. However, one fundamental distinction made by the common lawyer is between land and movable property, and although this distinction is recognised by civil law systems (CC art 516), it is not so fundamental in Romanist thinking. In the common law, it is fundamental because land and movable property give rise to two quite different legal regimes. There is a regime dealing with real property (land law) and a regime – or perhaps regimes – dealing with personal property. Within personal property, there is an important sub-division between goods, on the one hand, and things in action and money, on the other. The buying and selling of goods are subject in part to a specific statutory regime (Sale of Goods Act 1979; and now the Consumer Rights Act 2015).

77. GENERA NON PEREUNT

Generic things do not perish.

(Baldus, Comment on C.4.2.11 no 3)

Within the category of goods, a sub-distinction that is of particular importance is the one between consumable and non-consumable things. Again, this is a distinction that goes back to Roman law. If an owner of a particular book lends it to another, and this borrower refuses to return it, the owner, in any system based on Roman law, has a particular proprietary remedy by which he can reclaim the thing (an *actio in rem*). However, if the item lent is a consumable thing – someone 'lends' a bag of sugar or a loaf of bread – the lender cannot obviously ever reclaim the thing itself since it was lent for the borrower to consume and thus the borrower became owner as soon as he received it. All that the lender can do is to claim something equivalent or its value using a personal action (*actio in personam*) (D.12.1.3). The same is true of money in civil law thinking because money is a consumable item (D.7.5.5.1).

The distinction is important in English law as well, but perhaps not in such a fundamental way because, as we shall see, the common law does not have a special action for the recovery of goods. At common law, all that a lender has is an action in the tort of conversion for damages against a borrower who refuses to return the borrowed item, but the court can now order the return of the thing itself unless obviously it is a consumable item (Torts (Interference with Goods) Act 1977 s 3). This said, it is still important to distinguish between specific items (a book or a painting, for instance) and generic items since the first can be destroyed by accident – thus giving a borrower or bailee a defence – whereas the second cannot (*casus fortuna adversae non liberat generis debitorem* said Baldus, Comment on C.4.2.11 no 1). If a lender lends a loaf of bread, the borrower cannot claim that he is not liable for its value because, before being eaten, it was swept away in a flood. The same is true for money; the borrower cannot claim that he is not liable in debt to the lender because he has, after having received the money, lost his job through no fault of his own.

An associated distinction is one between specific and generic goods. One reason why the borrower remains liable for the swept-away loaf of bread is that it is a generic thing. One loaf of bread is no different from another given its consumable nature. Generic consumable goods could not perish, and thus the contractual obligation would not be destroyed with the accidental loss of such goods (*genera non pereunt*). Generic goods are not just consumables; a new car, as opposed to a second-hand one, is a generic item which does not become specific until it is identified, that is, extracted from stock and put aside for a particular purchaser (*Lazenby Garages Ltd* v *Wright* [1976] 1 WLR 459).

78. QUOD IURA REALIA SUNT IUS DOMINII DIRECTI, IUS DOMINII UTILIS, IUS QUASI DOMINII, IUS HEREDITATIS, IURA SERVITUTUM REALIUM ET PERSONALIUM

> *Real rights are direct ownership, practical ownership, quasi ownership, hereditary right, real and personal servitude rights.*

> (Baldus, Comment on C.2.3.28 no 19)

From a legal point of view, the most important aspect of property law is the legal relationships that are capable of existing between persons and things. Historically, Europe has seen two rather different legal models of these relations. The first is the Roman model, which is characterised by a notion of ownership founded on the idea of an exclusive power relation between person and thing (see maxim 79 below). This power relation – given expression by the Roman term for ownership, namely *dominium* – was all embracing in that it absorbed every aspect and every interest with respect to the item of property (Patault 1989: 17). The owner had complete power over the object, and this power was not dependent upon anything other than the existence of the relation of ownership. Thus, in a claim by a person for the return of his property, once the judge had found that the claimant was the owner, he had to order the defendant to return the object (D.6.1.9).

The second model is the feudal one. This, as we have already noted, made a fundamental distinction between land and movable property (chattels) because the whole structure of a feudal form of government was founded on the grant of land. The king was in theory deemed owner of all the land in his realm and he would then grant large parcels of this land to his lords who swore an oath of loyalty to him by way of contract. In turn, these lords would grant smaller parcels to tenants who in turn would grant even smaller parcels to sub-tenants and so on. "Repeated subinfeudation", writes one English legal historian, "resulted in a tenurial pyramid of uneven shape, from the king at the apex down to those who actually occupied and tilled the ground (the terre-tenants, or tenants in demesne)" (Baker 2019: 243). The basis of government and power in a feudal society was thus land, status and contract.

Accordingly, from a law of property point of view, the relationships between people and land were different from the Roman law model. There was not the notion of an exclusive *dominium* between a single person and a single piece of land; several different people had different interests in the same piece of land (Milsom 1981: 99–101). Thus, instead of viewing property relations in terms of an all-embracing relationship between person and a physical thing (*res corporalis*) the model was one of a relation between person and an abstract 'interest' in a piece of land, with this abstract interest being a form of intangible property (*res incorporalis*) that was related to the status of a person (Patault 1989: 48–50; Lawson & Rudden 2002: 79–80).

This feudal model was dominant in Europe in the late Middle Ages, but it gradually, though slowly, gave way in continental Europe to the Roman model. This was a gradual transformation, which actually involved, at first, a distortion of the Roman model. The medieval jurists made a distinction between two kinds of *dominium*: there was *dominium directum* and *dominium utile* (see Taitslin 2019: 350–352; Rüfner 2010). The vassal had *dominium utile,* while the feudal lord had *dominium directum*. This was almost entirely a creation of jurists such as Bartolus and Baldus, in that Roman law knew nothing of feudalism as such nor of split ownership. However, they did recognise the existence of a perpetual lease of land from municipal bodies that was given protection by an *actio in rem,* and this had the effect of turning it into a real (property) right (D.6.3.1.1). Bartolus used this lease as the basis of the thesis of split ownership

(see Comment on D.42.2.17.1 no 5). The next generation of jurists – the human-
ists – rejected this thesis and saw it as a corruption of Roman law; according
to Hugues Doneau, all that the vassal had was a real right in the land (*ius in re
aliena*) which were rights separate from ownership (Taitslin 2019: 351–352).
There was once again only a unitary notion of ownership.

In fact, the French Revolution was a revolution against the old feudal regime,
and so it should be of no surprise that the *Code civil* clearly and firmly re-
established the Roman model of property. According to the French Civil Code,
"ownership is the right to enjoy and to dispose of things in the most absolute
manner" (CC art 544). As a French writer explained, the importance of this
article was that it re-established ownership as a right to a tangible thing rather
than just being an intangible right (along with others in the same item of property). The jurists were able to do this because the Romans finally had two synonymous words for ownership, namely *dominium* and *proprietas* (D.41.1.13).
This allowed the jurists to merge ownership with the physical thing (*proprietas*, 'property') itself, thus making it a relationship between person and *res
corporalis* (Patault 1989: 219–210). The political implication is that only one
individual could be an owner of an item of property.

The English common law was, as we have seen (see, e.g., maxims 13 and
76), originally formed within a strictly feudal regime, resulting in English
property law still retaining many characteristics of the feudal model. Whereas
the Romanist systems have a single law of property subdivided into ownership, possession and rights in another's property, English law has one regime
for land, which still uses feudal concepts (despite the disappearance of feudalism centuries ago), and another for movable property. It even has a third
regime, according to some, for property like stocks and shares. Moreover, at
the level of remedies, it does not recognise any formal division into *in rem* and
in personam actions (see maxim 117). It largely uses the law of tort to protect
both real and personal property rights. Nevertheless, while it might be easy to
see the feudal model as unduly complex and scholastic when compared to the
Roman model, the position is not quite so simple. In the modern world, property law also serves as the basis of investment wealth and some 'feudal' ideas
– or at least conceptual ways of seeing property – have proved useful. The idea
of a strict and all-embracing relation between person and thing might well be
ideal when dealing with property as objects, but when dealing with property as
wealth, the ability to see property rights as abstract interests (*res incorporales*)
divorced from the thing itself and capable of being distributed amongst different persons has proved extremely useful (Lawson & Rudden 2002: 192–200),
as indeed has the concept of the trust (see Kahn-Freund 1949).

79.   [DOMINIUM] EST IUS DE RE CORPORALI
       PERFECTE DISPONENDI, NISI LEGE
       PROHIBEATUR

Ownership is the right in a physical thing of complete disposal unless legisla-
tion prohibits it.

(Bartolus, Comment on D.41.2.17.1 no 4)

Yet it would be idle to say that the term 'ownership' is not as much embedded in English law as it is in the civil law systems. Certainly, as an everyday
expression, 'ownership' and 'to own' are very familiar expressions both inside
and outside legal discourse in English law (see, e.g., Consumer Credit Act
1974 s 163; Torts (Interference with Goods) Act 1977 s 6(2): 'true owner'). Yet
what exactly is meant when common law lawyers talk of ownership? Given
the term's origin in Roman law, one would expect to find one answer in the
Roman sources, but this proves difficult because the Roman jurists neither
defined ownership as such nor, according to some, did they see it as a 'right'
(*ius*) (This thesis must, however, be treated with caution since the expression
iure dominii is to be found in the Roman texts). The Romans certainly distinguished between having full power (*plena potestas*) over a thing (J.2.4.4) and
rights (*iura*) that others might have in the property (such as a right of way) (*ius*
in re aliena). In other words, *dominium* (ownership) and *ius* (right) were separate notions even if ownership was seen as a *ius* (see maxim 76). But what were
the elements of this full power over the thing? It was the late medieval Roman
lawyers (the Post-Glossators) who, having trawled the Roman sources for all
references to the content of *dominium*, began to see ownership as a *right* (*ius in*
re) and to analyse it in terms of its constituent parts, namely a right to use the
thing (*ius utendi*), to the fruits of the thing (*ius fruendi*) and to freely dispose
of the thing (*ius abutendi*). This was the definition that was re-adopted by the
French Civil Code which, as we have seen (maxim 76), defines ownership as
the right to enjoy and dispose of property in the most absolute manner.

The problem with transposing this definition into English law is that the
latter has, at least with regard to land, split up the various *iura* into abstract
entities in themselves (Lawson & Rudden 2002: 90–100). Each of them has
become an 'estate' or 'interest' capable of being dealt with as an independent
entity. Thus, "the beneficial ownership of land may be divided in terms of time
as well as space, so that the right to enjoyment of the land for a limited period,
such as for life or a term of years, and the right to enjoy land after the expiry
of that period, can exist simultaneously as property interests in possession and
in remainder or reversion" (Lord Hoffmann in *Ingram v IRC* [1998] 2 WLR
90, at 93). Moreover, the trust has divided the right to enjoy and the right to

dispose of the property between two separate people, the beneficiary and the trustee, each of whom is nevertheless said to be 'owners' (one in equity and one at common law). In addition, a contract to possess real property for a term of years – that is to say, a lease – is regarded not just as a contract (personal right) but also as a real right that can be bought and sold as property (Law of Property Act 1925 s 1(1)(b)). It is extremely difficult to graft any Roman notion of ownership as an exclusive relationship between person and thing onto this land law structure, although the estate of fee simple in absolute is probably functionally equivalent to ownership. Thus, a person in principle has the right to do as he wants on his own land (estate) (*Bradford Corporation* v *Pickles* [1895] AC 587).

With regard to chattels, the position is seemingly different in that the idea of an exclusive ownership of a thing can be applied with less difficulty than with land. When goods are sold, what gets transferred from seller to buyer is 'property' in the goods (Sale of Goods Act 1979 ss 16–18) and this 'property' seems to be ownership, which in turn permits such an owner to dispose of the goods as she wishes. Indeed, it has been held that an owner of goods is entitled to be careless with his things provided that such carelessness does not cause physical damage to another (*Moorgate Mercantile Ltd* v *Twitchings* [1977] AC 890). Yet even with moveable property, the notion of ownership as a source of legal rights and remedies is not in truth that important. For "the English law of ownership and possession, unlike that of Roman law, is not a system of identifying absolute entitlement but of priority of entitlement" (Auld LJ in *Waverley BC v Fletcher* [1996] QB 334, at 345). Rather than ownership of property (real or personal), it is more accurate for common lawyers to talk of 'title' to goods or land.

How can ownership (or its nearest equivalent in the common law) be obtained? There are several principal ways: ownership can be acquired by succession (parents leave their house and chattels to their child), by gift, by sale and purchase and by loan when it is a consumable item being loaned. Succession and sale are major areas of substantive law governed by detailed rules; and mention has already been made of the loan of consumable items. However, with regard to sale, two models need to be mentioned. When S sells a piece of property to B, the question arises as to when title (ownership) in the property passes from S to B. In Roman law, there had to be, in addition to the contract of sale, a conveyance of title; the seller had formally to transfer ownership to the buyer, and the latter had to accept ownership. This conveyance was a property transaction quite separate from the obligation (contract) transaction, although in the case of sale of goods, the conveyance required little formality other than the mental intentions to transfer and to accept together, normally, with a handing over of the goods. German law has adopted this Roman model, and so has the English common law (as opposed to equity) with regard to land.

A separate conveyance (now registration at the Land Registry) of the land takes place after the exchange of contracts, although the purchaser acquires title to the land in equity on the exchange of contracts and so, functionally speaking, becomes owner thanks to the contract (Lawson & Rudden 2002: 59–60).

A second model is one where the contract and conveyance are not separate, and it is the contract itself (unless the parties decide differently) that passes ownership or title. This is the model to be found in French law and in English law with respect to goods provided the goods are ascertained (Sale of Goods Act 1979 ss 16–18). One problem with this model is that if the contract turns out to be void (non-existent), then title will not normally pass in English law because no one can give a better title than he or she has (*nemo dat quod non habet*) (D.50.17.54). The consequence is that if the purchaser resells the goods, the third party will not get title despite having paid for the goods (see e.g., *Ingram* v *Little* [1961] 1 QB 31). This problem is avoided in French law thanks to a provision that deems the possessor of a moveable item as the owner when he sells the goods (CC art 2276). Two dissenting judges in the House of Lords said that this kind of general rule ought to be adopted by English law (see *Shogun Finance Ltd v Hudson* [2004] 1 AC 919). But the position remains that only in limited circumstances will the third party get title to goods purchased from a person who turns out not to have title (for exceptions, see e.g., Factors Act 1889). It may be that the status of the person buying the goods will determine whether or not he gets title to them from a seller who has no title (*Stevenson* v *Beverley Bentinck Ltd* [1976] 1 WLR 483).

80.   NIHIL COMMUNE HABET PROPRIETAS CUM POSSESSIONE

Ownership has nothing in common with possession.

(Ulpian D.41.2.12.1)

A second major relationship between person and thing is possession. This, as Ulpian reminds us, has nothing in common with ownership, for possession is based on the idea of a factual, rather than a legal, relationship between person and thing (D.4.6.19; D.41.2.3). In fact, what Ulpian says is not entirely true, even in Roman times, but his comment is a most useful exaggeration since the two notions must be distinguished. Possession is the factual control by a person over a thing and can thus exist even when the person is not the owner of the property. The borrower of a book from a library will be in possession of the book while the library remains the owner of it. What was, and remains, important about possession as a legal concept is that it was protected by its own particular remedy that was different from the *rei vindicatio* that protected ownership. A dispossessed owner might therefore have two different actions against a wrongful possessor (D.44.2.14.3).

When is a person said to possess goods? According to the Roman jurists, what was required to possess was a physical (*corpus*) and a mental (*animus*) control of the thing (D.41.2.3.1; D.41.2.17.1), although physical control was construed quite widely. In fact, the Romans never really developed any single principle, and there are conflicting statements in the Roman sources as to the actual requirements of this notion. Moreover, the Romans also distinguished between possession and detention (*detentio*) of a thing (although the actual word *detentio* is medieval rather than Roman). This distinction was made because there was (and is) in fact an important relationship between possession and ownership; long possession in good faith can result in ownership of the property through prescription or, in English law, as a result of the Limitation Act 1980. In modern civil law, there is no single definition of possession. The Swiss Civil Code defines it as "one who has control of the thing" (Swiss CC art 919), but the French Civil Code says that it is the "detention or enjoyment of a thing or a right that we hold or that we exercise ourselves or through another who holds it or who exercises it in our name" (CC art 2228).

What is particularly interesting is the extension by the French to include not just physical objects but also an intangible 'right'. This certainly seems an extension beyond Roman law where it is clearly stated that the property had to be physical (D.41.2.3pr). Yet in later Roman law, the idea did begin to emerge that possession was a 'right' or a legal relation (*ius*) as much as a factual one, and thus one finds the expression *ius possessionis* in the sources (D.41.2.44pr). The importance of this shift of emphasis from the *res* (thing) to the *ius* (legal relation or right) is that the *ius* itself becomes a kind of *res incorporalis* (intangible thing) and this permits one to talk in terms of possession not just as an existing relationship but as a future relationship (a 'right to possession'). In other words, a *ius possessionis* could, like a right to a debt, form part of a person's goods or patrimony (D.41.1.52).

English law has long made use of the concept of possession partly because this notion reflected more accurately than ownership the relationship between person and land. As Milsom has explained, the relationship between a tenant and his land was founded on a feudal grant known as 'seisin' and like "*possessio* seisin became fundamentally a factual relationship between person and thing" (Milsom 1981: 119). Given this factual orientation and the absence of any notion of absolute ownership, rights with respect to land were always relative: who, as between two parties, had the better claim? This idea of property rights being a matter of relative title as between two people came to dominate the whole of English property law with the result that possession rather than ownership is the key concept. One should not be surprised by this because the common law system of remedies was one of personal actions (see maxim 116) and so all property disputes were a matter of a personal action by one person against another. If one combines this with the absence of any notion of Roman ownership, the "most that a person out of possession could claim was a better right to possession than the person in possession" (Baker 2019: 414). This remains true today. The modern torts of trespass to land and to goods and the tort of conversion do not require the claimant to prove that he or she is 'owner' as such; all that needs to be proved is that the claimant has a better right to possess than the defendant in the action.

As for possession itself, English law has not committed itself to any particular theory. As was observed in one case, it has never worked out a completely logical and exhaustive definition and the word depends upon the context in which it is used (*Towers & Co Ltd v Gray* [1961] 2 QB 351). In commercial law, the context may be wider than in criminal law, although much, again, will depend on the facts. Yet there must be some notion of physical control, even if this is more abstract on occasions than real, and there has equally to be a mental element with regard to the object (see Harris 1961). It is not easy to imagine a person possessing an object of which he has no knowledge whatsoever – although, of course, the law might presume such knowledge in a range of situations. The possessor of a piece of land might be deemed to possess everything on the land even if he is unaware of all the objects, and the same might be true of the possessor of a cupboard or other container (possessor of the genus is deemed possessor of the species). However, a passenger who found a necklace lying on the ground in an airport terminal and handed it in to the airport authorities was held to have a better right to it than the airport when it was never claimed (*Parker v British Airways Board* [1982] QB 1004). In contrast a person who trespassed into a local authority public park with a metal detector and found a valuable brooch was held not to have a better right to it than the local authority (*Waverley BC v Fletcher* [1996] QB 334).

At a general level, one can sum up by saying this: despite the various civilian theories based on the formal concepts of *corpus* and *animus*, English law has "employed possession as a flexible and functional concept, and emphasized different factors in different possessory rules, according to the dictates of justice and social policy" (Harris 1961: 106). Yet despite this flexibility, the concept is central to English property law. Uninterrupted possession of real property by a non-owner can result in the possessor obtaining ownership (or the best feudal equivalent) thanks to statute (Limitation Act 1980 s 15) and the transfer of possession (but not ownership) in chattels gives rise to a special proprietary relationship called bailment. This bailment relationship is of considerable importance in commercial and consumer law, for all contracts of hire of goods, transport, cleaning and repairing of goods and so on will involve this possessory relationship as well as a contractual one (but one must recall that the 'loan' of a consumable item to be consumed by the borrower will pass ownership in it). Indeed, in commercial law, the hire of movable property is linguistically treated as similar to that of a lease of real property; one talks of leasing a car or crane (Lawson & Rudden 2002: 115–117). Whether or not 'possession is nine tenths of the law' is an interesting question, but possession – and the right to possession – is of immense importance to English lawyers.

81. DOMINIUM EST IUS PLENUM, SED HYPOTHECA EST SEMIPLENUM

> *Ownership is a full right while a mortgage is less than a full right.*
>
> (Baldus, Comment on C.3.1.7 no 3)

Bailment is a good example of a person (the bailee) having a right (possessory) in someone else's thing. Now, if the thing (say, a motor car) has been transferred to the bailee for repair, the bailee will have more than a possessory right to the vehicle: he will have what is called a possessory lien, which will entitle him to keep possession of the vehicle until he is paid for the repairs (*Tappenden v Artus* [1964] 2 QB 185). This is an example of what is called real security – for the creditor has a right not just *in personam* but *in rem* – and there are several different types of such security.

In order to understand the conceptual basis of these real security rights, it is probably helpful to look at the stages in which they developed. The basic idea behind real security is that a piece of property acts as the guarantor of a debt, so if the debtor is unable to repay the money owed, the creditor can look to the property to recoup the debt. If Roman law is taken as the example, the development of this kind of security went through different stages (Johnston 1999: 90–95). The first stage was one where the debtor transferred both ownership and possession of the property acting as security. This, of course, had two major disadvantages for the debtor; he was deprived of the use of the property, and there was no guarantee that the creditor would retransfer ownership and possession. The second stage was where the debtor transferred only possession of the property, a contract known as *pignus* or pledge in Roman law. This contract still had the disadvantage that the debtor was deprived of the use of the property. The final stage was the *hypotheca* or mortgage, where the debtor retained both ownership and possession of the property, but the creditor gained a *ius in re* (through being granted an *actio in rem*) in the property (D.20.1.7). Both the pledge and the mortgage have passed into modern law and can be found in English law as well as in civil law.

Mortgages work well enough with respect to land – although the historical development stages were somewhat complex – and are the main method of financing the purchase of houses by most people in England and Wales

(Lawson & Rudden 2002: 141–144). The real right obtained by the mortgage lender is now registered at the Land Registry as a charge on the land acting as security. More complex are mortgages with respect to chattels for the obvious reason that it is extremely difficult to set up any kind of registration system with respect to movable items. Accordingly, while in form chattel mortgages are possible, in practice very restrictive legislation has completely discouraged such a form of security. Nevertheless, lawyers have managed to get around the legal difficulties involving chattels by developing the contract of hire purchase and contracts of sale with retention of title (on which see Lawson & Rudden 2002: 146–148). However, pledge remains an important form of chattel real security, but of course this involves transferring possession of the goods (bailment) to the pawnbroker.

82.   USUS FRUCTUS EST IUS ALIENIS REBUS UTENDI FRUENDI SALVA RERUM SUBSTANTIA

> *A usufruct is a ius of using and enjoying the things of another without infraction of the substance of such things.*
>
> (Paul, D.7.1.1).

Another form of real rights is servitudes. Again, this is an institution that goes back to Roman law, of which there were two kinds. There were those founded on the relationship between person (*persona*) and thing (*res*) – called personal servitudes – and those founded on a relationship between *res* and *res*, called real servitudes. Typical real servitudes were rights of way and rights to channel water over another's land (D.8.3.1) or, in towns, rights to light or to project a roof over another's land (D.8.2.2). These servitudes have passed into modern civil law and are defined in France as "a charge imposed upon one piece of land for the usage and the utility of a piece of land belonging to another" (CC art 637). Personal servitudes confer a real right in favour of a person, and some of the most important were called usufructs. These were real rights of using and enjoying the things of another, such as the right to quarry stone on another's land or to take fruit from certain trees. The usufruct also applied to moveable property and were assets in themselves in that they could be bought and sold as forms of intangible property (D.7.1.12.2). Modern civil law defines the usufruct as "the right to enjoy as owner things of which another has the ownership, but on the condition of conserving the substance of it" (CC art 578). Usufructs can be created in respect of movable property and even consumable items, the right owner of the latter being under an obligation to restore the same quantity and quality of goods (CC art 587).

Servitudes have also found their way into English law, of which there are two kinds, namely easements and restrictive covenants (Lawson & Rudden 2002: 153–158). Easements are much like the Roman real servitudes in that they are based on a relationship between two pieces of land (*res* and *res*); the easement – which might be a right of way, a right to light, or support for a building – attaches to the dominant tenement and is a burden so to speak on the servient tenement. English law also recognises a usufruct but does not call it by this name; they are called profits and entitle a person to take some profit – for example, fish, stones, sand and the like – from land belonging to another. Restrictive covenants are agreements restricting the use of land for the benefit of other land, and such agreements attach to (run with) the land rather than just existing as a right between persons. Thus, a certain piece of land might have a restrictive covenant prohibiting the building of industrial premises or limiting the range of activities that can be carried out on the property. As the name suggests, such covenants were originally contractual in nature but became real rights in the 19th century; as a result of their *in rem* nature, they need to be entered on the Land Registry.

CONCLUDING REMARKS

As has been mentioned, in Roman law itself the law of things encompassed not just what today we would call the law of property, but also the law of obligations (see next chapter). Debts were a form of property. However, from a 'rights' (*iura*) viewpoint, the separation between property and obligations is fundamental, and this was true of Roman law, although one has to be careful in translating *ius* as a 'right'. Yet, whatever the situation was in Rome, the distinction today is fundamental in continental law. It is more complex in the common law not just because of the distinction between legal and equitable rights, but also because the law of tort (law of obligations) provides many of the remedies that protect property rights. As in continental law, the common law equally distinguishes between ownership, possession and real rights in another's property, but one cannot assert with the same certainty that 'ownership has nothing in common with possession'.

8. Law of obligations (1)

In modern civil law the law of obligations is now the third generic category of private law. As we shall see, it covers three principal specific legal subjects: namely contract, tort (delict in civil and Scots law) and restitution. Like the law of property, these areas have much substance and, leaving aside restitution, are foundational legal subjects in any law programme. Again, like the law of property, many of the basic concepts and notions – and even some of the actual rules – go back to Roman law.

83. OBLIGATIO EST IURIS VINCULUM, QUO NECESSITATE ADSTRINGIMUR ALICUIUS SOLVENDAE REI, SECUNDUM NOSTRAE CIVITATIS IURA

> *An obligation is a legal bond by which we are bound by the need to perform something according to the laws of our state.*

(Justinian, *Institutes*, 3.13pr)

It has already been established that the notion of a law of obligations comes from Roman law (see maxims 41 and 73). Indeed, the Romans even provided a definition. However, this definition is rather meaningless as a proposition but is powerful in its metaphorical image of a *vinculum iuris* binding two persons; this image has proved extraordinarily influential and lies at the heart of all modern definitions of a law of obligations. For example, in French law, an obligation is still defined as a *lien juridique* (Fabre-Magnan 2024: 1–3).

The civilian law of obligations has two fundamental formal characteristics. First, it is a category that contains rights *in personam* (in Roman law it contained *actiones in personam*), rights *in rem* belonging to the separate category of the law of property (see Chapter 7). Secondly, the category of obligations formed, as we have seen, part of a highly coherent system of private law (see maxim 41). Rights *in personam* (personal rights) were defined in part by their opposition to rights *in rem* (real rights) and to personality rights (non-patrimonial rights forming part of the law of persons).

Gaius in his *Institutes* says that there were two sources ('birth') of obligations, namely contracts and delicts, but at the same time he admits that this duality is inadequate. There are some actions *in personam* that cannot be classified into one or the other of these categories (G.3.91). Thus, in a later work, he adds the third category of 'various causes' (D.44.7.1). This was hardly a satisfactory category for those with a systematic mind, and so Justinian in his *Institutes* identifies four sources, namely contracts, quasi-contracts, delicts and quasi delicts (J.3.13.2). These four categories have found their way into the French *Code civil*, although delicts and quasi-delicts are not distinguished; however, in the German Civil Code (BGB) both of the 'quasi' categories have been abandoned. Instead of quasi-contracts – which were seemingly justified in Roman law by the principle that 'no one should be unjustly enriched at the expense of another' (D.12.6.14) – there is the category of unjust enrichment (BGB § 812) (see maxim 112).

Modern civil law books on the law of obligations emphasise the distinction between the obligation as a legal bond (*vinculum iuris*) and the various subcategory sources by having a chapter on 'general theory of obligations'. At this level, the textbooks discuss for example the transmission of obligations and natural obligations, these latter, while giving rise to no actual legal obligation, having certain indirect effects in law (Fabre-Magnan 2024: 4–5). The Romans did not seem very interested in this kind of general theory, but a distinction between obligation and the various types of obligation certainly existed in Roman law. Yet, when the Romans talked of obligations in this general way, they usually had in mind contractual obligations; in other words, a contract was the paradigm obligation (D.5.1.20).

84. OBLIGATIONUM SUBSTANTIA NON IN EO CONSISTIT, UT ALIQUOD CORPUS NOSTRUM AUT SERVITUTEM NOSTRAM FACIAT, SED UT ALIUM NOBIS OBSTRINGAT AD DANDUM ALIQUID VEL FACIENDUM VEL PRAESTANDUM

> *The essence of an obligation does not consist in the fact that it makes something ours or a servitude ours, but that some other person is obliged to give, to do or to perform something for us.*

> (Paul, D.44.7.3pr)

Another way of understanding the law of obligations is from the position of legal remedies and legal rights. In Roman law, two fundamental types of remedy underpinned private law. An action *in rem* was a claim used to vindicate ownership or some lesser property right in a thing; it was a remedy aimed at the thing itself. The substantive area of law concerned with these real remedies was (and remains in modern continental law) the law of property (see chapter 7). The other type of remedy was an action *in personam*; these personal actions were aimed not at things but at another person, and the substantive area of law dealing with these claims was the law of obligations. Accordingly, as we have mentioned, the law of obligations is in part to be understood in contrast to the law of property. This contrast is today one of rights: real rights (*iura in rem*) are contrasted with personal rights (*iura in personam*) and the law of obligations is that area of law concerned with personal rights (to be distinguished from personality rights: see maxim 72). Perhaps this property and obligations dichotomy can be put another way: the law of obligations is about 'owing' while the law of property is about 'owning' (and its associated lesser rights and interests) (see maxim 73).

The importance of the distinction can be illustrated in relation to factual reality. If O lends B a book and B fails to return the object, O can recover the book by asserting his legal relation to the thing itself. In practical terms, this could mean that should O find 'his' book lying in the corridor outside B's room, he can in principle, simply retake possession of the object. If the book remained in the possession of B, and B refused to return it to O, the latter could – in Roman law – bring a vindication action, that is to say, an *actio in rem* aimed at the book itself. In short, the book remains his in the strict sense of an actual and direct *dominion* between *persona* and *res*. (In English law, O would have to bring a claim in the tort of conversion.)

However, if O lends B a loaf of bread, the ownership (*dominium*) relationship must come to an end the moment B eats the thing. In fact, Roman law took the view that the *dominium* relationship came to an end the moment O transferred consumable goods like wine, flour, or oil to another (unless perhaps O did this only for their safekeeping) (G.3.90). The only legal relation that existed from the moment of the disappearance of the ownership relationship was an obligation to return an equivalent amount of the property (D.12.1.3). If O, therefore, found a loaf of bread lying in the corridor outside B's room, he would not be entitled to take it. This property distinction reflected itself equally in the law of obligations. If O lent B a book and the book was destroyed in some accident for which B was in no way responsible, B may well have a defence to any contractual claim brought by O against him (D.13.6.18pr). However, such a defence would never be available in the case of goods to be consumed: *genera non pereunt* (see maxim 77).

What if O lent B a sum of money: is this property to be treated as consumable or non-consumable? The Romans gave a clear answer to this question: money was property to be consumed, and so when one person lent a sum of money to another, it could be recovered only via an *actio in personam* (D.7.5.5.1). Thus, if O lent B a sum of money for the weekend and on Monday found the sum lying on B's desk, O would not be entitled to retake it, even if the sum consisted of the same coins or notes (unless, again, the notes and coins were transferred only for their safekeeping). This is one reason why Roman lawyers found it necessary to develop a third category of obligations alongside contract and delict. If O paid money to B by mistake, perhaps thinking B was C, the payment could not be recovered by an *actio in rem* since money, like flour or wine, was a consumable item; ownership passed to the payee on payment. However, the payee could not keep the value of the money since there was no cause to justify the payment; he would be obliged to re-convey an equivalent amount on the basis that no one should be unjustly enriched at the expense of another (see maxim 112).

As we shall see, English law more or less conforms to this pattern of legal relations at the level of fact. However, there are exceptions, one of the most important being the equitable remedy of tracing. The Court of Chancery took the view that money might *not* be a consumable on occasions and thus could be reclaimed from another's patrimony on the basis of an *in rem* relation.

85.   PACTA SUNT SERVANDA

Agreements are to be kept.

(Baldus, Comment on D.2.14.1 no 1)

When one examines the various subject areas within the law of obligations, contract was, and possibly remains, the central one. The notion of contract is Roman in origin in the sense of a *vinculum iuris* based upon agreement, but the fashioning of a general theory of contract is post-Roman. The Romans themselves developed a detailed set of contractual ideas around a range of transactions such as sale, hire, partnership, loan and deposit; and each of these transactions had their own particular *actio* or legal remedy. The Romans did not stop with these transactional forms, for they equally developed some more general ideas of contracting. For example, formal promises (stipulations) were enforceable at law provided they were spoken in a particular form of words, and pacts and innominate (unnamed) contracts were also given legal enforceability where justice required (D.19.5.1). Ulpian summed up the importance of *pacta: quid enim tam congruum fidei humanae, quam ea quae inter eos placuerunt servare* (for what is more appropriate for trust in human affairs than making people keep to what they have agreed to) (D.2.14.1pr)? People must keep to the contracts that they have agreed to.

86.   NUDA PACTIO OBLIGATIONEM NON PARIT

No obligation arises from a bare pact.

(Ulpian, D.2.14.7.4)

Yet what the Romans did not do was fashion a general theory of contract based upon promise or agreement. As Ulpian famously asserted, bare pacts are not enforceable at law, a variation of this maxim being *ex nudo pacto non oritur actio* (no action arises from a bare pact). This said, the Romans nevertheless recognised that all the different contracts shared the common denominator of agreement (*conventio*) (D.2.14.1.3), and they were accordingly able to cat- egorise them within the single classification of actions *ex contractu*. Indeed, Ulpian suggests that if there was a sufficient ground (*causa*) this might be the basis for a 'synallagmatic' obligation (D.2.14.7.2), for contracts arise out of agreements (D.16.3.1.6).

In the later civil law, the medieval doctors of law and the canon lawyers began to develop the common denominator of *conventio* and *consensus* (also found in Roman law) into a general theory of contract. The first step was to reverse the 'bare pact' metaphor and turn it into a 'clothed pact' (*pactum ves- titum*); if a sufficient *causa* could be found, then the bare pact 'cohered' into a 'binding' contract (*pactum nudum vestitur cohaerentia contractus*, said the Post-Glossators). As one can see, the early medieval Roman lawyers felt very constrained by the authority of the Roman texts and thus 'bare pacts' had to be considered unenforceable. The canonists, in contrast, were more independ- ent in that the Church had other moral priorities than those inherent in Roman law. To break a promise was, in the Church's eyes, a sin, even if the promise amounted to a bare pact, and thus the canon lawyers tended to assert that a bare pact could nevertheless give rise to a legal action: *pactum nudum ligat de iure canonico*, said the canon lawyer Panormitanus (1386–1445). Or, put another way, *ex pacto nudo, de iure canonico oritur actio* (in canon law a bare pact gives rise to an action) (Decius, Comment on C.2.3.10). And so gradually the idea of a *nudum pactum* was by-passed, at first with the help of the *stipula- tio*, and later by ideas from customary and mercantile law, with the result that by the 17th century lawyers on the Continent recognised a general common principle that all consensually formed contracts should be kept (*pacta sunt servanda*) (see above maxim 85).

87. LES CONVENTIONS ÉTANT FORMÉES, TOUT CE QUI A ÉTÉ CONVENU TIENT LIEU DE LOI À CEUX QUI LES ONT FAITES

Agreements once formed, everything that has been agreed has the force of enacted law between those who have made them.

(Domat, *Les loix civiles*, First Book, First Part, Book I, Title I, Section II, § VII)

By the 17th century, a general theory of contract had been well-established in continental Europe. The famous statement of Domat's, saying that contract has the status of legislation between the parties (*tient lieu de loi*), which found its way into the French *Code civil* (art 1134, now art 1103), was based on an interpretation – or more likely a misinterpretation – of a comment by Ulpian, namely *contactus legem ex conventione accipunt* (D.16.3.1.6). This comment appears to suggest that a contract is a form of legislation (*lex*) arising out of an agreement, but Ulpian probably did not actually mean this as *lex,* as this was an ambiguous term. But be that as it may. *Consensus* had become the normative foundation of the contractual obligation, and there was no longer a need, at a theoretical level, for a law of contracts based on a set of empirical transactions and associated legal actions.

Yet, in some ways, this early *Code civil* axiom proved to be the high point of contractual theory in that many subsequent codes did not subscribe to the private legislation thesis. Indeed, the Dutch Code of 1992 makes it very clear that obligations arise from legislation and not vice-versa (Book 6 art 1). However, what has survived is the principle of *consensus* as the normative trigger for a contractual relationship; thus, the *Principles of European Contract Law* (PECL), one of the efforts of the last century to fashion a common European contract code, asserts that a contract is formed, provided the parties intend to be legally bound, if there is "sufficient agreement" (art 2.101). The Civil Code of Québec states that a "contract is formed by the sole exchange of consents" (art 1385). Most of these new codes recognise, however, that consent is not something that can be objectively gauged and thus it finds its formal expression through offer and acceptance (PECL arts 2.201, 2.204).

Yet this analysis model is much less empirical than it might at first seem, and so one is often forced back to the transactional categories – sale, hire, deposit, insurance, carriage and so on – that were typical of the old Roman approach. The result is that in the modern civil law, the starting point for a contract is not actually the general theory but the particular type of transaction in play. As Professor Rampelberg notes, the civilian jurist tends to start out "from the list of 'named' contracts, the unnamed contract playing only a marginal role". Indeed the "civilian jurists practically never work within the general category of contract; in particular, they never worry about knowing if a new agreement can or cannot be considered as a contract." For, "when faced with a new form of agreement, they deal with it either by combining existing agreements or adapting a quite different one" (Rampelberg 2005: 35).

88.   A VALUABLE CONSIDERATION IN THE SENSE OF THE LAW, MAY CONSIST EITHER IN SOME RIGHT, INTEREST, PROFIT, OR BENEFIT ACCRUING TO ONE PARTY, OR SOME FORBEARANCE, DETRIMENT, LOSS, OR RESPONSIBILITY, GIVEN, SUFFERED, OR UNDERTAKEN BY THE OTHER

(Lush J, in *Currie v Misa* (1875) LR 10 Ex 153, 162).

Professor Rampelberg continues by contrasting this civilian attitude with that of the common lawyers. As we shall see (below maxim 90), English lawyers did not develop a general theory of contract until the 19th century – for their thinking before then was dominated by the forms of action – but, when they did, they used this general theory as their starting point. Thus, according to Professor Rampelberg, the common lawyers "are not familiar with types of contractual agreement"; and from "the very moment an agreement has a pat-rimonial content, the English judge has to determine if there is a contract in starting out from the general notion of unnamed contract, the only category on which he can base himself". The professor interestingly warns that "when the civilians wish to convince the common lawyers to abandon the requirement of consideration they run the risk of doing away with the one authentic unifying element... in exchange for a mutilated general notion of contract" (2005: 35). The foundation of contract in the civil law would appear to be, then, the named transaction which acts as the *causa*; in the common law, by way of contrast, it is consideration which acts as the *causa*, operating within the general category of contract. And thus there is no such thing in English contract law as the 'gratuitous' contract; in order for a contract to be binding each party must gain a benefit and suffer a detriment. In most commercial and consumer contracts this requirement is rarely missing because one party renders goods or services (detriment) while the other party must pay a price (detriment); the party ren-dering the service is to receive payment (benefit) while the party having to pay is to receive the goods or services (benefit).

89. [I]F I BUY A HORSE FROM YOU, THE PROPERTY IN THE HORSE IS AT ONCE MINE AND THEREFORE YOU SHALL HAVE A WRIT OF DEBT FOR THE MONEY AND I SHALL HAVE DETINUE FOR THE HORSE UPON THIS BARGAIN

(Fortescue CJKB, in *Doige's Case* (1442), in Baker & Milsom, *Sources of English Legal History*, Butterworths, 1986, 391, 394)

So, how did a law of contract develop in English law given that the common law supposedly evolved free of Roman law? For many centuries the common law indeed remained largely uninfluenced by the categories of the Roman law of obligations. However, this does not mean that people were not contracting from the 11th century onwards (or before); undoubtedly they were, and this is why the Court of Chancery developed its remedy of specific performance (see maxim 118). What it means is that the common law itself did not at a formal level think in terms of a substantive law of contract based upon agreement and consent. It provided, instead, some remedies when a sale or some other kind of transaction went wrong. For example, as Chief Justice Fortescue indicated, the unpaid seller of a cow could bring a claim in debt, while a buyer who had not received the promised cow could bring an action in detinue. One has to recall that the common law was a series of forms of action. There was something of a defect before the 15th century in the rule that 'not doing is no trespass' which meant that it was difficult to bring a claim for damages against someone who had simply failed to do what he had promised (Ibbetson 1999: 126–129). However, this was overcome by a species of trespass on the case called *assumpsit,* which by the 17th century had become a form of action permitting a disappointed contractor to obtain damages for breach of a contractual promise (Ibbetson 1999: 147). Indeed a form of *assumpsit* could even be used for obtaining a debt on the basis that a person who failed to pay was in breach of his promise to repay (although at the level of pleading, the debt and damages distinction did not disappear: Ibbetson 1999: 147–151).

During the 18th century, the shape of the modern law of contract began to form, thanks in part to the appearance of doctrinal literature, much of it influenced by civilian thinking. In the 19th century, a fully formed general theory of contract had established itself in judicial thinking (see e.g. *Carlill* v *Carbolic Smoke Ball Co* [1893] 1 QB 256). Cases were now classified under the category of contract and tort rather than debt, damages, assumpsit and the like (see Bramwell LJ in *Bryant v Herbert* (1877) 3 CPD 389). Nevertheless, the debt and damages dichotomy and the debt and detinue one as well have not fully disappeared, and so Chief Justice Fortescue's observation about the sale of a horse retains a certain relevancy. Accordingly, if B buys a car from S, property (ownership) in the car is at once vested in B (Sale of Goods Act 1979 ss 16–18) and S will have an action for debt – which is different from an action for damages (see maxim 117). But if the car is not delivered to B, he or she will have a claim in 'detinue' (now conversion) against S, liability being in damages for the value of the car (although today B will also have an alternative action for breach of contract).

90.   THE BASIC PRINCIPLE WHICH THE LAW OF CONTRACT SEEKS TO ENFORCE IS THAT A PERSON WHO MAKES A PROMISE TO ANOTHER OUGHT TO KEEP HIS PROMISE

(Lord Diplock, in *Moschi* v *Lep Air Services Ltd* [1973] AC 331, 346)

There is no doubt that this general theory had been imported from civil law (see, e.g., the judgment of Lord Coleridge in *Ditcham v Worrall* (1880) 5 CPD 410 and Kekewich J in *Foster v Wheeler* (1887) 36 Ch D 695). As David Ibbetson puts it, one was "squeezing English rules into models developed elsewhere" (1999: 153). However despite the talk of contract being founded on 'agreement' this was, and probably remains, inaccurate both as a matter of history and theory. Liability in contract is based on the idea of a breach of promise rather than the non-performance of an agreement, as Lord Diplock indicates in his general principle. However, Lord Diplock went on to add that this "basic principle is subject to a historical exception that English law does not give the promisee a remedy for the failure by a promisor to perform his promise unless either the promise was made in a particular form, e.g., under seal, or the promisee in return promises to do something for the promisor which he would not otherwise be obliged to do, i.e., gives consideration for the promise" (Lord Diplock in *Moschi* v *Lep Air Services Ltd* [1973] AC 331, at 346). (As for contracts made under seal, see now Law of Property (Miscellaneous Provisions) Act 1989 s 1.)

The result is that a contract in English law is different from a contract in the civil law in several ways. First, it is not formed merely by 'sufficient agreement' (cf DCFR, Bk II, arts 4:101–103); there has to be a specific offer and acceptance (*Gibson* v *Manchester City Council* [1979] 1 WLR 294). Secondly, the existence of a mistake does not prevent a contract from being formed; a promise is a promise and only in exceptional circumstances will an error make a contract void (*Bell* v *Lever Brothers* [1932] AC 161). Thirdly, there does not necessarily have to be an 'object' to the promise; as a judge once said: "If a man covenant, for a valid consideration, that it shall rain to-morrow, he cannot afterwards say, 'I could not make it rain; I did all I could to make it rain; but it would not.' He chooses to covenant that such a thing shall happen, and if it does not, he has broken his covenant" (Maule J in *Canham v Barry* (1855) 24 LJCP 100, 106). Fourthly, a contract itself tends not to be seen as some kind of abstract single binding obligation (*vinculum iuris*) but more as a collection of promises called terms, which are traditionally divided into several kinds. There are express terms – which can give rise to problems of interpretation with respect to their language – and there are implied terms, which the courts sometimes have to read into contracts, or a class of contracts, in order to give them efficacy (*The Moorcock* (1889) 14 PD 64). Another dichotomy is the one between conditions and warranties. The former are terms fundamental to the contract which, if broken will permit the other party not just to claim damages but also to terminate the contract. Warranties are less serious terms which, if broken, give rise only to a claim in damages. So what is the general theory of English contract law? Lord Diplock expressed it this way: "Each promise that a promisor makes to a promisee by entering into a contract with him creates an obligation to perform it owed by the promisor as obligor to the promisee as obligee. If he does not do so voluntarily there are two kinds of remedies which the court can grant to the promisee. It can compel the obligor to pay to the obligee a sum of money to compensate him for the loss that he has sustained as a result of the obligee's failure to perform his obligation. This is the remedy at common law in damages for breach of contract". Lord Diplock then added: "But there are some kinds of obligation which the court is able to compel the obligor actually to perform. In some cases ... a remedy to compel performance by a decree of specific performance or by injunction is also available. It was formerly obtainable only in a court of equity ... But, since a court of common law could make and enforce orders for payment of a sum of money, where the obligation was itself an obligation to pay a sum of money, even a court of common law could compel the obligor to perform it" (*Moschi* v *Lep Air Services Ltd* [1973] AC 331, at 346).

Two valuable points arise from this description. The first is that to talk of damages as the main remedy for breach of contract (as many writers have done) is misleading since such claims are statistically quite rare. By far the most common claim in England and Wales for breach of contract is an action in debt for the price of goods sold, services supplied, or for unpaid rent or loans (see maxim 99). The importance of this statistic is that in substance ninety per cent of all claims in contract are claims for specific performance; that is to say, as Lord Diplock indicated, the claimant is asking the court to enforce directly the defendant's primary obligation (namely to pay a sum of money). Given that debts are a form of intangible property – they are choses in action – contract is really as much part of the law of property as the law of obligations. It is a means by which sellers or suppliers can create property for themselves, although if the debtor goes bankrupt, the value of this property might well disappear.

The second point is that, despite the statistical importance of debt claims, the rule that a non-performing contractor is also liable for damages for breach of a contractual promise remains important as a principle of liability. Thanks to the old action of assumpsit, which became a general action for any breach of promise, a breach of contract is a cause of action in itself. All that a claimant who suffers loss or damage has to show is that there was a binding contract between the claimant and the defendant, that the defendant was in breach of it, that the breach caused the claimant's damage, and that the damage was not too remote (*Hadley v Baxendale* (1854) 9 Ex 341; 156 ER 145). And in order for there to be a binding contract, the claimant has to show that there was offer and acceptance, consideration, and an intention to create legal relations (*Carlill* v *Carbolic Smoke Ball Co* [1893] 1 QB 256). In short, once a contract is established, liability to pay a debt or to pay damages attaches to the notion of 'contract' itself. Liability arises out of the breach of the contractual promise (term) broken and not out of facts giving rise to a particular class of contract.

91.   IF THERE IS ONE THING MORE THAN ANOTHER WHICH PUBLIC POLICY REQUIRES, IT IS THAT MEN OF FULL AGE AND COMPETENT UNDERSTANDING SHALL HAVE THE UTMOST LIBERTY OF CONTRACTING AND THEIR CONT- RACTS, WHEN ENTERED INTO FREELY AND VOLUNTARILY, SHALL BE HELD SACRED AND SHALL BE ENFORCED BY COURTS OF JUSTICE

(Sir George Jessel, in *Printing and Numerical Registering Co v Sampson* (1875) LR 19 Eq 462, 465)

One fundamental maxim or principle that attaches to the general theory of contract is freedom of contract. This principle of freedom of contract is affirmed in both the PECL (art 1.102) and UNIDROIT (art 1.1), although perhaps finding its most perfect expression in the French assertion that contracts are a form of private legislation between the parties (CC art 1103). In its heyday, this principle assumed not only that contractual parties were formally and substantially equal but that parties were free to make what a third party might consider unreasonable contracts. Contract, in other words, was a matter for the parties and not the courts. Yet this ideology of freedom – as expressed by Sir George Jessel – was to result in a paradox: a party had the freedom to insert in a contract a clause that stipulated whatever his behaviour he was in no circumstances to be contractually liable. Such freedom inevitably resulted in abuse where economically powerful parties were able to impose on weaker parties standard form contracts full of clauses limiting or nullifying the apparent rights of the weaker party.

Courts in the UK and continental Europe developed a number of tactics to deal with this abuse (strict interpretation, *contra proferentem* rule, good faith, abuse of rights, fundamental terms, and so on), but it was only with legislative intervention in the 1970s that the problem became fully regulated. This legislation, on the whole, tackled the paradox of freedom and abuse by formally making a distinction between consumer and non-consumer contracts (see now Consumer Rights Act 2015). Freedom of contract was maintained as between commercial parties able to look after their own interests; consumers, on the other hand, were given more or less full protection against abusive terms, although in England much will turn on what 'unfair' means to judges. Will this be judged from the consumer or the commercial perspective? The answer seems to be that consumer protection does not seem to be a high priority for the judges (see in particular *Arnold v Britton* [2015] UKSC 36; *ParkingEye Ltd v Beavis* [2015] UKSC 67).

This said, the control of unfair clauses is not confined to consumer contracts. Both in English law and at the European level (see PECL art 4.110), unfair clauses can be struck down in certain types of commercial contracts. Moreover, there is authority to the effect that a small commercial concern might even be treated, in certain circumstances, as a consumer (*R & B Customs Brokers Co Ltd v UDT Ltd* [1988] 1 WLR 321). As is typical with English law, much will depend upon the facts. One might note in addition that Equity can have a role with respect to certain types of abusive clauses. If such a clause imposes on the other party a 'penalty' for any breaches of contract – that is to say a clause stipulating that the contractor must pay a fixed sum of money that is in excess of any damage suffered by the party not in breach – it will be unenforceable, although there are exceptions. If the penalty is there to protect a 'legitimate interest' and is not excessive, it may now be enforceable (*ParkingEye Ltd v Beavis* [2015] UKSC 67).

92. LES CONTRATS DOIVENT ÊTRE NÉGOCIÉS, FORMÉS ET EXÉCUTÉS DE BONNE FOI

> *Contracts must be negotiated, formed and performed in good faith.*
>
> (*Code civil* art 1104)

One way in which abusive terms can be tackled in civil law systems is through the doctrine of good faith. To contract and not to contract at the same time, or indeed to contract on terms where one party is put at a significant disadvantage, could be seen as evidence of bad faith (cf PECL art 4.110).

The notion of *bona fides* has its origin in Roman law, where it required equity in contracts to the highest degree (D.16.3.31pr). Nevertheless, this general statement must be seen in the context that contracting parties were also free to take advantage of each other (D.4.4.16.4; D.19.2.22.3), and thus the exact scope of the duty of good faith in the context of commerce has never been easy to gauge. One Scottish Law lord has pointed out that good faith functioned at the level of the remedy rather than right and was not, therefore, "a source of obligation in itself" (*R (European Roma Rights Centre) v Immigration Officer at Prague Airport* [2005] 2 AC 1, at paras 59–60 per Lord Hope). Yet, in modern civil law, the requirement of good faith is to be found in all the codes; thus, for example article 1104 of the French civil code now states that agreements "must be negotiated, formed and performed in good faith." It is a general duty to be found in both the PECL (art 1.201) and UNIDROIT (art 1.7) ('good faith and fair dealing').

Certainly, the topic has attracted much literature. What makes the duty difficult is whether it is simply a passive duty – that is to say, a duty not to act in positive bad faith – or if it goes further and imposes active duties on contracting parties. Traditionally, in France, good faith has translated itself into two main obligations: the duty of loyalty (*devoir de loyauté*) and the duty of co-operation. Both of these raise interesting questions in themselves. However, more recently French doctrine and jurisprudence seem to have gone further, imposing a duty to inform and to collaborate, the latter specifically appearing as an independent duty in the PECL (art 1.202). Good faith is, in other words, being used to construct a new philosophy of *solidarisme contractuel* in which a contracting party has to further not just his own interests but, to an extent, the interests of his co-party (Derroussin 2012: 437–438; Fabre-Magnan 2024: 141–142). This said, the *Code civil* states that good faith is always to be presumed, and thus the burden of proving bad faith is on the person who alleges it (CC art 2274).

Whether good faith is to be found in English law has, traditionally, been a difficult question given that there are judicial dicta pointing in both directions. One writer has described it as an 'irritant' (Teubner 1998), while a Victorian Law Lord has claimed that it is a term implied in all mercantile contracts (Lord Watson in *Glynn Mills Curie & Co v East & West India Dock Co* (1882) 7 App Cas 591, at 615). However what is clear is that English law is very sceptical about any notion of *solidarisme contractuel* and the case law itself demonstrates that parties are expected to look after their own interests; they are not generally under a duty to inform (see, e.g., *Reid v Rush & Tompkins Plc* [1990] 1 WLR 212; *University of Nottingham v Eyett* [1999] 2 All ER 437). The only general duty is not positively to mislead (misrepresentation). Good faith has, in some civilian systems, extended itself beyond the contractual obligation and into the pre-contractual domain (as the new CC art 1104 indicates; and see also art 1112); this extension is reflected in the PECL in that negotiations broken off in bad faith may give rise to liability (art 2.301). But English law has seemingly rejected such a principle, although not without some dissent in the academic literature (*Walford* v *Miles* [1992] 2 AC 128). Yet, there is one case where a defendant who negligently failed to read the claimant's tender (offer) was held liable in damages for this failure (*Blackpool & Fylde Aero Club Ltd* v *Blackpool BC* [1990] 1 WLR 1195).

Perhaps the English position has best been summarised by Bingham LJ where he said of good faith that: "English law has, characteristically, committed itself to no such overriding principle but has developed piecemeal solutions in response to demonstrated problems of unfairness. Many examples could be given. Thus equity has intervened to strike down unconscionable bargains. Parliament has stepped in to regulate the imposition of exemption clauses and the form of certain hire-purchase agreements. The common law also has made its contribution, by holding that certain classes of contract require the utmost good faith, by treating as irrecoverable what purport to be agreed estimates of damage but are in truth a disguised penalty for breach, and in many other ways (*Interfoto Picture Library Ltd* v *Stiletto Visual Programmes Ltd*" [1989] QB 433, at 439). One might add to this list devices such as equitable estoppel and the (occasional) duty to behave as a reasonable contractor.

However, most importantly, there have been more recent developments since Bingham LJ's statement. Good faith might be implied in contracts that are relational or long-term, as opposed to instantaneous contracts such as buying a cup of coffee or a newspaper. In one relatively recent case involving relational contracts, the judge said this: "Firstly, a term requiring good faith does not mean honesty. That emphasised sentence in the passage in *Chitty* is, in my judgment, simply wrong, and ignores statements in the cases explaining what a term requiring good faith means. There is more to a duty of good faith than a requirement to act honestly. It includes honesty, but there is more to it than that. Secondly, by stating that English law generally *rejects* a legal requirement of good faith, the passage at 1–058 uses its opposition to the doctrine as a justification for why that doctrine is said not to be of application".

However, the judge went on to say, this is "a wholly circular argument, and ignores a number of cases". And so, he said that he did "not consider that, on the authorities… identified, English law rejects a legal requirement of good faith." But he added that "the cases make clear is that such a duty will not be routinely applied to all commercial contracts" (Fraser J, in *Bates* v *Post Office* [2019] EWHC 606, para 710). The judge then went on to add: "I therefore consider that in this respect, the learned editors of *Chitty* do not correctly summarise the jurisprudence in this area of the law. I consider that there is a species of contracts, which are most usefully termed 'relational contracts', in which there is implied an obligation of good faith (which is also termed 'fair dealing' in some of the cases). This means that the parties must refrain from conduct which in the relevant context would be regarded as commercially unacceptable by reasonable and honest people. An implied duty of good faith does not mean solely that the parties must be honest" (para 711).

Does this judicial statement now represent English law? Great care must be taken here since a retired Supreme Court judge (Lord Neuberger) has cast doubt on the judgment (see Hyde, *The Law Society Gazette*, 12 June 2024). Yet what was unfortunate about Lord Neuberger's intervention was that it was centred on the *Bates* case in which Fraser J's judgment, whether right or wrong, helped lead to the exposure of one of the United Kingdom's worst ever miscarriages of justice concerning sub-postmasters wrongfully convicted of fraud. The retired Supreme Court judge thus found himself on the wrong side of history and having to justify his apparent support for the Post Office which had wrongfully prosecuted these sub-postmasters (the convictions had to be overturned by statute). It will be difficult for any future court to say that Fraser J was wrong since not only was his decision evidently on the side of justice (giving a boost to good faith and relational contracts) but the judgment itself has become celebrated amongst those who fought against the prosecutions and convictions.

93. VERBA ITA SUNT INTELLIGENDA UT RES MAGIS VALEAT QUAM PEREAT

> *[Contractual] words should be interpreted so as to preserve rather than destroy.*
>
> (Baldus, Comment on D.45.1.80; Coke, Litt 42a)

Implied terms could be regarded as an aspect of contractual interpretation: the court is, in effect, interpreting a contract in order to decide if the parties had impliedly agreed that there should be an obligation of good faith. In fact, the courts have asserted that implied terms and contractual interpretation must be kept separate since the two exercises involve different principles and approaches (*Marks & Spencer plc v BNP Paribas* [2015] UKSC 72). But this seems a special common law rule and so, when looking at Roman texts, it is by no means easy to distinguish between implying certain meanings and interpreting words of a contract. As for interpretation itself, the maxim *verba ita sunt intelligenda ut res magis valeat quam pereat* is one that has long been recognised in the civil law – it has its roots in Roman law (D.45.1.80, as interpreted by Baldus: *stipulatio est interpretanda ut valeat, non pereat*) – and has been translated as "the contract should be interpreted so that it is valid rather than ineffective" (Staughton LJ in *Lancashire County Council v Municipal Mutual Insurance Ltd* [1997] QB 897, 910). In other words, the aim is to uphold contracts wherever possible (see also Civil Code of Québec art 1428; DCFR art II-8:106). One, more recent, UK example where this principle has – seemingly – been applied is *RTS Flexible Systems Ltd v Molkerei Alois Müller GmbH & Co KG* [2010] 1 WLR 753.

What, then, are the general principles regarding the interpretation of contracts? In France, the fundamental principle is the common intention of the parties, and this intention means that the judge must not stop at a literal interpretation of the words; the judge must go beyond the words themselves (CC art 1188). However, if it is not possible to determine this common intention, then the contract must be interpreted according to the sense that a "reasonable person" placed in the same situation would give to the contract, a test that (once again) seemingly goes back to Roman law and the case of the good man and the implied term (*vir bonus*) (D.19.2.58.1).

In English law, the test at first sight seems the reverse of the civilian one. The judge can look only at the words used in the contract and must not go beyond these words. That said, the difference may not be so wide since the test used for interpretation is that of the reasonable man. As Lord Hoffmann has put it: it "is agreed that the question is what a reasonable person having all the background knowledge which would have been available to the parties would have understood them to be using the language in the contract to mean" (*Chartbrook Ltd v Persimmon Homes Ltd* [2009] 1 AC 1101, para 14). Where there is a difference is with respect to the evidence of intention. As Lord Hoffmann went on to explain (in para 39): "Supporters of the admissibility of pre-contractual negotiations draw attention to the fact that continental legal systems seem to have little difficulty in taking them into account. Both the *Unidroit Principles of International Commercial Contracts* (1994 and 2004 revision) and the *Principles of European Contract Law* (1999) provide that in ascertaining the 'common intention of the parties', regard shall be had to prior negotiations: articles 4(3) and 5(102) respectively. The same is true of the United Nations Convention on Contracts for the International Sale of Goods" (1980). The Law Lord continued:

But these instruments reflect the French philosophy of contractual interpretation, which is altogether different from that of English law. As Professor Catherine Valcke explains in an illuminating article ("On Comparing French and English Contract Law: Insights from Social Contract Theory" (16 January 2009) Social Science Research Network), French law regards the intentions of the parties as a pure question of subjective fact, their volonté psychologique, uninfluenced by any rules of law. It follows that any evidence of what they said or did, whether to each other or to third parties, may be relevant to establishing what their intentions actually were. There is in French law a sharp distinction between the ascertainment of their intentions and the application of legal rules which may, in the interests of fairness to other parties or otherwise, limit the extent to which those intentions are given effect.

And he concluded:

English law, on the other hand, mixes up the ascertainment of intention with the rules of law by depersonalising the contracting parties and asking, not what their intentions actually were, but what a reasonable outside observer would have taken them to be. One cannot in my opinion simply transpose rules based on one philosophy of contractual interpretation to another, or assume that the practical effect of admitting such evidence under the English system of civil procedure will be the same as that under a continental system.

94.   LA CONVENTION EST NULLE, S'IL Y A DOL, VIOLENCE GRAVE OU ERREUR SUR LA QUALITÉ DE LA CHOSE

> *The agreement is void if there is deceit, serious duress or mistake as to the quality of the thing.*

(Cambacérès, *Projet de code civil*, art 717; see also Code civil, art 1130)

Returning to the formation of a contract, in the civil (continental) legal systems, a contract is based on agreement and consent. As Cambacérès asserted in his *Projet,* "[w]ithout consent and the meeting of the minds, no agreement" (art 709). The foundation for this thesis is Roman law where, despite the lack of a general theory of contract, Ulpian nevertheless noted that all the different contracts had a common denominator, namely agreement (*conventio*) (D.2.14.1.3). This being the case, it logically follows that if there is an obstacle preventing the coming together of two minds in agreement, there cannot be a contract; there is, in other words, no true consent (CC art 1130).

Before looking at the 'vices' that undermine consent, something needs to be said about English law because it is by no means evident that English contract law is based on the same thesis. In fact, a close look at the 19th-century cases reveals that the English law of contract was, in its formative days at least, founded on two ideas. First, there was a general principle that "if a man has made a deliberate statement, and another has acted upon it, he cannot be at liberty to deny the truth of the statement" (*McCance* v *L & N W Ry* (1861) 31 LJ Exch 65, 71). Secondly, there was the principle that any contractual promise was *prima facie* actionable even if it lacked an object and a cause in the civil law sense of these terms. Accordingly, if a person was contractually to promise that it shall rain the next day, he would be liable on the basis not only that he ought not to be allowed to go back on his word (*Canham* v *Barry* (1855) 24 LJCP 100, 106) but also that he has assumed a risk and must bear the consequences (*Hall* v *Wright* (1860) 29 LJQB 43, 46). These two ideas give rise to a law of contract in England which is based, historically at least, more on the effect of words than upon the coming together of two wills. This is not to say that *consensus* is irrelevant; it is not. Nevertheless, the cause of action for a breach of contract does not arise out of any agreement as such but out of the promise either to pay a debt or to perform some act; the language is one not of 'non-performance' but of 'breach'. English contract law is, then, built upon the notion of enforceable *promise* rather than agreement and this distinction is more than academic. In the civil law tradition, the emphasis on consent (*consensus*) and agreement (*conventio*) has given rise to an idea of contract that is essentially subjective (see above Lord Hoffmann, para 39, and maxim 90). The contractual bond is based on the coming together of two wills. In the common law, in contrast, the idea of promise is much more objective; it is a 'thing' that once launched assumes a life of its own and upon which others might well rely.

This distinction between agreement and promise matters when it comes to the effects of deceit, duress and mistake. In a system based upon *conventio*, the existence of fraud, mistake, or duress will logically act as an obstacle to the formation of a contract because they act as obstacles to the coming together of two minds. No contract is formed. In a system based on promise, although the law might not be prepared to enforce a contract tainted by a vitiating factor, such a factor does not, as a matter of conceptual logic, prevent the formation of a contract. A promise can still have an objective existence even if it has been induced by fraud, error, or duress. This explains why, as will be seen, a judge once pointed out that fraud in English contract law does not vitiate consent. Fraud is dealt with by remedies coming from outside contract (damages in tort and rescission in equity). It equally explains why there never really developed, within the common law (as opposed to equity), a general theory of mistake in contract. There is simply no principle at common law similar to the one to be found in the Québec Civil Code, which states that error "vitiates consent of the parties or one of them where it relates to the nature of the contract, the object of the prestation or anything that was essential in determining that consent" (art 1400). The result is that it is by no means easy for a party to escape from a contract, where the other party is guilty neither of fraud nor misrepresentation, on the basis that had he known of certain facts he would not have contracted (*Bell* v *Lever Brothers* [1932] AC 161). The same is true for duress. It does not usually make the contract non-existent (void); if proved, it makes the contract voidable – that is to say the victim has the option to rescind the contract.

There is, then, in operation here a distinction between contractual rights and available remedies. An emphasis on granting remedies illustrates an external approach to the problem of error, duress, or fraud: the law can provide remedies independent of contract for the innocent contracting party. This is the approach found in Roman law in respect of fraud and duress, for these were wrongs giving rise to non-contractual delictual actions, and thus were designed to protect victims against loss by allowing them to sue for damages. Another possibility was for the law to grant an action in restitution (see maxim 112), which indeed, if available, would take precedence over an action for *dolus malus* (D.4.2.14.1).

This remedies (rescission) approach is an important characteristic of the common law as well. It was the Court of Chancery that provided the remedy of equitable rescission to relieve a party who had been induced to enter a contract as a result of a false statement (misrepresentation) or duress (which includes undue influence). A misrepresentation is traditionally defined as an untrue statement of existing fact which induces the representee to enter into a contract with the representor. The word 'statement' is not confined literally to speech; various other kinds of acts and omissions can be construed on occasions as representations. And the word 'fact' now includes, as a result of a major House of Lords decision in the law of restitution, an untrue statement of law (*Kleinwort Benson Ltd v Lincoln CC* [1999] 2 AC 349). If the misrepresentation was made fraudulently, this also gave rise to a damages action in tort for deceit and today this tort is available to a contracting party even in the absence of fraud (Misrepresentation Act 1967 s 2(1)). One might note here how the emphasis is not on error or fraud as such, but on the words uttered by a party to induce a contract. This is why an English judge has observed that "there is... no general principle of law that fraud vitiates consent". The "effect of fraud is simply to give the innocent party the right, subject to certain limits, to rescind the contract" (Goff LJ in *Whittaker v Campbell* [1984] QB 318, at 326–327; confirmed in *Shogun Finance Ltd v Hudson* [2004] 1 AC 919, at para 7).

95. NON VIDENTUR QUI ERRANT CONSENTIRE

They do not consent those who are in error.

(Ulpian, D.50.17.116.2)

What if there is an error but no misrepresentation? The leading authority on mistake is the House of Lords decision in *Bell v Lever Brothers* ([1932] AC 161). A company, which had made termination contracts with two of its directors, brought an action to have the contracts set aside after subsequently discovering that the directors had committed breaches of their contracts of employment while working for the claimant company. The company equally sought return of the compensation payments they had made in performance of the termination contracts. The jury returned a verdict that the two directors had not fraudulently concealed their breaches. The trial judge, the Court of Appeal and two Law Lords thought that the termination contracts were void for mistake, but the majority of the House of Lords thought that the contracts were valid. Lord Atkin stressed two fundamental points. First, that it was vital to keep in mind the jury verdict acquitting the directors of fraudulent misrepresentation or concealment; and, secondly, that the company got exactly what it bargained for, namely the retirement of the directors. "It seems", said the Law Lord, "immaterial that [the company] could have got the same result in another way" (at 224). Lord Atkin went on to give a number of analogous examples. Most of these involve buying something that either the buyer or both parties believed to be of much better quality than it turned out to be; provided that the seller has made no representation or warranty, the contract is not void. This may be unjust to the buyer, but, said the Law Lord, the example "can be supported on the ground that it is of paramount importance that contracts should be observed, and that if parties honestly comply with the essentials of the formation of contracts – i.e., agree in the same terms on the same subject-matter – they are bound, and must rely on the stipulations of the contract for protection from the effect of facts unknown to them" (at 224). This mention of stipulations does, however, provide an insight into how the courts can declare a contract void for mistake even if there is no misrepresentation. If a fact is so fundamental to the whole transaction, it is possible for a court to imply a condition into the contract to this effect.

The rigour of this common law position was, until recently, partly mitigated by the equitable remedy of rescission, which was held to be applicable to mistake as well as misrepresentation. According to a decision given in 1950, equity could set aside a contract for mistake (*Solle* v *Butcher* [1950] 1 KB 671), but the Court of Appeal has now ruled that this decision is wrong and that there is no such equitable jurisdiction (*The Great Peace* [2003] QB 679). This decision by the Court of Appeal is itself wrong both from an historical and a precedent point of view and so can only be justified as one of policy (Macmillan 2010: 316). This said, it would nevertheless appear that the remedy of rescission in equity is no longer available for mistake. However, equity is still not entirely excluded. Another important remedy for mistake is rectification of a contract, and this is available to correct a written contractual document that wrongly records what was clearly agreed between the parties, for example, a £200,000 price stated as £20,000. What the court does here is order that the document itself be corrected. This remedy of rectification in equity is not one that strictly allows a party to escape from the contract, but it does allow the party to escape from the contract as recorded in a contractual document.

96.   THE CREDITOR IS ENTITLED TO DAMAGES
       FOR LOSS CAUSED BY THE DEBTOR'S NON-
       PERFORMANCE OF AN OBLIGATION, UNLESS
       THE NON-PERFORMANCE IS EXCUSED

Draft Common Frame of Reference, art III-3:701(1)

Once a person has entered into a valid contract which is not open to voidabil-
ity, then, with some statutory exceptions, the contractor is bound to perform
his contractual promise or promises. What if the promisor fails to perform?
The principle which comes into play is one that finds its latest, and simplest,
manifestation in the European Draft Common Frame of Reference (DCFR).
The promisee (creditor) is entitled to compensatory damages. In fact, this general principle, in a longer form, found expression in the original *Code civil* of
1804 (ancient art 1147), but it is not one that can be described, at least in its
generality, as directly coming from the Roman sources as such since there was
no general theory of contract. But, this said, there are texts which at a lower
level of abstraction come close to expressing the same idea (see e.g. the situations in D.45.1.91). What is important about the Roman texts is their emphasis
not just on non-performance but also on fault (see also D.45.1.23). In the civil
law tradition, the non-performance must be the result of some fault on the part
of the non-performer, unless the contract itself was one where liability would
be strict (one, in other words, where the promise was for a result come what
may). This requirement of fault is inherent in the DCFR principle since it states
"unless the non-performance is excused". The most recent manifestation of
this principle is now to be found in the reformed articles of the French *Code
civil*. Article 1231–1 says that damages will be payable on a non-performance
if the debtor cannot show that the non-performance has been prevented by a
force majeure. What is interesting to note here is that the burden of proving an
absence of fault is on the non-performer.

97.   EI QUI AFFIRMAT NON EI QUI NEGAT INCUMBIT
       PROBATIO

He who asserts must prove, not he who denies.

(Paul, D.22.3.2)

Does the DCFR (or the *Code civil*) principle regarding non-performance of
a contract apply in English law? One would have thought that the answer
would be affirmative, given that a non-performance is prima facie a breach of
the contractual promise. Yet, in terms of precedent, the position seems more

complicated, thanks to another principle that states that he who asserts must prove the allegation. The focal point is the idea of a *force majeure* – that is to say, a supervening event that prevents performance of the contract. As we have just seen, such an event would provide a defence in French law for non-performance, but the onus is on the non-performer to prove a *force majeure*. The intervening event must not be caused by the fault of the non-performer.

In English law, the rule is that if an outside event intervenes to prevent the performance of a contract and this intervention destroys the commercial basis of the agreement, the contract is automatically terminated, and both parties are accordingly released from their promises. Frustration, as this rule is known, "kills the contract" (*Constantine (Joseph) SS Ltd* v *Imperial Smelting Corporation* [1942] AC 154, 163). The frustration rule is of course subject to a number of conditions, one of which is that the frustration must not be self-induced. Thus, if the intervening event has been 'induced' by the non-performer, he will not be free from liability to pay damages. For example, if C contracts with D for the hire of D's hall for a social event on a specific date in the future and, before this date but after the signing of the contract, the hall is destroyed by fire owing to D's negligence, D will be guilty of self-induced frustration.

However, a question arises as to the burden of proof, which may be illustrated by the following case. The claimant had contracted to hire a ship to transport its cargo of ore from Australia to Europe, but on the required contractual date, the ship was not available. The reason for this failure was that the ship in question had been destroyed by an unexplained explosion in the boiler room. The hirer claimed damages for non-performance of the contract, but the owners of the vessel argued that there could be no liability as the contract itself had been destroyed by frustration (*Joseph Constantine*, above). In the Court of Appeal, Lord Justice Scott declared that this was a "very simple case" ([1940] 2 KB 430, at 432), and that unless the defendants could prove that the ship had been destroyed through no fault on their part, they would be liable in damages for non-performance of the charterparty. In effect, the Lord Justice was applying the old *Code civil* rule (art 1147). However this decision was overruled by the House of Lords, with one of the Law Lords responding to Scott LJ by saying that the case was "not... a very simple one" ([1942] AC at 160 per Viscount Simon LC). What, then, made the case difficult? The short answer is the maxim *ei qui affirmat non ei qui negat incumbit probatio,* which was quoted by Viscount Maugham in *Joseph Constantine* (at 174). It was the claimant alleging self-induced frustration, and thus it was incumbent on this person to prove the allegation. In truth, the House of Lords had reversed the effect of the maxim set out in the old CC article 1147.

Was the House of Lords right in its approach to this issue of *force majeure* and the burden of proof? However, this perhaps is the wrong question. It is wrong because the nature of a contractual obligation is different from one in the law of non-contractual harm (see maxim 101). The obligation in a contract is to perform, whereas the obligation in delict (tort) is not to cause damage through one's fault. In this latter situation, fault is a central constituent of liability and thus must be proved by the one alleging it. In contract, the central constituent of liability is the failure to perform the contractual obligation; all that needs to be proved by the claimant is the non-performance ('you have not done what you promised to do'). If the defendant wishes to escape paying damages, then the onus should be on him to prove that the non-performance was due to some frustrating (*force majeure*) event for which he was in no way responsible. The defendant is alleging that he is not responsible and thus it seems rational to argue that he should prove it. In short, it was Scott LJ who, arguably, was right.

98.   GENERALITER CAUSA DIFFICULTATIS AD INCOMMODUM PROMISSORIS, NON AD IMPEDIMENTUM STIPULATORIS

> *In general difficulty of performance is a burden on the person making the promise not an impediment on the other party.*

(Venuleius, D.45.1.137.4)

A *force majeure* is, accordingly, an event which can relieve the promisor of his obligation to perform the contract. Yet what amounts to a *force majeure* or, in English law, a frustrating event? Here, a distinction needs to be made. This is the distinction between an event that destroys the contract and an event that merely makes performance more difficult or onerous. As Lord Simon said: "Frustration of a contract takes place when there supervenes an event (without default of either party and for which the contract makes no sufficient provision) which so significantly changes the nature (not merely the expense or onerousness) of the outstanding contractual rights and/or obligations from what the parties could reasonably have contemplated at the time of its execution that it would be unjust to hold them to the literal sense of its stipulations in the new circumstances; in such case the law declares both parties to be discharged from further performance" (*National Carriers Ltd* v *Panalpina (Northern) Ltd* [1981] AC 675, 700). As Lord Simon makes clear, an increase in expense or onerousness (*difficultas*) does not amount to a frustrating event, and a similar conclusion was reached in French private law. Thus, a long-term fixed price contract was held to be binding in French private law even when inflation had made the fixed price economically unrealistic. Contracts, like statutes, were binding, and severe inflation did not amount to a *force majeure*.

However, in French administrative law, the theory of unforeseen change of circumstances (*la théorie de l'imprévision*) was adopted in the famous *Gaz de Bordeaux* case of 1916 on the basis that the public interest takes precedence over the binding nature of the contract; it was not in the public interest that the lighting company should go bankrupt as a result of the huge rise in costs, which made the fixed-price contract economically ruinous (CE 30.3.1916). Interestingly, English law has reached a similar result as the *Gaz de Bordeaux* case in *Staffs Area Health Authority* v *South Staffs Waterworks Co* ([1978] 1 WLR 1387), although for the majority of the Court of Appeal, this result was simply a matter of interpretation of the contractual document. Lord Denning, however, went beyond the interpretative approach and based his decision both on frustration and on a *rebus sic stantibus* (things remain the same) implied clause giving rise to a right to have the contract renegotiated (the expression itself originates with the Post-Glossators: see Bartolus, Comment on D.12.4.8). In fact, Denning's approach, although rejected by the other judges, now finds expression in codes such as the PECL (art 6.111) and UNIDROIT (arts 6.2.1–6.2.3). Indeed, the reformed French *Code civil* now permits a contract to be renegotiated if performance has become "excessively onerous" (art 1195), moving French private law more towards the position adopted in French administrative contract law.

99. THE CREDITOR IS ENTITLED TO RECOVER MONEY PAYMENT OF WHICH IS DUE

(Draft Common Frame of Reference, art III–3:301(1))

What if there is no impossibility or difficulty in performing a contract as such, but the debtor still fails to perform? The general rule expressed in many textbooks is that a breach of contract (and an unjustified failure to perform amounts to a breach in English law) gives rise to a claim in damages. This is misleading. Many failures to perform involve a promise to pay a price or other fixed sum of money. One only has to think of the number of contracts a person – a consumer often – makes every day where the consumer's promise is to pay. Where such a person fails to pay, the creditor has a claim not in damages but in debt, this latter claim being not just a remedy distinct from damages (see maxim 116) but a separate cause of action as well (*Overstone Ltd v Shipway* [1962] 1 WLR 117). It is in effect a form of specific performance at common law; the debtor is being forced to perform his primary obligation, the promise to pay. Ninety percent of all claims for breach of contract begun in the English courts are claims in debt and not damages.

100.   LE DÉBITEUR N'EST TENU QUE DES DOMMAGES ET INTÉRÊTS QU'ON A PU PRÉVOIR

The debtor is liable in damages only for what he was able to foresee.

(Pothier, *Traité des obligations*, § 160)

However, in those cases where the claimant is suing for damages, the question arises as to how such compensation is to be calculated. The general rule is that the victim of a breach of contract is entitled to be put into the same position as if the contract had been performed. Nevertheless, there is a limitation to this principle expressed in the maxim that the defendant contractor in breach will be liable in damages only for the damage that was foreseeable at the time of entering the contract. This foreseeability rule, as expressed by Pothier, was incorporated into the French civil code (art 1150, now art 1231-3) and it was equally incorporated into English law in the case of *Hadley v Baxendale* ((1854) 9 Ex 341), although the term 'contemplation' was used rather than 'foreseeability'. The damage incurred by the claimant contractor must have been in the contemplation of the party in breach.

This principle is, however, also subject to modification in that the damage or loss suffered must be of a kind that was in the reasonable risk to be contemplated. Thus, a breach of contract that causes a loss or damage of a kind that is way outside the risk to be imposed on the contractor in breach will not be recoverable (*Transfield Shipping Inc v Mercator Shipping Inc* [2009] 1 AC 61). Perhaps another way of stating this is that the claim must not be totally unreasonable (*Ruxley Electronics Ltd v Forsyth* [1996] 1 AC 344). In the past, damages could be claimed only for actual physical damage or proved economic loss, but today damages can also be claimed, in certain circumstances, for mental distress arising from the breach of contract (*Ruxley*; *Farley v Skinner* [2002] 2 AC 732).

CONCLUDING REMARKS

The maxims considered in this chapter do not by any means cover all the legal rules and principles of the law of contract. They do, however, cover some of the main focal points of the subject. They will hopefully provide something of an overview of what is a central subject in private and commercial law, although the word 'private' must be treated with great care as the law of contract is equally applicable, in English law, to public bodies. As will be seen (maxim 118), contract is an area of the common law where the distinction between law and equity remains of some importance.

9. Law of obligations (2)

In this chapter, one turns from principles concerning contractual obligations to those of non-contractual obligations. Generally speaking, non-contractual obligations embrace two specific subject areas, namely tort (or delict) and restitution (or quasi-contract or unjust enrichment). In Roman law, the subdivision of the law of obligations, at least in Justinian's time, was into four subject areas. These were contract, quasi-contract, delict and quasi-delict. The distinction between delicts and quasi-delicts is not entirely clear and has been the subject of considerable debate. It may represent a distinction between fault and strict (non-fault) liability, but it would be dangerous to attribute this distinction to the Romans; it could well be due to the invention of later interpreters of the *Corpus Iuris*. The distinction between contract and quasi-contract has, however, survived into modern times but, again, is a disputed category and is being replaced by a general principle of unjust enrichment.

101. QUILIBET VULT SIBI DAMNUM AB ALIIS DATUM RESARCIRI; RESARCIAT ALIIS

Whoever wishes that damage done to him by others be repaired; so, he should repair [damage] done to others.

(Thomasius, *Larva legis Aquiliae*, § II)

The other principal category within the law of obligations, that is the law of delict or tort, is based on the causing of loss or damage by one person to another. Not all such caused damage is actionable, and so one can basically say that the law of delict or tort is about determining when a person is liable and when he (or she or more often it) is not. The subject is complex for several reasons. First, because of its history; secondly, because of its complexity on occasions, something that has been exacerbated in modern times by technology and by insurance; and thirdly, because it is not easy to find some underpinning and all-embracing general theory that will explain tort as a coherent category. Indeed, one tort expert once wrote that tort law "is what is in the tort books, and the only thing holding it together is their binding" (Weir 2006: ix).

One reason for this 'theory' issue is that the history of delict in civil law was a little like the history of contract law in that, as with contract, there was in Roman law itself no general notion of delict as a singular term, other than 'wrongdoing'. Just as there were different types of contract, so there were different kinds of delict. Accordingly, in Roman law, a number of legal actions had been developed to deal with harm arising outside of contractual transactions and, if there was any general foundational idea, it was, according to Gaius, the notion of wrongfulness (*ex maleficio*) (D.44.7.4). Thus, obligations arose from theft (*ex furto*), damage (*ex damno*), robbery (*ex rapina*) and insult (*ex injuria*) (D.44.7.4). In order to be actionable, the harm suffered had to fall within one of these categories, and although Gaius tells us that they share the common denominator of wrongfulness, the Romans did not fashion any general theory of delictual liability at the level of the generic category itself. What the Romans did do, however, was to lay the foundations for a claim for wrongful damage based upon fault (*culpa*) (see maxim 101). During the second life of Roman law, this idea of damage caused by fault – based on the Roman action for wrongful damage established by an old statute called the *Lex Aquilia* (187 BC?) – was developed more or less as a general theory of liability (see maxim 102).

In England, the development of tort liability was, by way of analogy, not dissimilar, for the foundation of both contract and tort was a number of distinct forms of action. The basis of the modern law of tort is to be found in the writ of trespass and its offshoot, trespass on the case. As David Ibbetson notes, trespass "lay for invasive interferences to land, goods, or the person" while trespass on the case "covered a range of situations where the loss had been caused wrongfully" (1999: 154). The distinction between trespass and case was not clearly rationalised for several centuries, but later the difference was expressed in terms of liability based on the invasion of a right and liability based on damage arising from a wrong (Ibbetson 1999: 155–158). A further development, which had little actual support in legal history, was to be found in the distinction between direct and consequential damage. If the injury had been directly caused by the defendant, it was trespass, but if it was indirectly caused, it was case (*Scott v Shepherd* (1773) 96 ER 525).

These distinctions are still of some importance today. Thus, trespass will not lie in, say, a pollution case unless the damage was directly caused (see Denning LJ in *Esso Petroleum Ltd* v *Southport Corporation* [1954] 2 QB 182, 195–196) and the difference between liability based on the invasion of a right and liability based upon a wrong remains an analytical tool (*Three Rivers DC v Bank of England (No 3)* [2003] 2 AC 1, 229). However, the main thrust of development has been the importance of fault as the foundation of liability (Weir 1998). Now, in the civil law, as mentioned, the modern law of fault liability is founded upon the Roman delict of wrongfully caused damage (*damnum injuria datum*) which, in the later civil law, became the basis for the whole category of delict (see generally Descheemaeker 2009). This is not to say that strict liability (liability without fault) did not exist; there are examples in Roman law and in French law there was a major expansion focused on the *Code civil* article dealing with damage caused by persons and things under the control of another (CC art 1384, now art 1242) (see maxim 104). But fault became a central moral principle and a means of balancing freedom to act with the causing of damage, an increasingly fraught issue with the industrial revolution. Not surprisingly, the same was true of English law: throughout the 18th and early 19th centuries, tortious liability became ever more dependent upon the existence of fault (Ibbetson 1999: 164).

Nevertheless, the forms of action approach to liability resulted in a situation where the notion of 'fault' did not actually act as a starting point in itself of liability. And so, even in situations where it could be shown that the defendant had intentionally caused economic loss or harm, there would be no liability unless the claimant went further and indicated a particular category of tort (*Bradford Corporation* v *Pickles* [1895] AC 587). The claimant had to show the constituents of one of the old forms of action that had become causes of action with the abolition of the forms of action. Thus, a claimant had to allege trespass, nuisance, deceit, or whatever (*Mogul SS Co* v *McGregor, Gow & Co* [1892] AC 25; *Esso Petroleum Ltd* v *Southport Corporation* [1954] 2 QB 182, cf [1956] AC 218). Even with the development of the tort of negligence from 1932 onwards, this tort was just another one alongside a range of others.

This means that the category of tort is also significantly different from that of contract. As we have seen, a breach of 'contract' is a cause of action in itself. However, there is no such notion as a 'breach of tort duty' (*Bradford Corporation* v *Pickles* [1895] AC 587). In order for there to be liability in tort, a claimant must show either that the defendant is in breach of a general duty of care owed to him (tort of negligence) or that there exists within the facts a cause of action of some other tort (for example, nuisance or defamation). Nevertheless, this formal dimension to the law of tort hides a statistical reality. Just as most contract claims are actions in debt (maxim 99), so most tort claims are actions for personal injury arising primarily out of accidents on the road or in the workplace, although medical negligence claims are beginning to become important as well. Such statistical realities have given rise to the thesis that tort is simply a means of accident compensation and not a very efficient one at that.

Yet, tort does have other important roles even if the statistics suggest otherwise. Torts such as trespass to the person (which includes false imprisonment), malicious prosecution, misfeasance in public office and of course negligence have an important public law role. They are the means by which governmental bodies like the police and local authorities can be held to account for their actions. In addition, the tort of nuisance can have a role in protecting the environment (*Barr v Biffa Waste Services Ltd* [2012] 3 WLR 795), although statute is diminishing the tort's importance (but see now *The Manchester Ship Canal Company Ltd v United Utilities Water Ltd (No 2)* [2024] UKSC 22). However, the tort of defamation has perhaps a more negative contribution in the way that it can seriously restrict freedom of speech. That said, defamation can be used to protect certain personality rights such as dignity and even privacy. Tort also provides the remedies for protecting property rights. Trespass to land and trespass to goods are the remedies to be used against those who interfere with possession of property; and conversion is the nearest claim that English law has to a *rei vindicatio* in respect of goods. Intellectual property rights, actually protected for the most part by a statutory regime, are given extra protection by torts such as passing off, while the economic torts (for example, inducing a breach of contract) protect business interests. The law of tort, in short, provides the remedies for whole areas of the English common law, and these remedies are not restricted to damages. The equitable remedy of an injunction can often be used in conjunction with a cause of action in tort to prohibit acts which would invade a personality or property right. Indeed, the use of such injunctions has attracted criticism (https://www.bbc.co.uk/news/articles/cjeegzv09l3o).

102. TOUT FAIT QUELCONQUE DE L'HOMME, QUI CAUSE À AUTRUI UN DOMMAGE, OBLIGE CELUI PAR LA FAUTE DUQUEL IL EST ARRIVÉ À LE RÉPARER

> *Any fact whatsoever of a man which causes damage obliges the man by which the fault has occurred to repair it.*

(Code civil art 1240, formerly art 1382)

The delict of wrongfully caused damage, based on fault (*culpa*), is, as we have seen, Roman in origin. However, it was just one of several delicts. During the second life of Roman law, it became the central principle of delictual liability, which found its most abstract expression in the French code of 1804. In France, therefore, all that needs to be proved is damage, fault, and causation, fault embracing both intentional and negligent harm. It is the legal fact of causing damage which triggers the obligation to make reparation.

There was no such general principle in the UK until the case of *Donoghue v Stevenson* ([1932] AC 562). Before 1932, negligence was an important constituent of other torts and in certain specified duty situations, but there was no tort of negligence as such. The starting point for the modern UK tort of negligence is, therefore, this precedent. Despite being a Scottish case, it is equally an English precedent because the House of Lords stated that they were declaring the law of England as well as that of Scotland. Mrs. Donoghue brought an action for damages against the manufacturer of a bottle of ginger beer which, so she alleged, had caused her personal injury damage as a result of containing a decomposed snail. She had drunk the beer in a café after it had been bought for her by a friend. The manufacturer sought to have her claim struck out on a preliminary point of law: even if he had been careless in allowing the snail to get into the beer, he owed no duty of care to Mrs. Donoghue. A majority in the House of Lords held that a duty did exist. Why is the case so important? The answer is to be found in a number of factors.

The first factor is the actual facts themselves. The immediate facts were (and to some extent still are) important in that they extended the structural symmetry of consumer protection. Before the decision, a consumer injured by a defective product could sue only if he or she had actually purchased the product (Sale of Goods Act 1893 (now 1979) s 14); the advantage of such a contract claim, however, is that a consumer did, and does, not have to prove fault (*Frost* v *Aylesbury Dairy Co Ltd* [1905] 1 KB 608). *Donoghue* establishes that a consumer, even one who did not buy the product, injured by a defective product can sue the manufacturer. The seeming disadvantage is that the consumer must prove fault, but this is less of a burden than it might seem thanks to a later case establishing that the defect itself is prima facie evidence of negligence (*Grant v Australian Knitting Mills Ltd* [1936] AC 85). Legislation has further improved the position of the third-party consumer in that he or she may now be able to sue in contract (Contracts (Rights of Third Parties) Act 1999). A separate product liability statute, anyway, allows consumers suffering personal injury and property damage to sue for damages without having to assert negligence (Consumer Protection Act 1987 Part I).

The second factor is the 'neighbour principle'. Normally, a case is rarely an authority beyond its own material facts, and thus it was argued in *Grant v Australian Knitting Mills* (noted above), which involved defective underpants, that underpants were materially different from a bottle of ginger beer. Not surprisingly, the argument was rejected (but was it such a daft argument for a lawyer to make?), and this was not just because both pants and ginger beer are 'products'. Lord Atkin in *Donoghue* famously said:

> The rule that you are to love your neighbour becomes in law, you must not injure your neighbour; and the lawyer's question, who is my neighbour? receives a restricted reply. You must take reasonable care to avoid acts or omissions which you can reasonably foresee would be likely to injure your neighbour. Who, then, in law is my neighbour? The answer seems to be – persons who are so closely and directly affected by my act that I ought reasonably to have them in contemplation

as being so affected when I am directing my mind to the acts or omissions which are called in question ([1932] AC 562, at 580).

This is what lifts negligence liability out of its imprisonment within specific factual categories and establishes the tort as a general cause of action prima facie applicable, seemingly, to any set of facts where damage is caused, by a careless act, to anyone within the 'neighbour' range of 'proximity'.

A key limiting factor, then, is the notion of 'proximity', a term used and developed by Lord Atkin himself in *Donoghue*. Yet, and this is a third factor, if 'duty' is based on 'proximity', what is the actual difference between these two notions? First, the former is *normative*, that is to say, a concept that expresses a pure *ought* situation. To say that someone is under a 'duty' to do something is a moral and legal way of expressing what he ought to do. Proximity, in contrast, is purely *descriptive*; to say that one person is proximate to another is simply to describe a factual (an 'is') situation and implies in itself no 'ought' dimension. Secondly, the two terms are not synonymous even when viewed from the standpoint of liability; there can be situations of proximity but no duty (see e.g. *Marc Rich & Co v Bishop Rock Marine Co Ltd* [1996] 1 AC 211). Where 'proximity' and 'duty' are valuable is that the former can be used within a factual situation to organise the facts in such a way that the imposition (or non-imposition) of a duty becomes almost a natural consequence; it is, in other words, a valuable reasoning tool since it functions within the facts. Duty, in contrast, functions only in a world of normative rules.

However, the neighbour principle was not to be as abstract as it might first have appeared, and so a fourth factor is the scope of the duty of care. One material fact was the damage suffered by Mrs. Donoghue: the decomposed snail made her physically ill, and it was for this damage that Stevenson might potentially have been liable. However, this was not the only harm suffered by Mrs. Donoghue; she had also 'lost' the value of a bottle of ginger-beer. Later cases, citing earlier ones, identified the 'interest' forming the object of the manufacturer's duty as the threat to health, not the threat to wealth. Put another way, the physical injury suffered by Mrs. Donoghue and her economic loss are two quite different types of 'damage'. Thus, the 1932 case is important in establishing (if retrospectively) the financial loss rule in the tort of negligence. There is, in principle, no duty of care if the careless act causes economic but no physical damage (see, e.g., *Spartan Steel & Alloys Ltd v Martin & Co* [1973] 1 QB 27).

A fifth factor concerns a procedural aspect of the case. It is often said that it was never proved whether or not there was a snail in the ginger-beer bottle, and this is because the case never went to trial (see *Freeman v Home Office (No 2)* [1984] QB 524, at 555–556). The appeal that reached the House of Lords was a 'striking out' action; that is to say the defendant asked the court on a preliminary question of law to strike out the case as disclosing no cause of action. Even if, argued the defendant, all the facts, including negligence, were proved by the claimant, these facts would still not make him liable since they disclosed no duty of care. What the House of Lords had to decide, then, was whether they did disclose a duty of care and, in order to decide this question, it was assumed that there was a snail in the bottle. Having lost the preliminary question of law action, Stevenson settled the case. Many subsequent duty of care cases are striking out claims; thus to say, for example that the Home Office was found liable in negligence in *Home Office* v *Dorset Yacht Co* ([1970] AC 1004) is not exactly true. These striking out claims have proved problematic from a human rights position since they can appear arbitrarily to deny the claimant a remedy if not a fair trial (see *Barrett v Enfield LBC* [2001] 2 AC 550; *Z v UK* [2001] 2 FLR 612).

From a comparative law position, *Donoghue* can be linked to CC art 1382 (now art 1240) in the way it lays down a general principle based on negligence. Indeed when put beside intentional physical damage to the person, it is now possible to talk in terms of a general *culpa* liability (*Letang* v *Cooper* [1965] 1 QB 232). Yet there is one fundamental difference. The mere fact of causing harm to another through a negligent act is not in itself enough to generate liability; there has to be a breach of a duty of care. The actual negligence issue is, therefore, a question of fact which must be proved (and would once have been a question for the jury); the second issue is one for the judges because it is a pure question of law. This question of law issue suggests English law, given the limitation on liability imposed by the duty of care control device, is really closer to the German Civil Code paragraph 823 which requires, in addition to fault, cause and damage, the invasion of a specific interest ('life, body, health, freedom, ownership or any other right'). Duty of care is, in practice, a means by which the tort of negligence protects only certain interests.

The next major development in the tort of negligence was the decision in *Hedley Byrne & Co* v *Heller & Partners Ltd* ([1964] AC 465). The case itself involved a favourable credit reference letter gratuitously given by a bank in respect of a company that subsequently proved unable to pay its debts. The recipient of the reference, who had extended credit to the company on the strength of the letter, lost heavily when the company went into liquidation and they brought an action in negligence for their loss against the bank. Although the claimant lost its action because of a disclaimer in the credit reference letter, the House of Lords indicated that a duty of care could in principle exist between the bank and the claimant. This decision thus extended liability to damage done by careless words (misrepresentation) and although it looks at first sight a major extension of *Donoghue v Stevenson* it is probably more accurate to see the case as a development in the area of the tort of deceit, perhaps with the idea of filling gaps in the law of contract rather than in extending

Donoghue as such (*Peek v Derry* (1887) 37 Ch D 541 (CA); cf (1889) 14 App Cas 337 (HL)). Those suffering loss as a result of a misstatement need no longer prove fraud provided they can establish a *special relationship*. In the words of Lord Steyn, "the rule was established that irrespective of contract, if someone possessed of a special skill undertakes to apply that skill for the assistance of another person who relies upon such skill, a duty of care will arise" (*Hall (Arthur JS) & Co v Simons (a firm)* [2002] 1 AC 615, 676).

What makes the case particularly special is that it appears to be a major exception to the established idea that *Donoghue v Stevenson* was concerned with physical rather than economic interests. However, the key to the case is a *voluntary assumption* of responsibility by the defendant together with *reliance* by the claimant (see e.g. *Lennon v Comr of Police of the Metropolis* [2004] 1 WLR 2594). Yet it may be that 'reliance' will be interpreted quite generously when the duty problem is closely associated, directly or indirectly, with a contractual relationship and thus liability can attach to a reference from an ex-employer and to a breach of contract by a solicitor where only a third party (and not the contracting party) suffers loss as a result of the breach (*Spring v Guardian Assurance Plc* [1995] 2 AC 296; *White v Jones* [1995] 2 AC 207). What is particularly important about *Hedley Byrne* is its central place in the law of obligations in as much as it both straddles the divide between contract and tort and acts as one starting point for recovering pure economic loss through the tort of negligence.

103.   CULPAM AUTEM ESSE, QUOD CUM A DILIGENTE PROVIDERI POTERIT, NON ESSET PROVISUM

Fault, then, is what a diligent person ought to foresee, but has not foreseen.

(Paul, D.9.2.31)

When does an act amount to a negligent one? One key notion here is foreseeability. Any act which a reasonable person might have foreseen as being a danger to others but fails to foresee is prima facie a careless act. Thus, a pruner who throws down branches onto a place where he ought to have foreseen that people might pass underneath, and fails to shout a warning, will be guilty of *culpa* according to a well-known Roman text (D.9.2.31). In English law, a definition of negligence was provided in the middle of the 19th century which is not dissimilar in substance to the Roman one. Negligence "is the omission to do something which a reasonable man, guided upon those considerations which ordinarily regulate the conduct of human affairs, would do, or doing something which a prudent and reasonable man would not do" (Alderson B in *Blyth v Proprietors of the Birmingham Waterworks* (1856) 11 Exch 781, 784).

Foreseeability is not, however, sufficient in itself to determine whether an act or a failure to act is negligent. There is also the question of risk. It may be that an activity that is a perfectly legitimate one carries with it some remote, yet foreseeable, possibility that it could cause damage to another, and so the question of fact is not actually whether the damage was foreseeable but whether the defendant, in the circumstances, acted reasonably. One does not have to obsessively guard against every conceivable risk if doing so would involve excessive expenditure. The leading case here is *Bolton v Stone* ([1951] AC 850), which was an action for damages by a bystander in the street against a cricket club for an injury sustained by the bystander when she was struck on the head by a cricket ball hit out of the ground by a batsman. Cricket balls had been hit out of the ground before, and so if one were to apply the foreseeability test, it could be said that the accident was foreseeable. Did this mean that the cricket club did not behave reasonably in failing to provide a system of fencing that would ensure that cricket balls never reached the street? The House of Lords held that the cricket club need not have gone to these lengths, given that the risk was small and thus held that the club was not negligent. Perhaps if the activity had been something other than cricket, the decision might have been different.

Foreseeability also has a role in causation. A claimant has to show that the defendant's careless act caused the damage, and this involves two levels of operation. There is cause in fact where actual causation must be established as a fact, which once would have been decided by a jury, and there is cause in law where damage that is considered too remote is disregarded. The test for the latter is one of foreseeability. It has already been seen that this foreseeability test has a long history in the law of contract (see maxim 100), but in the law of tort, the test was introduced into English tort law only in 1961 (*The Wagon Mound (No 1)* [1961] AC 388). If the harm suffered by the victim is unforeseeable, the negligent actor can escape liability.

Nevertheless, foreseeability can be deceptive here in that this test can end up excluding certain types of harm for reasons that are not strictly relevant in terms of risk. This point is well illustrated by a particular difficulty that arose after the adoption of the foreseeability test. A farmer carelessly allowed his farm to become infested with rats, with the result that a farm worker became infected with a very rare disease contracted from rats' urine (Weil's Disease). The farmer was held not liable since this particular damage was unforeseeable; had the worker been infected through a rat's bite, he would have recovered (*Tremain v Pike* [1969] 3 All ER 1303). What foreseeability (of the actor) has done here is to introduce a problem of genus and species: one must foresee not only damage (genus) but the particular species of harm. Breach of duty (reasonableness) becomes intertwined with remoteness.

The courts had begun to grapple with this genus and species problem in a case where a small boy entered a shelter erected by the defendants over a manhole in the street and started to play with a paraffin warning lamp; the lamp fell down the manhole and exploded, causing the boy serious burns. The defendants argued that while injury by fire was foreseeable, injury by explosion was not, but the House of Lords rejected this defence on the ground that the harm was of a recognised type (*Hughes* v *Lord Advocate* [1963] AC 837). The problem surfaced again some time later when two friends decided to repair an old boat which had been left on local authority land. The boat collapsed on one of the boys, causing him very serious injury, yet his damages claim was rejected in the Court of Appeal on the ground that it was unforeseeable that the boys would jack up and prop up the boat; in other words, the species of accident was unforeseeable. This decision was overturned in the House of Lords: "foreseeability is not as to the particulars but the genus", said Lord Hoffmann (*Jolley v Sutton LBC* [2000] 1 WLR 1082, 1091).

One area which seemingly remained untouched by the foreseeability test was the principle that a tortfeasor must take his victim as he finds him. A worker was burnt on the lip by some molten metal, an injury that might have been prevented had the employer not been negligent; however, the burn turned cancerous owing to the plaintiff's special susceptibility to cancer and he died. The employer was held liable for the death (*Smith v Leech Brain & Co* [1962] 2 QB 405; and see also *Robinson v Post Office* [1974] 1 WLR 1176). Again, as with the genus and species issue, this kind of damage simply cannot be excluded by reference to the foreseeability test. If it is to be excluded, it should be on the basis of a more structured and objective relationship between the category of damage suffered and the risk attaching to the actor. In other words, the foreseeability test is by no means as exclusionary as it might at first seem.

104. ON EST RESPONSABLE NON SEULEMENT DU DOMMAGE QUE L'ON CAUSE PAR SON PROPRE FAIT, MAIS ENCORE DE CELUI QUI EST CAUSÉ PAR LE FAIT DES PERSONNES DONT ON DOIT RÉPONDRE, OU DES CHOSES QUE L'ON A SOUS SA GARDE

> *One is liable not only for damage that one has caused through his own action, but also for damage caused by the actions of persons for whom one is responsible or for things that one has in his keeping.*

> (*Code civil* art 1242, formerly art 1384)

In addition to liability incurred through an individual's negligent act, France developed, particularly during the last century, a whole regime of strict liability (liability without fault) based on a liability for people and for things. CC art

1242 imposes a liability for damage done by a thing under the control (*sous sa garde*) of another. For well over a century, this statement was thought to be simply a general introduction to the then articles 1385 and 1386 and thus restricted to damage resulting from dilapidated buildings and from animals. However, during the 20th century, the *Cour de cassation* used this principle to develop a liability for things in general, and one particular landmark was the application of this strict liability article to motor vehicles in the famous *Jand'heur* decision in 1930. Such general liability is found in few other systems, although many do now have special traffic accident regimes (including France since 1985). Instead, the tendency is to create specific areas of liability, one of the most important being the EU-inspired liability for defective products.

As we shall see (maxim 106), English law has equally developed a liability for people for whom one is responsible in an employment sense. However, a liability based on damage done by things is more fragmented and the level of duty variable. Liability without fault attaches to dangerous animals and, in certain circumstances, to non-dangerous ones as well (Animals Act 1971 s 2). In addition, there are one or two other strict liabilities. The tort of private nuisance can make a landowner liable for damage arising from the unreasonable use of his land and 'unreasonable' in this context is not confined to fault. Public nuisance can be used in respect of dangerous structures that injure members of the public, and it can equally extend to vehicles parked on the highway (*Benjamin* v *Storr* (1874) LR 9 CP 400). A landowner or occupier may also be liable under the rule in *Rylands* v *Fletcher* ((1866) LR 1 Ex 265; (1868) LR 3 HL 330) for the escape of a dangerous thing brought onto the land, although it seems that this rule has to some extent been subverted by the torts of negligence and nuisance (*Transco plc* v *Stockport MBC* [2004] 2 AC 1). Factory machinery and other things that are dangerous may well entail an employer in liability through the tort of breach of statutory duty (actually now no longer strict) or negligence, and there are a number of statutory strict liability regimes. An employer may also be liable for injury caused by defective equipment (Employers' Liability (Defective Equipment) Act 1969). Contract also has a central role to play in respect to liability for things. Thus, the victim of defective goods may well have a contractual claim and, even if he does not, all EU systems now have delictual liability regimes in place.

In fact, products liability is central to the tort of negligence in as much as the foundational case of *Donoghue* v *Stevenson* ([1932] AC 562) was, of course, a products case. Damage arising from a defective product also transcends the contract and tort divide, in that a purchaser of goods that are not reasonably fit for their purpose and (or) not of satisfactory quality can sue the seller for damages without having to prove fault (Consumer Rights Act 2015 ss 9–10). Similar provisions apply where goods are hired. In addition to these existing claims, there is now a statutory regime (Consumer Protection Act 1987), itself the result of a European Directive in respect of dangerous products. The key provision states that "where any damage is caused wholly or partly by a defect in a product" the producer "shall be liable for the damage" (s 2). The Act goes on to lay down that "there is a defect in a product... if the safety of the product is not such as persons generally are entitled to expect" (s 3). The statutory regime follows the common law negligence position with respect to the type of damage remedied. The regime does not apply to pure economic loss and thus the defective product must cause either personal injury or physical damage to property (s 5(1)) other than to itself (s 5(2)).

It may seem odd that animals are subjected to a statutory regime at a time when their importance in terms of transport had been completely eclipsed by motor vehicles (see *Mirvahedy v Henley* [2003] 2 AC 491). One might, instead, have expected a 'Motor Vehicles Act' perhaps along the lines of the French Law of 1985, which aimed to ameliorate the legal position of victims injured on the roads. For, alongside accidents at work, traffic accidents are the other great source of personal injury litigation. Yet English law has, on the whole, refused to establish a no-fault liability regime for motor vehicles, with the result that civil liability for accidental harm is entirely dependent on the tort of negligence. Indeed, even the tort of breach of statutory duty – once applicable to things in the workplace – was excluded from things on the road (*Phillips* v *Britannia Hygienic Laundry Co* [1923] 2 KB 832) and its role in workplace accidents has been severely reduced (Enterprise and Regulatory Reform Act 2013 s 69). Thus a victim must prove fault before damages can be obtained (*Mansfield v Weetabix Ltd* [1998] 1 WLR 1263). This said, there is one case which suggests that those who put commercial vehicles on the road that cause damage through a defect in for example the brakes might be put into a position where they virtually have to disprove fault (*Henderson* v *HE Jenkins & Sons* [1970] AC 282). But such a principle – summed up in the maxim *res ipsa loquitur*, if in fact there is such a principle – probably does not in general extend to private vehicles.

105.   SIC UTERE TUO UT ALIENO NON LAEDAS

And so use what is yours so as not to harm others.

(Broom's maxims 365)

Where damage has been caused by things on land, the position becomes complex because the sources of such liability are complex. Statute plays a fundamental role, yet not only are several different statutes to be considered, but the common law continues to have a background role as well (see *Gwilliam v West Hertfordshire Hospital NHS Trust* [2003] QB 443, paras 35–44). Before 1957, the position with regard to persons injured on land belonging to another was particularly complex because of the differing kinds of status of all those connected with the land. Occupiers might well have to be differentiated from landlords, and those coming onto land might enter under a contract (for example, football spectators) or because they were invited (guests), or because they were given an implied licence to enter (for example, travelling salesmen). The common law once had different levels of duty attaching to these different classes of people. The aim of the Occupiers' Liability Act 1957 was to simplify the position, and it did this by reducing all the duties owed by an "occupier" to a "visitor" to a "common duty of care" (s 2(1)).

In effect, then, it is the law of negligence that applies to persons lawfully on the land of another. As for uninvited persons (trespassers), they were once owed either no duty or a limited duty of care. However, the position has been modified (seemingly) by the Occupiers' Liability Act 1984. An occupier owes a duty to "persons other than his visitors in respect of any risk of their suffering injury on the premises by reason of any danger due to the state of the premises or to things done or omitted to be done on them" (ss 1(1)(a), 1(3)). But the occupier must be *aware* both of the *danger*, or have reasonable grounds to believe that it exists, and of the *uninvited person* being "in the vicinity of the danger" (s 1(3), emphasis added). It is unlikely that this 1984 statute will actually be of much help to trespassers even if the occupier is aware both of the danger and of the trespassers, since the decision of *Tomlinson v Congleton BC* ([2004] 1 AC 46). In this case, Lord Hoffmann said that he thought that "it will be extremely rare for an occupier of land to be under a duty to prevent people from taking risks which are inherent in the activities they freely choose to undertake upon the land" (para 45).

Occupiers' liability, as expressed in the 1957 and 1984 legislation, is concerned with the liability of an occupier to those on the land under his control. However, dangerous premises can equally injure or damage people off the premises. A collapsing wall might fall onto a passer-by, or an activity carried out by the occupier might seriously annoy, if not physically damage, a neighbour (*Mint v Good* [1951] 1 KB 517; *Fearn v Tate Gallery* [2023] UKSC 4). An activity attached or associated with a particular piece of land can, of course, physically spread itself beyond the premises and spill onto the public highway. And this can cause problems for neighbours, if not the community in general (*Att-Gen v PYA Quarries* [1957] 2 QB 169; *Lawrence v Fen Tigers Ltd* [2014] AC 822).

Several specific torts are of importance when it comes to the liability of an occupier and/or owner of premises to those off the land. The most important are trespass, private nuisance, public nuisance and the rule in *Rylands v Fletcher*. One must not, of course, forget negligence since one foundational case involved injury to a person on the highway (public road) as a result of an activity (cricket) carried on by an occupier (*Bolton* v *Stone* [1951] AC 850). This case also raised the difficult issue of the relationship between the torts of nuisance and negligence. In many ways, it is a sterile exercise to try to compare the so-called strict liability torts like nuisance with negligence at the formal level; it is more often a question of the nature of the damage suffered and the activity producing this damage, not forgetting, either, the remedy and interests (public or private) in issue. For example, it would appear that very wealthy people who live (literally) in glass houses (or more specifically apartments) have a right not to be looked at by members of the public on the Tate Gallery viewing balcony (*Fearn* v *Tate Gallery* [2023] UKSC 4). The interest in play here is seemingly privacy, but the decision seems to raise some interesting questions about urban living. Be that as it may – the UK Supreme Court can move in mysterious ways – the actual requirements of many of these torts have been set out by Denning LJ in *Esso Petroleum Ltd* v *Southport Corporation* ([1954] 2 QB 182). One might note that torts such as private nuisance can no longer be employed where the damage is personal injury.

106.   QUI FACIT PER ALIUM EST PERINDE AC SI FACIAT PER SEIPSUM

He who acts through another is as if he acted himself.

(*Liber Sextus*, regula 72)

The idea of a liability for things is balanced, symmetrically speaking, in CC art 1242 (formerly 1384) by the further idea of a liability for people. We have seen that English law does give some expression to the idea of a liability based on the control of a thing. Does it also give expression to the idea of a liability arising out of the control of a person? As with liability for things, the answer is not entirely negative by any means, but the conceptual structure of English tort law can make comparison with French law complex. Accordingly, there is no general principle in English law similar to the liability for persons in CC art 1242. Instead, there are a number of specific situations where one person will be liable for a tortious act committed by another person. The most important, in the law of tort, is vicarious liability.

The starting point of liability for another's tort is the well-established principle of vicarious liability whereby an employer ('master') is liable for torts committed by an employee ('servant'). The liability is based on three sub-rules: (i) there must be a tort, (ii) committed by a servant, (iii) acting within the course of his employment. All of these rules have given rise to case law.

First, then, the claimant injured by an employee must establish a tort; that is to say, he must establish that the employee's act that has caused the damage amounted to trespass, negligence, conversion, defamation, or whatever. If there is no tort, there is no employer's liability. Most of the torts committed by employees are unintentional ones – normally negligent behaviour or breach of a statute – but an employer can also be liable for wilful behaviour. Thus, an employer has been held liable for harassment by one employee towards a co-employee (*Majrowski v Guy's and St Thomas' NHS Trust* [2007] 1 AC 224).

Secondly, the individual who has committed a tort must be a 'servant', that is to say, an employee and not an independent contractor. Thus, a business enterprise will be liable for the careless driving of a driver on the payroll but not for a taxi driver who drives some of the managers to the railway station. There are some ambiguous situations, however. Some firms hire out not just vehicles but also drivers; and so if the driver carelessly injures a third person, it may not always be clear whether it is the owner or hirer of the vehicle who is to be vicariously liable. More recently, however, the Court of Appeal has held that both companies may be vicariously liable since there is nothing in the precedents that definitively restricts the concept to one employer (*Viasystems (Tyneside) Ltd v Thermal Transfer (Northern) Ltd* [2006] QB 510). Another difficulty is that some contracts of employment specifically state that employees are not 'servants' but independent contractors; here, the courts may or may not be influenced by form depending on the facts and the nature of the contract between the employer and the person who has caused the damage. Nevertheless, a relationship that is akin to an employment one can suffice (*Various Claimants v Catholic Child Welfare Society* [2013] 2 AC 1; but cf *Armes v Nottinghamshire CC* [2017] UKSC 60).

The third requirement is perhaps the most difficult, since there is a large grey area between acting for one's employer and acting for oneself (a 'frolic of one's own'). For example, the company van driver who carelessly injures another road user while delivering his employer's goods will involve the employer in liability. However, if the driver was using the company van to take his family out to a picnic one Sunday, the employer will probably not be liable. The test used to be summed up in this question: was the actor doing something he was employed to do? Applying this test, a bus company was held not liable for an assault by a bus conductor on a passenger since assaulting passengers was not what he was employed to do (*Keppel Bus Co v Sa'ad bin Ahmad* [1974] 2 All ER 700). But in another case, the House of Lords insisted that an employer of a security guard would have been liable (but for an exclusion clause) for his criminal act in deliberately burning down the premises of a client whose factory he had been sent to guard (*Photo Production Ltd v Securicor* [1980] AC 827).

The position over criminal behaviour has now (at least seemingly) been put on a more solid basis. Such behaviour, even if it involves a very serious crime such as child abuse or grievous bodily harm, can involve the employer in liability. The test now is the 'connection' between employment duty and the tortious act, and if there is a sufficient connection, there will be liability (*Lister v Hesley Hall Ltd* [2001] UKHL 22). Thus, a supermarket was held liable to a member of the public, who was legitimately on the supermarket premises, and who was viciously attacked by a supermarket employee (*Mohamud v Morrison Supermarkets plc* [2016] UKSC 11). However, the position has become some-what confused after another Supreme Court case involving the same super-market. An employee of the supermarket deliberately and wrongfully leaked details of thousands of fellow employees, and the latter unsuccessfully brought a claim against the supermarket. The Supreme Court held that as the employee was acting in vengeance (he had a grudge against his employer) and entirely in his own interest, he was on a 'frolic of his own' and so his act was not con-nected to his employment (*Morrison Supermarkets plc v Various Claimants* [2020] UKSC 12). This is a somewhat bizarre holding given the previous deci-sions involving the connection test – cases where it could equally have been said that the employee was acting on a 'frolic of his own'. But the UK Supreme Court can on occasions move in mysterious ways.

107. TENENTUR AUTEM, PRAETER IPSUM QUI PER SE ET ἈΜΕΣΩΣ DAMNUM DAT, ALII QUOQUE FACIENDO AUT NON FACIENDO

> *Besides he who directly causes damage himself, others are also held liable either by doing or not doing.*
>
> Grotius, *De Jure Belli Ac Pacis*,
> Book II, Chap 17, § 6

Vicarious liability cannot apply where an independent contractor commits a tort since he is not a 'servant' (employee). Yet there appear to be cases that contradict this logic; there are decisions where an employer of an independent contractor is seemingly held liable for the tort committed by the contractor. For example, in *Rylands* v *Fletcher* ((1866) LR 1 Ex 265 (Ex); (1868) LR 3 HL 330 (HL)), the owner of land who hired a firm of independent contractors to build a reservoir on the property was held liable for the negligent work carried out by the contractor. However, the liability of the employer in these excep-tional cases is not vicarious; it is based on the breach of a direct *non-delegable* duty between the victim and employer. In addition to any statutory duties, such a duty can arise from the keeping of a dangerous thing, an extra-hazardous act (*Honeywill & Stein* v *Larkin Brothers* [1934] 1 KB 191), a bailment relation-ship (*Riverstone Meat Co* v *Lancashire Shipping Co* [1961] AC 807), a pub-lic nuisance (*Tarry* v *Ashton* (1876) 1 QBD 314) and of course a contractual relationship between the victim and employer (*Wong Mee Wan v Kwan Kin Travel Services Ltd* [1996] 1 WLR 38).

This last relationship is of particular importance because it so clearly indicates how the law of obligations can become distorted by the relationship between legal personality and liability. When a company contracts to do something, it can perform the contract *only* through its employees, and thus vicarious liability is irrelevant. If an employee fails to perform his employer's contractual promise, the employer cannot claim that the employee's act (or failure) is not *their* act; it is they, the employer, who have promised, and thus it is they who will be in breach of contract. In other words, the contractual performance and duty cannot be delegated, in the sense of freeing the employer of his contractual responsibility, to an employee.

Land can also give rise to a non-delegable duty attaching to the owner or occupier. In one case, a local authority was held liable for a nuisance caused by a group of travellers who had occupied land belonging to the council; as one judge pointed out, this was not a matter of vicarious liability, but a matter of whether the council had *adopted* the nuisance in as much as it was connected with their land (*Lippiatt v South Gloucestershire Council* [2000] 1 QB 51). The key question for the employer, contractor, or landowner is whether he can use the person who actually commits the tort to isolate himself from liability. Thus, the householder who hires a reputable firm of contractors to build, say, a garage will probably not be liable if the contractors commit a public nuisance (*Rowe v Herman* [1997] 1 WLR 1390). But the employer cannot always isolate himself from a general duty to provide safe premises simply by hiring a firm of independent contractors (*Gwilliam v West Hertfordshire Hospital NHS Trust* [2003] QB 443). The Occupiers' Liability Act 1957 imposes a direct duty on the part of an occupier towards visitors, and this means that if an independent contractor working on the occupier's land creates a danger resulting in injury to a visitor, the occupier may well be liable for breach of this direct statutory duty of care. An occupier who does employ an independent contractor may also be under a duty to check that the contractor has adequate insurance (*Gwilliam*).

One notable case in recent times involving a state school suggests that the Supreme Court might be developing the direct duty notion a little further, although it is always difficult to tell with the UK Supreme Court. A schoolgirl suffered serious brain damage as a result of an accident in a swimming pool; the swimming session had been organised by her local school but supervised by an independent contractor. An action by the girl was brought against the local education authority responsible for the school, but this claim failed in the Court of Appeal on the basis that the person who had caused the damage was an independent contractor. The case law, as it stood then, seemed to support this result. Nevertheless, the Supreme Court reversed this decision and held the school (education authority) liable (*Woodland v Swimming Teachers Association* [2014] AC 537). Lady Hale justified the decision in an interesting way (para 30):

> Consider the cases of three 10-year-old children, Amelia, Belinda and Clara. Their parents are under a statutory duty to ensure that they receive efficient full-time education suitable to their age, ability and aptitude, and to any special needs they may have (Education Act 1996, section 7). Amelia's parents send her to a well-known and very expensive independent school. Swimming lessons are among the services offered and the school contracts with another school which has its own swimming pool to provide these. Belinda's parents send her to a large school run by a local education authority which employs a large sports staff to service its schools, including swimming teachers and life-guards. Clara's parents send her to a small state-funded faith school which contracts with an independent service provider to provide swimming lessons and life-guards for its pupils. All three children are injured during a swimming lesson as a result (it must be assumed) of the carelessness either of the swimming teachers or of the life-guards or of both. Would the man on the underground be perplexed to learn that Amelia and Belinda can each sue their own school for compensation but Clara cannot?

Lady Hale and Lord Sumption (who also held the school liable) were perhaps ahead of their time – Lord Sumption thinks that a negligence approach to personal injury is outdated (see Samuel 2022a) – and so it is unlikely, especially now that these two judges are retired and replaced by more conservative ones, that this non-delegable duty liability will be developed further. Indeed, it may be restricted.

108. NON VIDETUR VIM FACERE, QUI IURE SUO UTITUR ET ORDINARIA ACTIONE EXPERITUR

> *It does not seem to be the employment of duress when one uses one's right to bring an ordinary action.*
>
> (Paul, D.50.17.155.1)

Threatening or indeed bringing a legal action is not a form of unlawful duress. One is perfectly entitled, one might say, to vindicate one's legal rights. Nevertheless, English law recognises that on rare occasions this entitlement – this right to bring an action – can be abused and such abuse can be a tort. Abuse of the criminal process can give rise to the tort of malicious prosecution, and this tort has now been extended to the civil process (*Willers v Joyce* [2016] UKSC 43). Abuse of the civil process is also a tort in itself and one that seemed to be an extension by analogy of malicious prosecution. Whether there is a need for a separate tort of abuse of the civil process is an interesting question, but it is possible that the tort of abuse of the legal process is wider in scope (see *Crawford Adjusters (Cayman) Ltd v Sagicor General Insurance (Cayman) Ltd* [2014] AC 366, para 149). In *Gibbs v Rea* ([1998] AC 786) it was established that the malicious procurement of a search warrant is actionable if four conditions are fulfilled. These conditions, set out in a recent case, are: "(1) a successful application for a search warrant, (2) lack of reasonable and probable cause to make the application, (3) malice, and (4) resultant damage arising from the issue or execution of the warrant" (Kennedy LJ in *Keegan v Chief Constable of Merseyside Police* [2003] 1 WLR 2187, at para 13). What is interesting about this tort is that it seems to be a cause of action independent of malicious prosecution, abuse of public office, and even perhaps abuse of civil process (see *Crawford Adjusters*, para 149), thus confirming that an alphabetical list of causes of action is still the approach when it comes to intentional damage.

As for malicious prosecution itself, this is a well-established tort. One key element, as the tort indicates, is malice. In *Martin v Watson* Lord Keith quoting, *Clerk & Lindsell on Torts*, said:

> the plaintiff must show first that he was prosecuted by the defendant, that is to say, that the law was set in motion against him on a criminal charge; secondly, that the prosecution was determined in his favour; thirdly, that it was without reasonable and probable cause; fourthly, that it was malicious.

And he added that the "onus of proving every one of these is on the plaintiff" ([1996] AC 74, 80). One might note here that malicious intention is not enough; the prosecution itself must be objectively unreasonable. However, although the tort is, in practice, one that is used mainly against the police and is thus an aspect of what a continental lawyer would call administrative liability, it can also be brought against private individuals if such an individual is the person who "set the law in motion" (Lord Keith). As for the extension of this tort to civil claims, Lord Clarke in *Willers v Joyce* said:

> The question here is whether there is a tort of malicious prosecution of a civil claim. For my part I can see no sensible basis for accepting that the tort of malicious prosecution of a crime exists in English law, whereas the tort of malicious prosecution of a civil action does not. Not only are the ingredients the same, but it seems to me that, if a claimant is entitled to recover damages against a person who maliciously prosecutes him for an alleged crime, a claimant should also be entitled to recover damages against a person who maliciously brings civil proceedings against him. The latter class of case can easily cause a claimant very considerable losses. They will often be considerably greater than in a case of malicious prosecution of criminal proceedings (para 86).

109.   VOLENTI NON FIT INJURIA

Consent negatives wrongdoing.

(Baldus, Comment on J.4.4).

109A. SCIENTI ET CONSENTIENTI NON FIT INJURIA

Knowledge and consent negatives wrongdoing.

(*Liber Sextus*, regula 27)

What defences are available to those facing a tort claim? An action in tort can fail to get off the ground if the defendant can show that the claimant consented to the damage. Thus, the surgeon is not liable in trespass for the invasion of the patient's body because the patient will have consented to the operation; equally, the victim of a legitimate tackle in sport will be taken to have consented to the injury, and this may even extend to horseplay (*Blake v Galloway* [2004] 1 WLR 2844). Of course, just what amounts to consent can on occasions be difficult, and one old case which suggests that submission can amount to *volenti* is no longer good law (*Latter v Braddell* (1881) 50 LJQB 448). Equally, the surgeon who fails to inform a patient of the full risks associated with any operation can undermine any consent. But such a situation may not result in a trespass claim, for the law takes the view that the patient consented to the invasion so to speak; it may give rise, instead, to liability in negligence if a risk materialises.

A particular difficulty arises in this area of medical law where the patient, perhaps through unconsciousness, is unable to give consent. Here the courts have applied the notion of the patient's 'best interests' adding also the presumption that the medical profession, and thus a matter of public policy, is under an obligation to save life. However, where absence of consent is very clear, the doctors cannot act. One distinction that is fundamental is that between knowledge and consent: mere knowledge of a risk will not act as a defence (*Smith v Baker & Sons* [1891] AC 325). The risk has to be 'willingly accepted' (see, e.g., Occupier's Liability Act 1957 s 2(5)).

110. NECESSITAS FACIT LICITUM QUOD ALIAS NON EST LICITUM

Necessity makes legal what would otherwise be illegal.

(10 Coke's Reports 61)

Another defence that, in medical law, is often associated with consent is necessity. "That there exists in the common law", said Lord Goff, "a principle of necessity which may justify action which would otherwise be unlawful is not in doubt" (*In re F* [1990] 2 AC 1, 74). The emergency treatment of a patient without his or her consent can be justified as a matter of necessity if such treatment is reasonable and in the best interests of the patient; and such a defence will extend to, for example, a sterilisation operation on a mentally weak person provided it is reasonable and in her own best interest (*In re F*). More difficult is the problem that arose in one case where the police, in order to recapture a dangerous criminal, ended up by destroying, through the use of CS gas, the shop in which the criminal had barricaded himself. If the police had not been negligent – for necessity is not a defence to negligence – the owner of the shop would not have succeeded in any of the strict liability torts because the police would have had the defence of necessity (*Rigby* v *Chief Constable of Northamptonshire* [1985] 1 WLR 1242). One can speculate if such a defence will today always be valid in such situations now that the Human Rights Act 1998 is in force, for it seems harsh that an individual should have to suffer an invasion of his property and perhaps family life for the benefit of the community (cf *Dennis v MOD* [2003] EWHC 793). But much might much depend upon the insurance position.

111. EX TURPI CAUSA NON ORITUR ACTIO

No action arises out of an illegal cause.

(Cowper's Reports 343; inspired by D.12.5.8 and D.17.1.6.3)

A defendant may also escape liability if it can be shown that the claimant was engaged in an illegal activity when he sustained the damage. The maxim *ex turpi causa* was originally one that was confined, at least in English law, to contract, but extended to tort in more recent times. In contract, such a defence functions more at the level of the remedy rather than the right – the contract is unenforceable rather than void – but in tort one can say that it is a matter of actionability. The courts will not enforce a right if such enforcement can be regarded 'as sufficiently anti-social and contrary to public policy' (*Pitts* v *Hunt* [1991] 1 QB 24; and see now *Patel v Mirza* [2016] UKSC 42).

112. IURE NATURAE AEQUUM EST NEMINEM CUM ALTERIUS DETRIMENTO ET INIURIA FIERI LOCUPLETIOREM

By natural law it is just that no one should be made richer through the loss and wrong to another.

(Pomponius, D.50.17.206)

Roman law, as has been seen (maxim 83), subdivided obligations into four categories, one of which was quasi-contract. This category included actions that were designed to reverse what is described in a celebrated *regula iuris* as unjust enrichment. Examining this quasi category in the context of the law of obligations, one might say this: delictual (tortious) liability is, on the whole concerned with damage and loss incurred by a claimant. The object of the action is to secure compensation, and this is achieved through a liability to pay damages. It is a question of corrective justice, although in certain situations policy considerations might require an appeal to distributive justice. Quasi-contractual (unjust enrichment) liability is different; here, the emphasis is not on the claimant's loss or damage (although these may well be relevant) but on the defendant's gain. When viewed through the eyes of a common lawyer, the nature of the claim is more likely to be debt rather than damages since one is often seeking the repayment of a specific amount of money, although, of course, other remedies might well be relevant. In terms of moral philosophy, the remedy often responds more to distributive rather than corrective justice, and this is one reason why the legislator has intervened in an attempt to reverse unjustified enrichment resulting from criminal behaviour (Proceeds of Crime Act 2002).

The general principle governing liability in respect to a gain, since Roman times, is this: no one should be unjustly enriched at the expense of another. This principle would appear to contain several essential elements. There must be (i) an enrichment that (ii) is unjust and (iii) gained at the expense of another (*Benedetti v Sawiris* [2014] AC 938, para 10). As with delictual liability, two approaches can be discerned. First, liability can be approached through a number of specific remedies or causes of action, each of which is governed by its own set of rules. This was the Roman approach, where liability depended on the availability of particular types of *actio*; and it is more or less the Roman approach that is found in the *Code civil* (*quasi contrats*: CC art 1300). However, in addition to the specific quasi-contractual claims, French law now formally recognises the normative general principle of unjust enrichment (CC art 1303).

The use of the word 'contract' in this quasi-context comes from the idea that this kind of liability arises out of a situation 'as if' there was a contract between the parties. This 'as if' idea, however, was to be problematic for some later civilians. Either a meeting of the minds existed, or such a meeting did not exist; and if there was no *consensus,* there could be no contract. Accordingly, a second approach – which has just been noted with regard to the reformed French law of obligations – is one where liability rests directly on the unjust enrichment principle itself. In German law, for example, liability is based on such a general principle (BGB § 812), although the practical application of this code paragraph has proved difficult.

English law recognised towards the end of the last century these enrichment claims as falling under a liability that is neither contractual nor tortious (see e.g., *Kleinwort Benson Ltd v Glasgow CC* [1999] 1 AC 153). Nevertheless, contract, tort and unjust enrichment can overlap in situations where a defendant has, for example profited from a breach of contract or a tort. If the claimant has suffered damage equivalent to the gain, there is no problem since the remedy of damages will normally solve the problem (corrective justice). Difficulties occur when the claimant has suffered no damage. In this situation, the English judges have turned to equity: a person who profits from a wrong but causes no damage to the victim of a breach of contract or a tort might be held liable in equity via its remedy of account of profits (distributive justice) (*Att-Gen v Blake* [2001] 1 AC 268). Some commentators regard this situation as an example of restitutionary damages, but this is an error since account is an equitable debt claim rather than a damages remedy.

This approach to unjust enrichment liability through the principle itself is, as far as the common law is concerned, rather misleading. The subject has been, and to an extent still is, very much remedy-driven, which means that rules attach as much to damages, debt, account, subrogation, tracing and the like as to any substantive law of obligation relationship. In turn, these remedies can cut across, say, the frontier between owing and owning, between contract and tort, and between law and equity. Quasi-contract in English law has, for example, traditionally focused on the three non-contractual debt remedies of an action for money had and received, an action for money paid, and an action on a *quantum meruit.* While these debt actions are clearly *in personam*, they can sometimes be based on an *in rem* (proprietary) substantive right because a debt, as a chose in action, is a form of property (*Lipkin Gorman v Karpnale Ltd* [1991] 2 AC 548). Additionally, equity offers its own independent *in rem* claim called tracing; a claimant can reclaim money in another's bank account on the basis, not of an obligation, but of ownership (*Agip (Africa) Ltd v Jackson*

[1990] Ch 265 (ChD); [1991] Ch 547 (CA)). The claimant simply asserts that the money in another's patrimony is his property.

In addition to the quasi-contractual debt claims, equity has a number of other remedies available, in addition to tracing, that can be used to prevent unjust enrichment. Indeed, it might be said that the idea of unjust enrichment is one of the great motivating principles of Chancery and so each time equity intervenes in the area of contractual obligations it could be said that it is preventing a means of justified enrichment being turned into, because of, say, undue influence or misrepresentation, a vehicle of unjustified enrichment. Such intervention can be positive or negative in operation. It is positive when equity grants a remedy such as rectification, rescission, or injunction; it is negative when it refuses to grant, for example, specific performance or injunction. In other words, equity can simply refuse to order the performance of a contract and this will have the effect of forcing the contractor demanding performance to sue for damages at common law. If such a contractor cannot show damage, or is deemed to be the cause of his own loss, the common law court, again perhaps reflecting the principle of unjust enrichment, will award only nominal damages.

What equity cannot normally do, although there are statutory exceptions, is to award damages since it does not appear to have any inherent jurisdiction to award this remedy (*Jaggard v Sawyer* [1995] 1 WLR 269). Accordingly, it cannot restore an enrichment through the protection of the restitutionary interest by means of a compensation claim as such. What it has is the remedy of account, which can be used to extract unjustified profits or receipts of money. Indeed, the remedy of account has been specifically described as an equitable debt claim and is of use in situations where the parties are in a fiduciary relationship (*English v Dedham Vale Properties* [1978] 1 All ER 382). It may also be available as an alternative to an action for money had and received where one person has profited from a wrong at the expense of another or in exceptional situations where other normal remedies prove inadequate (*Att-Gen v Blake* [2001] 1 AC 268).

The principle of unjust enrichment can cut across such established boundaries as the one between common law and equity and property and obligations. Another boundary is the one between tort liability in damages and unjust enrichment liability in debt. Where a victim suffers damage as a result of a breach of contract or a tort by more than one defendant, the victim can sue any particular defendant for all their damage (unless the damage itself is causally apportioned between two or more defendants: *Rahman v Arearose Ltd* [2001] QB 351). However, the defendant condemned to pay has a statutory right to "recover contribution from any other person liable in respect of the same damage" (Civil Liability (Contribution) Act 1978 s 1). This contribution right is not, strictly speaking, an equitable remedy since its source is statute.

Yet the principles are based on what is 'just and equitable' and so it is not unreasonable to see the claim for contribution as being one closer to account than quasi-contract.

Another area where equity, restitution and tort come together is subrogation, which has been described as a remedy rather than a cause of action (*Boscawen v Bajwa* [1996] 1 WLR 328). However, it would be better to see it as an institutional structure rather than as a remedy defined and governed by rules. Subrogation is based on a formal relationship either between two persons or between a person and a thing, and is a means by which one thing or one person is substituted for another thing or person without the actual form of the relationship changing. There are thus two forms: real subrogation is where one object is substituted for another object, and personal subrogation is where one person 'stands in the shoes' of another person. Take for example the situation where D owes C a debt, and this debt is secured on D's house. If S pays off C with his own money, the law may on occasions allow S to become subrogated to C's position, with the result that S 'stands in the shoes' of C and takes over the security attached to D's house. The form of the legal structure stays the same, but an individual part changes.

Subrogation plays a central role in the English law of obligations since it is the means by which an insurance company is able to gain access to the courts. Thus, in many tort cases, the real plaintiff or defendant is not the named party but an insurance company subrogated to the rights of the insured named party. However, as we have mentioned, this can be problematic because subrogation is not a tort remedy as such but belongs in the law of restitution. It is a device supposedly preventing unjust enrichment. Yet, when used by an insurance company to recoup insurance money paid out to a victim of a tort, the principles of fault and unjust enrichment can become confused. The loss-spreading aim of tort can be undermined by the desire, on principles of unjust enrichment, to place final liability on the individual at fault (*Lister* v *Romford Ice & Cold Storage Co Ltd* [1957] AC 555).

Given all the different quasi-contractual and equitable remedies which appear to be designed to prevent unjust enrichment, it is not difficult to claim that there exists in England the general principle of unjust enrichment. This claim becomes even stronger when one looks at the historical basis of the common law, which for many centuries thought in terms of debt and trespass (damages) rather than in terms of a strict dichotomy between contract and tort. Debt, as Lord Atkin pointed out, "was not necessarily based upon the existence of a contract" (*United Australia Ltd v Barclays Bank Ltd* [1941] AC 1, 26). However, the problem became one of looking for a conceptual basis upon which one could found a duty to repay a debt in situations where there was no wrong as such. Such a conceptual basis was found in the existing law of contract: "for there was no action possible other than debt or assumpsit on the one side and action for damages for tort on the other." And the "action... for money had and received... was therefore supported by the imputation by the Court to the defendant of a promise to repay" ([1941] AC 1, 27). This notion of an implied contract no doubt worked well enough in a range of cases, but it could create logical difficulties in certain situations. For example, if an enriched defendant was, as a matter of law, incapable of making contracts through a lack of capacity, it logically followed that no contract could be implied and thus no quasi-contractual action allowable (*Sinclair v Brougham* [1914] AC 398).

There is no doubt now that the principle of unjust enrichment exists as the basis for a category within the law of obligations quite independent of those of contract and tort (*Benedetti v Sawiris* [2014] AC 938). Accordingly, the principle seems to have been used as the basis for decisions in a few cases, and it even appears in a modern statute. Yet it would be wrong to say that the principle exists as a *direct* source of obligations in all common law countries. Some jurisdictions, such as Australia are sceptical. What does exist are a number of *in personam* and *in rem* remedies that can be used, *inter alia*, to prevent unjust enrichment. In other words, if there is a principle of unjust enrichment, it is a principle that operates, at least in some jurisdictions, only through the existing categories of substantive law. It operates through contract, tort, equity, or bailment and through certain 'empirical' remedies belonging to the law of actions (action for money had and received, tracing, subrogation and the like) (see maxims 117–118). Yet what is valuable about unjust enrichment is that it provides a substantive idea to underpin non-contractual debt actions in much the same way as 'tort' provides a basis for non-contractual damages actions. Tort, however, is not a normative idea in itself; it is simply a general category or common denominator containing, or underpinning, a range of independent causes of action (trespass, negligence, nuisance, defamation and so on). Unjust enrichment can be viewed in a similar way. Consequently, what is important from a normative position is the remedy or cause of action (or even 'process') that is relevant to the factual situation. This means, in turn, that, from a law of obligations position, it continues to be important to think both in abstract (unjust enrichment) and in concrete terms (remedy, cause of action). But this, of course, is typical of English law.

Perhaps the final word might be given to Evans LJ, who has provided a useful and succinct history of the emergence of the restitution principle. He observes that:

> The principle of unjust enrichment is recognised in English as in other systems of law. It requires the recipient of money to repay it when the circumstances are such that it is contrary to "the ties of natural justice and equity" for him to retain it; cf Lord Mansfield CJ's celebrated dictum in *Moses v Macferlan* (1760) 2 Burr 1005,

1012. How those circumstances may be identified has been the subject of countless judicial decisions over the centuries. A number of recognisable forms of action emerged from the mists of legal history. These entitled the plaintiff to recover, not damages, but a quantified sum from the defendant who was not necessarily a wrongdoer and who was not bound by any contract or express undertaking to pay the sum claimed by the plaintiff. The circumstances in which such a non-contractual obligation can arise are various; the recovery of money paid under a mistake of fact..., or where the consideration in return for which the money paid has failed, are well-established examples. Now, the mists have cleared still further. It is recognised that these different forms spring from a single underlying principle, which is described as the right to recover on grounds of unjust enrichment; that is to say, the defendant has been unjustly enriched by the payment made to him and which the plaintiff seeks to recover (*Kleinwort Benson Ltd v Birmingham CC* [1997] QB 380, 386).

113.   NEMO EX SUO DELICTO MELIOREM SUAM CONDICIONEM FACERE POTEST

No one is to be allowed to improve their condition from their own wrong.

(Ulpian, D.50.17.134.1)

The principle of unjust enrichment has found expression, as indeed has been seen in English law (Proceeds of Crime Act 2002), in the more precise maxim that no one should be allowed to profit from their own wrong. The application of this principle lies at the heart of Ronald Dworkin's theory about the operation of principles (as opposed to rules) in common law reasoning (1977: 23–28). Thus, a beneficiary under a will who murders the testator is not entitled to inherit, even if a literal reading of a statute governing wills appears to state that the beneficiary can inherit. This is a fairly straightforward case, but there are situations that can prove more difficult. In *Tinsley v Milligan* ([1994] 1 AC 340), a majority of the House of Lords decided that a woman who had transferred her share in a jointly purchased house to her partner, in order that the two of them could facilitate a social security fraud, could reclaim her equitable interest in the property despite the illegality of the contract. The dilemma facing the court was this: if the judges had refused to aid the claimant in *Tinsley*, the private interest and enrichment of one of the fraudsters would have been much enhanced, thus affirming that, for her, crime pays. In other words, if the court had allowed the party effectively to escape from the contract, it would have resulted in an unjustified benefit for the fraudster. The majority decision meant only that the status quo was restored; or, to put it another way, the majority of the judges chose the lesser of two evils.

114.   CUM PAR DELICTUM EST DUORUM, SEMPER ONERATUR PETITOR ET MELIOR HABETUR POSSESSORIS CAUSA

When both parties are in the wrong, the claimant's position is weaker and that of the possessor stronger.

(Ulpian, D.50.17.154)

Tinsley v Milligan concerned another maxim associated with the principle of unjust enrichment – or at least associated in a somewhat negative way. This is the maxim *in pari delicto potior est conditio defendentis (possidentis)* (where both parties are equally in the wrong, the position of the defendant (or possessor) is stronger) (see Broom's maxims 718–728). This maxim is not Roman in its actual verbal form, but in substance, money or property transferred under an illegal or immoral transaction could not be recovered (D.12.5.3), and Ulpian's *regula* expresses the maxim in substance. Moreover, the Romans also said *in pari causa possessor potior haberi debet* (where the legal cause is equal, the position of the possessor should be considered as better) (D.50.17.128pr). What this means in practice is that in an illegal transaction where one party has transferred possession of money or property, the party who has received such things is in a stronger position because the courts will not provide an *actio* for the transferor to recover the money or property (*ex turpi causa non oritur actio*). The person receiving the property cannot, in other words, be legally forced to make restitution, and thus he finds himself enriched thanks to this rule. No doubt the enrichment is unjust, but then one could say that the transferor has only himself to blame.

CONCLUDING REMARKS

It would be idle to think that the maxims set out in this chapter have provided comprehensive coverage of the law of tort. What they have done is to emphasise some of the major focal points – often those with long histories – of this area of the law. Perhaps one overriding difficulty with the law of tort is a plural, and sometimes confusing, set of aims and objectives that have become associated with the subject as a result of history rather than rationality. Individual responsibility as a philosophy finds itself in conflict with the personal injury costs – often statistically predictable – arising from certain activities, in particular accidents on the road and in the workplace. Thus, accident compensation has become in recent centuries a major purpose, and one that overshadows individual responsibility in that both road and work accidents are covered by compulsory insurance. There are also important constitutional rights and interests protected by the law of tort, which endows the subject with an important public law element. The subject equally provides many of the remedies for protecting property rights. The idea, then, that tort can somehow isolate itself as a discrete area of the law is one that does not stand up to scrutiny the moment that one views law in terms of protected and conflicting interests.

As for the law of restitution or unjust enrichment, the subject still has a distinct remedies flavour in that the principle of unjust enrichment is too vague to have an independent normative force and thus expresses itself, in its detail, only through remedies such as debt (quasi-contract), account and a range of other equitable remedies. This said, distinguishing claims for wrongful enrichment from wrongful damage is sensible in that the legal policies and principles may well be different from those underpinning contract and tort. Yet a too-rigid separation, at least in the common law, between contract, tort and restitution is also inadvisable because the frontiers between these subjects are very fluid.

10. Law of actions

The third generic category in Gaius' scheme is the law of actions. Today this area, at least in the common law world, is better known as remedies and, again in the common law world, it still has important relevance in that the nature of the remedy claimed in any legal case is often as important as any 'right' in issue. That said, a complete separation from substantive areas of the law, such as contract, tort, property and public law is unrealistic, and this is particularly true with regard to the law of restitution, which is based on an old maxim from Roman law (maxim 112).

115. UBI IUS IBI REMEDIUM

Where there is a right there is a remedy.

(Broom's maxims, 191)

This is stimulated perhaps by *Nihil aliud est actio quam ius quod sibi debeatur, iudicio persequendi* – an action is nothing but a right that is owed to one to be pursued by a judgement.

(Celsus, D.44.7.51; J.4.6pr)

An article once stated in its abstract that the "ancient Roman legal maxim ubi ius [ibi] remedium reminds us that the law provides many types of remedy for the breach of legal wrongs, including an inherent power of superior courts, in some situations, to fashion novel remedies where existing ones are inadequate to redress particular violations of rights" (11 MJ 3 233). As to the meaning of the maxim, one perhaps cannot complain, but the expression *ubi ius* appears nowhere in the Roman sources and is not to be found (probably) until much later in legal history. This said, the spirit of the maxim is possibly stimulated by an observation from the Roman jurist Celsus that an *actio* is simply a means of vindicating our 'right' (*ius*). The importance of the maxim is that it puts the 'rights' before remedies, that is to say, it considers remedies to be secondary and just a procedural means of giving expression to a person's pre-existing rights. The spirit of the maxim can, then, be located in the work of the humanist jurist who was one of the first to insist on the separation between rights and remedies, namely Hugues Doneau (1527–1591).

116.   UBI REMEDIUM IBI IUS

Where there is a remedy there is a right.

(reversal of maxim 115)

A number of contemporary writers have reversed the maxim *ubi ius ibi reme-dium* in order to explain how both Roman classical law and the common law before the nineteenth century thought in terms of actions (remedies) rather than rights. The distinctions between the various contracts and delicts in Roman law were defined in terms of different kinds of actions. Equally, in the pre-19th century common law, substantive law was determined by different forms of actions. Henry Maine summed up the historical development by say-ing that "substantive law has at first the look of being gradually secreted in the interstices of procedure" (1890: 389). Even today, it seems that it is the remedy that still defines the right. As an English judge noted:

> In the pragmatic way in which English law has developed, a man's legal rights are in fact those which are protected by a cause of action. It is not in accordance, as I understand it, with the principles of English law to analyse rights as being something separate from the remedy given to the individual.... [I]n my judgment, in the ordinary case to establish a legal or equitable right you have to show that all the necessary elements of the cause of action are either present or threatened (Sir Nicolas Browne-Wilkinson in *Kingdom of Spain* v *Christie, Manson & Woods Ltd* [1986] 1 WLR 1120, 1129).`

Freerick Maitland had also observed at the beginning of the last century that the "forms of action we have buried, but they still rule us from their graves" (1909:1).

117.   ACTIO IN PERSONAM INFERTUR: PETITIO IN
        REM: PERSECUTIO IN REM VEL IN PERSONAM
        REI PERSEQUENDAE GRATIA

*An action is brought against a person: a vindication claim against a thing: a
lawsuit against a thing or against a person in pursuit of a thing.*

(Papinian, D.44.7.28)

In Roman law, there were two fundamental types of legal action. There was
a claim against a thing (*in rem*), for the enforcement of a property right, and
a claim against a person (*in personam*) for the enforcement of an obligation
right. This distinction at the level of remedies was to give rise to the fundamental dichotomy between a real right (*ius in rem*) and a personal right (*ius in
personam*), a distinction that was probably in the minds of the Roman jurists
themselves but became more developed in the time of the medieval jurists who
frequently used the expressions *ius reale*, *ius proprietarii* and *ius obligationis*
(some of which are to be found in the Roman sources). These distinctions
remain fundamental in modern civil law.

In common law the distinction between real rights and personal rights is
equally fundamental. Thus, a contractual right is a personal one, while a mortgage involves a real right in the property mortgaged. In other words, a mortgage involves both a contractual right (*in personam*) and a real right (*in rem*)
acting as the security for the contractual debt. However, what English law does
not have is a distinction between actions *in rem* and *in personam*; as a result of
history, all actions are personal actions at common law.

The personal actions at common law were very different from the *actiones*
to be found in Roman law and were based on the system of writs. The original
formulation of each action was a response to an empirical problem that existed
in English society at the time of formulation (such as people not paying what
they owed). However, some of the actions subsequently became enlarged, if
not deformed, through development by lawyers and courts, often through the
use of fictions. The main actions which were to survive into the 19th century
(if not later) are worth noting because they have left their imprint on Anglo-
American legal thought.

The action of *account* was a writ ordering the defendant to render an
account of the plaintiff's money. The action was less an actual claim than
an accounting process aimed at identifying money in the defendant's possession 'belonging' to the plaintiff. Account "was not primarily concerned with
the obligation to pay money, which sounded in debt, but with the antecedent
obligation to enter into an account in order to discover what, if anything, was
owing" (Baker 2019: 387). By the 16th century, the common law action for

an account had declined into oblivion, but in form, the remedy survived in the Court of Chancery, and by the 19th century, account was regarded as an equitable, rather than common law, remedy (see *London, Chatham & Dover Railway Co* v *S.E. Railway Co* [1892] 1 Ch 120, 140).

The action of *assumpsit* was a development of trespass on the case and was used as a means of claiming damages for a breach of promise. Viewed from a modern perspective, it can be seen as the remedial basis for a theory of contractual liability. The Court of King's Bench developed a particular type of *assumpsit* to be able to attract debt claims that were normally brought in Common Pleas. Thus, two types of *assumpsit* were established: there was the general action in damages for damage arising from an unperformed promise and a debt-like claim for the recovery of a specific sum of money (Ibbetson 1999: 147–151). As both claims were technically for damages, the debt and damages distinction ought, perhaps, to have disappeared. Yet it did not. Indeed, the distinction not only survived but a claim in debt is regarded as a different cause of action than a claim in damages (*Overstone Ltd* v *Shipway* [1962] 1 WLR 117). One might add that in order for *assumpsit* to lie, there had to be some kind of *quid pro quo* (reciprocity); this requirement subsequently developed into the doctrine of consideration (Ibbetson 1999: 142) which in turn became one of the fundamental requirements for an enforceable contract at common law (see maxim 88).

Another 'contractual' action was *covenant,* which was a claim for damages arising out of the breach of a 'covenant', that is a promise given under seal. It had several procedural disadvantages and as a result never really developed into a general claim for breach of contract. Yet the action has to some extent survived into the modern world in that a unilateral promise executed as a deed will still be binding (see Law of Property (Miscellaneous Provisions) Act 1989 s 1).

A further action used by a disappointed 'contractor' was the writ of *debt,* which was an action for a specific sum of money alleged to be due to the plaintiff and generally arising out of some 'contract' between the parties. This action was one of the oldest in common law and was actually as much a 'property' claim as a contractual one (Ibbetson 1999: 18). However in the 17th century, as mentioned, debt got eclipsed to a certain extent by the special form of *assumpsit* called *indebitatus assumpsit,* but it nevertheless survived as a separate remedy into modern law and must therefore be distinguished from an action for damages (*Jervis* v *Harris* [1996] Ch 195). Indeed, the action was not limited to contractual situations, and three particular forms of debt developed as restitution (or quasi-contract) remedies (see maxim 112). These are the action for money had and received, the action for money paid, and the *quantum meruit* action (see Lord Atkin in *United Australia Ltd* v *Barclays Bank Ltd* [1941] AC 1). These three quasi-contractual debt claims were originally rationalised on the basis that there was an implied contract between the parties, but this theory has now been abandoned. They are now based upon the Roman principle of unjust enrichment (D.50.17.206; Ibbetson 1999: 284–293) (see maxim 112).

If debt was a claim for a specific sum of money, *detinue* was an action for a specific movable thing. It was accordingly the nearest action that the common law had to an *in rem* claim and was once the remedy used by the owner of a chattel (bailor) who had transferred possession of it to another (bailee) such as a transporter of goods or cleaner of clothes (*Building and Civil Engineering Holidays Scheme Management Ltd* v *Post Office* [1966] 1 QB 247; *Morris* v *C W Martin & Sons Ltd* [1966] 1 QB 716). The transfer of possession gave rise to a relation called bailment which was a property relationship independent of any contract between the two parties; the bailee was under a strict duty to return the goods to the bailor and failure to do this would result in liability for damages in detinue, unless the bailee could show that the goods were lost through no fault of his own. Detinue survived as a cause of action in tort until 1977 when it was abolished by statute (Torts (Interference with Goods) Act 1977 s 2(1)). Its role has been taken over by the tort of conversion (1977 Act s 2(2)).

Another type of property claim was the writ of *ejectment,* which lay where lands or tenements were let for a term of years but the lessee was ejected from the premises. In substance, this writ was a real action, but in form, it was a personal claim developed by the use of a fiction to avoid the technicalities of an actual real action. The action is still available to anyone, including now a mere contractual licensee, wrongfully dispossessed of land (*Manchester Airport Plc* v *Dutton* [2000] 1 QB 133).

The Writ of *Error* was a means by which a disappointed litigant could 'appeal' against a court decision on the basis of an error on the face of the record. It was not properly an appeal since the case was never re-heard as such; questions of fact or law, a misdirection of the jury, a perverse verdict, or whatever could only be considered by a Court of Error if such a basis for 'appeal' formed part of the court record. To make matters worse, there was no proper Court of Error until Parliament established the Court of Exchequer Chamber in 1830. Before then, there had been other Court of Exchequer Chambers, and the House of Lords could also act as a final Court of Error; but the system of 'appeal' before 1830 was, to say the least, complex, somewhat haphazard and procedurally narrow and unsatisfactory (the court could only re-examine the record).

An action for *replevin* lay where goods had been distrained (seized by a creditor) and was the claim by which the owner sought their recovery. However, the most important claim in respect of interference with goods or with the person was the writ of *trespass.* Along with debt, this was another of the common law's oldest writs and is seen as the ultimate source of most of our present-day compensation claims (tort). An action for trespass was, in origin a claim for damages against a person who had harmed the plaintiff in breach of the king's peace (*contra pacem nostram*) and by a forcible wrong (*vi et armis*). "The word 'trespass'", notes Ibbetson, "meant no more than 'wrong', and its legal use had no predetermined boundaries" (1999: 14), but there were three distinct varieties which were to develop, namely trespass to the person (*vi et armis*), to goods (*de bonis asportatis*) and to land (*quare clausum fregit*). These three varieties have survived into the modern law of tort and have an important constitutional and private law status since they are the torts that effectively protect the individual against the state and ensure quiet possession of property.

The writ of trespass subsequently gave rise to an offshoot action called *trespass on the case,* which was a more general form of trespass where the facts did not disclose a forcible wrong and thus fell outside the Writ of Trespass (direct action). There is some debate over why actions on the case developed, the traditional learning being that when the Register of Writs became closed, statute authorised Chancery to issue writs on an analogy with trespass (*in consimili casu*). Whatever the situation, the action on the case became the means by which 'trespass' was transformed, from the 14th century onwards, into a more general liability action through the development of 'special cases'. Case thus became both general and particular at the same time in that it consisted of a series of actions based on model special facts which later developed into particular types of actionable wrongs such as *assumpsit, trover,* public nuisance, negligence and so on (see e.g., Denning LJ's judgment in *Esso Petroleum Ltd v Southport Corporation* [1954] 2 QB 182). However, one oddity of case was that trespass and trespass on the case remained independent personal actions whose difference was rationalised, in the 17th century, on the basis of direct (trespass) and indirect (case) damage (see *Scott v Shepherd* (1773) 96 ER 525).

Trover was an action for damages brought against a defendant who had 'converted' to his own use the plaintiff's goods and chattels. It later became known as conversion and is still the main tort for recovering movable property (Torts (Interference with Goods) Act 1977). As we have seen, conversion can now be used in situations that were once covered only by the tort of detinue; it is the remedy that a bailor uses to recover his goods from a bailee.

One can see, then, that Papinian's assertion about the nature of actions does not fully represent English law. It is possible to regard the torts of trespass and conversion as functionally fulfilling the role of actions *in rem* in Roman law. Yet they remain torts and thus, technically, part of the law of obligations rather than the law of property. Or, put another way, it is the law of obligations in England that provides the remedies for protecting and enforcing property rights. Moreover, from this remedies point of view, notions such as ownership are of little importance. Trespass and conversion are, essentially, based upon the notion of possession (see maxim 80). Who has the better right to possess?

118.   REMEDIUM EXTRAORDINARIUM NON INCURRIT CUM ORDINARIO

The extraordinary remedy does not conflict with the ordinary.

(Baldus, Comment on D.4.4.16)

In addition to the common law remedies, the Court of Chancery developed, from the 15th century, a series of remedies to complement the actions of damages and debt. Whether these remedies can be described as 'extraordinary' is today a moot point. But there was no doubt in the early centuries of the common law courts there were real problems with the remedies on offer from these courts. In particular, they could, with the one exception of repossession of land, grant only monetary remedies (debt and damages). The Court of Chancery offered a range of alternative ones. However, as the jurist Baldus seemingly recognised, the development of actions in addition to the ordinary ones did not mean that there would be a conflict and the Court of Chancery saw its relief not as a competitor as such to the common law remedies (not that Baldus was talking of the common law). Perhaps a later adaption of the Post-Glossators' view of extraordinary remedies – and one incorporated into the common law – sums up the situation: *Ubi cessat remedium ordinarium ibi decurritur ad extraordinarium* (where ordinary remedies prove wanting extraordinary ones come into play) (4 Coke's Reports 92). These equitable remedies remain distinct and often attract their own procedural, if not substantive, principles. Moreover, given the existence of debt and damages at common law, the majority of the remedies developed in Chancery were non-pecuniary and the principal ones remain of central importance in modern law.

An *injunction* was and is Chancery's most important remedy and, in its paradigm form, is a negative order. That is to say, it is an order not to do something which acts *in personam* against a defendant. It is, like all equitable remedies, said to be discretionary, although this is not to be taken to mean that judges have complete discretion, for the exercise is governed by equitable principles and, of course, all decisions have to be properly reasoned. There are particular kinds of injunctions, including a *mandatory injunction,* which is a positive order requiring the defendant to do something (see, e.g., *Kelsen* v *Imperial Tobacco Co* [1957] 2 QB 334), and an *interlocutory injunction* (emergency injunction), which is a special emergency form of injunction, where the "object... is to protect the plaintiff against injury by violation of his right, for which he could not be adequately compensated in damages recoverable in the action if the uncertainty was resolved in his favour at the trial" (*American Cyanamid v Ethicon* [1975] AC 396, 406). In the latter half of the 20th century, two particular forms of this remedy were developed. A *Mareva injunction* (freezing order) is one granted to restrain a defendant facing litigation from removing his assets so as to frustrate the claimant (*Mareva Compania Naviera v International Bulkcarriers* [1980] 1 All ER 213). What is important with respect to this injunction is that, although it operates in theory *in personam* (a remedy against the person), the reality is that its effects are *in rem* in that it affects the defendant's property (*Allen v Jambo Holdings* [1980] 2 All ER 502). Despite it attracting debate, the existence of this particular remedy has been confirmed by statute (Senior Courts Act 1981 s 37(3)) and is now the subject of considerable case law. An *Anton Piller* (search) order, again supposedly acting only *in personam* against the occupier of premises, is really nothing less than a civil search warrant (*Anton Piller KG v Manufacturing Processes Ltd* [1976] Ch 55); it was developed to combat intellectual property abuses and is usually applied for *ex parte*, that is to say in secrecy and without the defendant being present in court (*Columbia Picture Inc v Robinson* [1987] Ch 38).

An order for *specific performance* is another type of mandatory order that the Lord Chancellor could make with respect to the enforcement of contracts. However, he would only do this in situations where damages at common law were inadequate, and this is the reason why equitable specific performance is often described as an exceptional contract remedy. It is not available 'as of right'; although, in the case of the sale of land, there is a presumption that such a contract will be specifically enforced because land is a unique item, and, anyway, the purchaser becomes an equitable owner once contracts are exchanged. As one of its principles, equity looks on that as done which ought to be done, and so it will force the seller to make the purchaser the owner at common law. There are a number of principles that attach to specific performance; for example, equity will not enforce a contract if it would require constant supervision by the court (see e.g., *Co-operative Insurance Society Ltd v Argyll Stores Ltd* [1998] AC 1), or if the contract lacks mutuality of obligation (*Price v Strange* [1978] Ch 337), or again if it is a contract for personal services. It may well refuse the remedy if it would cause serious economic inefficiency (*Co-operative Insurance*, above).

In addition to these two leading non-monetary equitable remedies, there are several others. The remedy of *rescission* was developed by the Chancellor in order to set aside contracts where the defendant was guilty of certain kinds of unconscionable behaviour such as misrepresentation, fraud, or duress (including undue influence: for a good example, see *Credit Lyonnais Bank Nederland v Burch* [1997] 1 All ER 144). It was for a while thought that rescission would be available in certain circumstances for contractual mistake, but this has now been denied by the Court of Appeal (*The Great Peace* [2003] QB 679).

Another contractual remedy issuing out of the Court of Chancery that remains of importance in the law of contract is *rectification* of a contractual (or other) document. Rectification will be ordered if the document clearly does not reflect what was agreed upon between the parties. Being an equitable remedy, rectification allows a court to go beyond the text of a written contract (prohibited at common law) and to examine the pre-contractual negotiations (*Daventry DC v Daventry & District Housing Ltd* [2012] 1 WLR 1333). Rectification problems (in equity) may well now find now themselves intermixed with contractual interpretation issues (common law), leading to something of a conflict between the two systems.

In the area of restitution, *subrogation* is available where one person 'stands in the shoes' of another person and takes over certain rights of the latter. It has been described as a genuine remedy rather than a cause of action, with the result that it can be used in a variety of situations to protect property rights or to prevent unjustified enrichment (*Boscawen v Bajwa* [1995] 4 All ER 769) (see maxim 112). It is of particular importance in insurance and the law of obligations, in that once an insurance company has paid out on a policy, it is entitled to be subrogated to any rights the insured might have against third parties responsible for the event that triggered the insurance claim. Such a right does not always work efficiently, in that it can be a means of transferring losses from an insurance company (paid to take the risk) to a person who is uninsured.

Another important claim is *tracing,* which in its origin was a remedy in which Chancery recognised that a person could have a right *in rem* in money (or other property) in another person's patrimony (something which is not possible in civilian thinking since money is a consumable item). Whether tracing is an actual remedy is now in question since it has been described as a 'process' rather than a 'remedy' (*Boscawen v Bajwa* [1995] 4 All ER 769), but it certainly was once seen as a kind of *actio in rem*. It remains a proprietary remedy for reclaiming money in another's bank account, although it is normally available only where there is a special equitable 'fiduciary relationship' between the parties (see *Agip (Africa) Ltd v Jackson* [1990] Ch 265 (ChD); [1991] Ch 547 (CA)). In civilian thinking, once money has been transferred, title normally passes with the transfer because, as mentioned, money is a consumable item; allowing a person to claim money in another's bank account on the basis of 'ownership' is, then, a genuine Chancery innovation. One might add that it is questionable whether this remedy or process is a non-monetary claim since the end result is the retransfer of the money from defendant to claimant. It might be better therefore to see tracing as a non-monetary process supporting what became the equitable monetary remedy of account.

In addition to these purely equitable remedies, there are a number of well-established procedural remedies whose equitable origin has now largely disappeared behind civil procedural rules. *Declaration* is where a court is asked merely to declare the rights of the parties and is now a remedy well established in the rules of procedure (see, e.g., *In re S* [1995] 3 WLR 78). However, it originated in the Court of Chancery. Similarly, *discovery of documents* (disclosure) is one of the common law tradition's most famous pre-trial remedies (although it is to be found in Roman law; see D.2.13), yet it originated in the Chancellor's power to make *in personam* orders against a litigant. The remedy is normally associated with a substantive claim for damages or whatever and is a pre-trial procedural order to produce all documents relevant to the substantive claim (see now CPR part 31). However, it has also become an independent remedy and can be used, for example, to order a journalist to produce his or her sources (*X Ltd v Morgan-Grampian (Publishers) Ltd* [1991] 1 AC 1).

Finally, regarding non-monetary remedies, a person with an interest in property which is endangered by the defendant's business behaviour could apply to Chancery for the appointment of a *Receiver* to manage the affairs of the defendant. This is an important remedy in bankruptcy law. This equitable nature of bankruptcy law is equally found in the idea that a bankrupt's assets now become the property of a trustee in bankruptcy.

As we have seen, monetary remedies are normally associated with the common law courts, but they do have importance on occasions in equity. An action for an *account of profits* was originally a common law personal action (as has been seen), but its procedural nature made it an ideal process for Chancery jurisdiction. The remedy has recently undergone a renaissance in that it is now available as a restitution claim against a defendant who has obtained an unconscionable profit in situations where the claimant has suffered no corresponding provable loss (*Att-Gen v Blake* [2001] 1 AC 268).

Account is essentially a claim in debt rather than damages. As for damages, it is a matter of debate whether or not Chancery could award damages (rather than account). However, thanks to statute, damages can now be awarded in lieu of an injunction or specific performance (Chancery Amendment Act 1858 s 2; now Senior Courts Act 1981 s 50). Damages can also be awarded in lieu of rescission for non-fraudulent misrepresentation (Misrepresentation Act 1967 s 2(2)).

119.   ACTUS JUDICIARIUS CORAM NON JUDICE IRRITUS HABETUR, DE MINISTERIALI AUTEM A QUOCUNQUE PROVENIT RATUM ESTO

A judicial act given by a non judge is void, although a ministerial act is authoritative.

(Lofft's Reports 458)

Turning from what might be generally termed as private law actions to remedies available in public law, one has to qualify the earlier statement that the common law courts could issue, on the whole, only monetary remedies. It seems obvious that a decision made by a person who has no judicial authority is one that would seem to be null and void. Yet there are many public officials who make administrative decisions about all kinds of matters – tax, planning, social security and so on. Can such decisions be challenged in the courts and, if so, how?

In the domain of what today would be called administrative law, the starting point of a history of public law remedies is a group of actions known as the 'prerogative writs' (see maxims 61–62). The origin of these actions is to be found in the royal power of the *Curia Regis* to control all lesser authorities exercising power in the name of the king. This power passed to the judges of the King's Bench, and this court assumed a jurisdiction to assure that any judicial or administrative decision should conform to the common law. This jurisdiction was exercised via the prerogative writs, which were originally ordinary procedural processes but which, in the 16th–17th centuries, became a means of judicial control of administrative power (*R (Cart) v Upper Tribunal* [2010] 2 WLR 1012, paras 44–50). As with the 'private' law personal actions at common law, the prerogative writs can be presented simply in terms of a list.

The Writ of *Habeas Corpus* started life as a way of ensuring that a defendant appeared in court, but from the 16th century, it evolved into a remedy that did almost the opposite. The writ was used to determine if the imprisonment of a subject was valid in law. Thus, it became the means of giving expression to the liberty of the subject, a right which itself had been expressed in Magna Carta 1215. In the 18th–19th centuries, the scope of the writ extended beyond imprisonment by a public official or body to, for example the incarceration of wives by husbands and questions about the custody of children (family law). Habeas Corpus remains an independent remedy today, but its scope has been drastically reduced by a whole range of statutes that give powers to the police and sometimes other bodies to detain individuals without trial. It was once a powerful remedy but has been largely neutered by the legislator.

The *Writ of Prohibition* was the oldest of the prerogative writs and was originally used to prevent ecclesiastical courts from hearing cases involving temporal matters. Later, it was employed by King's Bench against any inferior court or tribunal that was considered to have been acting beyond its jurisdiction. In the 19th century, it was extended even further; it lay against statutory bodies and government departments, and thus became a means of controlling administrative, as well as judicial, decisions.

Two writs of particular importance were *mandamus* and *certiorari*. The word *mandamus* means 'we command' and the writ carrying this name was used to restore public offices to those deprived of them. In the 17th century, it developed into a means of controlling local authorities: the writ commanded the authority to act or to show cause why it did not. In the 20th century, the writ became the means of forcing a public body to exercise its statutory duties. The Writ of *Certiorari* was originally used to remove a case from an inferior court to King's Bench and thus acted as a means not just of assuming jurisdiction but also of reviewing cases (although only criminal). It was later extended to administrative bodies, and thus Certiorari became a general procedure for reviewing criminal cases from inferior courts and orders issued by public officials or bodies. It could not be used as a method of appeal as such since the review applied only to an examination of the record to ensure that an order or conviction was not *ultra vires*. But in the 20th century, the huge growth in administrative tribunals resulted in a renewed life for Certiorari; it became the procedural means for Queen's or King's Bench to examine the decisions of administrative bodies and to correct errors in law. If such errors were found, the decision of the public body could be quashed. In other words, it was a remedy by which the judges of the common law could review, and quash if necessary, the judicial (as opposed to administrative) decisions of public bodies and public officials.

These writs survived the abolition of the form of action in 1852 and 1875, but, with the exception of habeas corpus, became 'orders' in 1938 (Administration of Justice (Miscellaneous Provisions) Act 1938 s 7). In 1977 these orders were combined to form a single action of *Judicial Review,* and this term has now largely eclipsed the old labels such as mandamus and certiorari (Senior Courts Act 1981 s 31), although habeas corpus has survived as an independent writ as a result of its constitutional and ideological importance. Procedure is now governed by Part 54 of the Civil Procedure Rules 1998. Interestingly, case law has suggested there is a difference between public and private law that applies to the distinction between judicial review on the one hand and the ordinary other remedies such as debt and damages on the other (*O'Reilly* v *Mackman* [1983] 2 AC 237), but this has been rejected by doctrine as being historically and conceptually inaccurate (see Oliver 2001). Many of the principles of

administrative law have actually been taken from areas of private law such as
trusts and company law.

In addition to these prerogative writs, the Court of Chancery, as has been
seen, developed a series of non-monetary remedies, two of which became particularly important in the area of 'public law'. The Court of Chancery seemingly always had an inherent power to issue a declaratory judgment, that is to
say, a judgment that simply declared a right but did not follow it with any specific relief (*Guaranty Trust Co of New York v Hannay & Co* [1915] 2 KB 536,
568). However, because of the reluctance of English judges to issue advisory
opinions, this remedy did not become important until the 19th century and
after. Nevertheless, in the field of public law, the declaration was of particular
importance with respect to disputes against the Crown because the judges felt
that they could not issue coercive remedies against their own 'employer', so
to speak. Declarations were different. And indeed it seems that this remedy
may have been used by the common law courts, as well as Chancery, perhaps
as early as the 16th century (Lawson 1980: 234). Whatever the historical situation, the declaration became a general public law remedy in the 20th century thanks to the Crown Proceedings Act 1947 s 21. Declaration, it should
be noted, is wider than Certiorari (see *Pyx Granite Co v Ministry of Housing*
[1958] 1 All ER 625, 632). Moreover, it is a remedy adopted by the Human
Rights Act 1988 (s 4).

The second Chancery remedy is, of course the *injunction*. This remedy,
because of its flexibility, "made it a weapon particularly suitable for checking
the action of public authorities encroaching on property rights". Indeed "it is
not at all surprising that the principles on which judicial control was exercised,
namely, the so-called rules of *natural justice* and the doctrine of *ultra vires*,
were first expressed and expounded in cases relating to an action for injunction as well as, or even earlier than, in cases concerning prerogative writs"
(Galeotti 1954: 31). In the 19th century, the injunction, along with declaration, became an important public as well as private law remedy. However from
the 18th century, an individual could not claim an injunction against a public
body unless some 'private' interest of his was in issue (private right or special
damage); the individual had to claim the remedy via the Attorney-General in
a Relator Action (see generally *Gouriet v Union of Post Office Workers* [1978]
AC 435). Today, an injunction against a public body is claimed by way of judicial review proceedings if the matter in issue is one of public law.

The prerogative writs, with the exception of habeas corpus, have been abolished in form but remain – along with the two equitable remedies (declaration
and injunction) – as remedies available in an action for judicial review. The
grounds for obtaining such a review were summed up by Lord Diplock: the
"first ground [is] 'illegality', the second 'irrationality' and the third 'procedural impropriety'" (*Council of Civil Service Unions v Minister for the Civil*

Service [1985] AC 374, 410) (see maxim 61). These grounds should not be seen as watertight compartments since administrative law is always developing; but they do help one to distinguish between an action for judicial review and an appeal against a decision of a court or tribunal. An action for judicial review does not concern itself with the substance of a decision but only with its legality. It is not for the judges to judge the fairness of the administrative decision under review, and so they cannot substitute their decision in place of the decision taken by a public official; all they can do is to quash the decision. In contrast, when appeal judges allow an appeal, they substitute their decision for that of the court below. Nevertheless, the two procedures do share something of a common history, and, of course, the continental review of a judgment by a *Cour de cassation* seems closer to a judicial review process than to an appeal (see maxim 33).

Three important requirements for judicial review need to be mentioned. The first is that the person bringing the action must have 'sufficient interest' in the matter (Senior Courts Act 1981 s 31(3)) (see maxim 121). A second fundamental requirement is that the defendant is a public body: the remedy of judicial review is not available against private persons or entities. However, the test for a public body is not a formal one but a functional one, and so a private body may be open to an action if it is performing a public function (*R (Beer) v Hampshire Farmers' Markets Ltd* [2004] 1 WLR 233). The third requirement is that judicial review is a remedy of last resort. It should not be permitted "if a significant part of the issues between the parties could be resolved outside the litigation process" (*R (Cowl) v Plymouth CC (Practice Note)* [2002] 1 WLR 803, para 14).

A final question that needs to be considered with respect to judicial review is whether or not the action includes a claim for damages. The answer is both yes and no, as has been seen (maxim 61, and see maxim 121 below). The actual formal remedy of judicial review does not in itself permit a claim for damages because the old prerogative writs were not damages actions. Accordingly, a claimant must prove that he has a cause of action in contract or tort before damages can be awarded. However, a claimant does not need to bring a separate claim, and so the judicial review proceedings can be used to claim damages; but, of course, they will only be awarded if they would have been awarded in a separate claim.

In addition to all of these remedies, essentially developed historically by the courts, statute has introduced many remedies of its own. It is a moot point whether these statutory actions are public or private in nature, but as they are the result of legislation, it is at least possible to say that they have a public law flavour. Sometimes legislation makes use of existing remedies such as injunctions, damages, or even tracing (see, e.g., Proceeds of Crime Act 2002 s 305); sometimes it introduces its own remedy of statutory orders, powers of cancellation or variation, or other measures. In particular such statutory orders are found in family law legislation and in the Acts regulating the financial, employment and consumer sectors of the economy. Equally, statute might take an existing remedy such as damages and extend it to certain heads of damage or interests which might not normally be protected in the ordinary law of contract and tort (see, e.g., Disability Discrimination Act 1995 s 28V(2); Equality Act 2006 s 68(4)). Often, when statute introduces a new cause of action, it will lay down provisions as to the remedies available and what interests are protected by the remedies deemed available (see, e.g., Protection from Harassment Act 1997), but it may also deny a particular remedy by establishing certain defences. One notable statutory remedy introduced by the Human Rights Act 1998 (s 8) is that of damages against a public authority that has invaded the human right of the claimant; another notable statutory provision is the granting of a power to use the self-help remedy of reasonable force in certain situations (see, e.g., Education and Inspections Act 2006 s 93).

120.   NAM ADVERSUS PERICULUM NATURALIS RATIO PERMITTIT SE DEFENDERE

For natural reason permits one to defend oneself against danger.

(Gaius D.9.2.4pr)

Although they do not strictly form part of the law of actions (since they are not legal actions as such), mention must nevertheless be made of remedies that are available without the aid of the court. These are called self-help remedies, of which the most well-known is probably the 'right' of self-defence. One can use force to repel a trespass, but only if the force used is reasonable in the circumstances. If it is not reasonable, then the person using self-help will himself be liable in trespass (*Revill v Newbery* [1996] QB 567).

However, in addition to this self-defence remedy, there are others which are, perhaps, less dramatic but actually of considerable importance. The victim of a breach of contract has, if the breach is fundamental, the right to terminate the contract, and if the breach amounts to a complete non-performance, the other party may be entitled to refuse to pay the price (*Bolton* v *Mahadeva* [1972] 1 WLR 1009). As with self-defence, care must be taken because if the breach was not fundamental, the person who terminates the contract will himself be in breach and may be liable in damages for any losses caused by the termination. Set-off is also a self-help remedy. Where two contracting parties owe each other money, one party can, if the debts are connected, set off against what he owes to his creditor what this latter owes to him. Thus, if D owes C £500 and C owes D £200, D need pay only £300 to C (for a history of set-off see *Eller v Grovecrest Investments Ltd* [1995] QB 272). An unpaid repairer of, for example, a motor car can use the self-help remedy of keeping possession of the vehicle until the owner pays for the repairs; this remedy is known as a lien (see *Tappenden v Artus* [1964] 2 QB 185). Another self-help remedy is the abatement of a nuisance; a neighbour can, for example, cut off the branches of a tree that encroaches onto his property and is a nuisance.

121. ALTERIUS CIRCUMVENTIO ALII NON PRAEBET ACTIONEM

> *A deceit on one person does not give rise to an action by another person.*
>
> (Ulpian D.50.17.49)

121A. PAS D'INTÉRÊT, PAS D'ACTION

> *In the absence of an interest there is no action.*
>
> (inspired also by D.47.23.3.1; D.47.2.10)

121B. L'ACTION EST OUVERTE À TOUS CEUX QUI ONT UN INTÉRÊT LÉGITIME AU SUCCÈS OU AU REJET D'UNE PRÉTENTION

> *The action is available to all those who have a legitimate interest in the success or rejection of a claim.*
>
> (French *Code de procédure civil*, art 31)

What are the procedural limits attaching to legal actions? One central limitation to be found in French law is the requirement that the parties to an action have a 'legitimate interest' in any legal claim, either in pursuing or defending an action. The idea that a claimant must have an interest goes back to Roman law, where it became a requirement that a person wishing to bring an *actio populationis* for things thrown or falling from a building ought normally to have an interest in the matter (D.9.3.5.5; D.47.23.3.1). It was also a requirement for an action of theft (*actio furti*) (D.47.2.10).

Is this interest requirement one that is a general rule attaching to all actions in any system? On the whole, the requirement need not be expressed since nearly all claims by their very nature will involve an obvious interest. The claimant is usually seeking a debt, compensation for loss or injury, an order to prevent a person from continuing a nuisance, a vindication of a property right, or some other decision that will advance their personal or economic interest. Indeed, in English law, it is a specific requirement of most torts that the claimant has either suffered actual damage or loss or that some important, often constitutional, right has been infringed. In contract, a claimant must equally show loss of some sort or another or that he or she is entitled to a specific sum of money. If such a claimant cannot prove loss, he will normally obtain only nominal damages and may end up having to pay costs. In other words, nearly all legal actions are based on the parties either asserting or defending an identifiable interest – often described as a 'right' – and so a general rule about having a legitimate interest is unnecessary. It is subsumed under other requirements.

This being said, in administrative law there is a specific rule attaching to the action for judicial review that the claimant must have a sufficient interest in the matter. If, then, a claimant can show no connection with the contested decision then such a person will be barred from bringing the action for lack of *locus standi* (legal standing). Does an environmental body such as Greenpeace have sufficient interest in a ministerial decision to allow, say, nuclear waste to be discharged into the atmosphere? One can see that such a procedural question has an enormous impact on environmental 'rights' (*R v Inspectorate of Pollution, ex p Greenpeace (No 2)* [1994] 4 All ER 329). In fact, one can reverse the situation in order to indicate that a person does not have to have a 'right' before he can claim judicial review. A citizen only has to have an interest or, better, a 'legitimate expectation' and thus it could be said that English law shares with continental law the idea that private law is about protecting rights, whereas as administrative law is about protecting interests and expectations.

Accordingly, one area where this individual interest or individual damage question can be of importance is where there is what might be termed a class or community interest at issue. Such an issue is usually associated not just with the interest but also with the definition of who can be a legitimate legal subject. An entity's activity that contributes to climate change might not cause any actual damage to living individuals but threatens the interest of future generations: how can such a generation's interest be protected – if at all – in the courts? What if a corporation enriches itself through illegal activity but causes no discernible damage to any individual? Some kind of class action (see maxim 70) might be one answer. Another possibility is to allow (by statute) a local or national public body to seek an injunction on behalf of the community.

CONCLUDING REMARKS

The law of actions might not today, in the civil law tradition, have a place in the civil codes as such since legal procedure is no longer based on the form or type of action. Actions have been relegated (so to speak) to codes of civil procedure. Nevertheless, in the common law world, the law of remedies continues to have a force and remedies such as the injunction attract their own specific rules, as do other remedies like specific performance, rescission, and rectification. The law of damages needs a whole textbook if it is to be adequately expounded in all its detail. Whatever the situation regarding a law of actions today, when it comes to dissecting a legal case in the common law world, the remedy in issue remains one vital focal point.

11. Legal method and reasoning

In this final chapter, the emphasis will be on method and reasoning in law. When one examines the history of Roman law in Europe from the 11th century to contemporary times, the different eras are delineated by changes in approach and methods regarding the Roman texts. This is not to say that one method always replaces another; there tends to be a change in orientation with the result that, today, there are different theories and methodological approaches within the discipline of law. Many of these methods are acquired through the study of positive law and the judgments in the relevant cases. Contributions by legal academics can also help (at least sometimes). An appreciation of different legal theories is necessary as well since approaches and methods can reflect different theoretical orientations.

122. EX FACTO IUS ORITUR

Law arises out of fact.

(Bartolus, Comment on C.3.9.1 no 4; Baldus,
Comment on D.9.2.52.2 and on C.2.1.3)

One of the most famous texts from the Roman law of delict is the case of the wagons on Capitoline Hill in which one wagon rolls back into another wagon behind it and in turn, this wagon runs over a slave boy. The owner of the slave asks the jurist against whom he might bring a legal action, and the jurist replies that it all depends on the causal circumstances: *in causa ius esse positum* (D.9.2.52.2). The jurist Alfenus then considers a number of alternative situations:

> For if the drivers who were supporting the wagon got themselves out of the way on their own accord and it was as a result of this fact that the mules were not able to hold the wagon and were themselves dragged back by the load, then no action could be brought against the owner of the mules. However with respect to the men who were holding up the tilted wagon a claim under the *lex Aquilia* could be brought; for it is no less the doing of damage he who voluntarily lets go of something he is holding up so that it hits something; for example if someone who steers an ass does not restrain it, he would do wrongful damage in the same way as if he had discharged a

204

spear or anything else from his hand. But if the mules behaved in the way they did because they were frightened by something, and the drivers left the wagon fearing they would be crushed, while no action could be brought against the men, an action could be brought against the owner of the mules. However if neither mules nor men were the cause, but the mules could not hold up the weight, or while trying slipped and fell and the wagon went backwards and the men had been unable to bear the weight of it when the wagon tilted over, neither the owner of the mules nor the men would be open to an action. What is indeed certain, whatever the situation in this affair, is that no claim could be made against the owner of the mules pulling the wagon behind, for they did not go back on their own accord but because they were hit and pushed backwards.

The medieval jurist Baldus added a single pithy comment to this section: *ex facto ius oritur.* He did not invent this comment – it is to be found in the works of several Glossators and Post-Glossators – but its application to this case is arguably particularly appropriate since it sums up what might be termed a 'bottom-up' approach to legal reasoning. One examines the facts in order to discover the correct legal solution. There is, of course a rule (*regula*) which is contained in the *Lex Aquilia* dealing with damage wrongfully caused, but the jurist mentions it only in passing.

The idea of law arising out of facts can be found in several English cases. One of the relatively more recent ones is *Blackpool & Fylde Aero Club Ltd* v *Blackpool BC* ([1990] 1 WLR 1195) in which a local authority invited tenders to manage and run a small airport. This tendering process was governed by strict rules and conditions, one of which was that tenders must be received by the local authority before a strict date and time. The claimants spent time and money preparing a tender and posted it directly into the local authority's own letter box a few hours before the deadline. However, owing to the negligence of the authority, the letterbox was not cleared for twenty-four hours, and when it finally was emptied the claimants' tender was assumed to be late. As a result, the tender was not considered by the local authority, and the contract was awarded to another tenderer. The question that arose in the case was this: can the disappointed tenderer bring an action for damages against the local authority for failing to give consideration to its tender?

Before considering the decision in more detail, it might be useful to approach this liability question in the abstract; that is to say, to look at the precedents as set out in the textbooks and to consider this factual problem from the position of textbook knowledge. Assuming that these facts have not yet reached any court, what would an experienced practitioner or indeed a law academic have made of this liability problem on the basis of the then existing textbook law? Despite the undoubted presence of fault on the part of the local authority, it is not unreasonable to suppose that the practitioner would have had reservations about the chances of liability being imposed on these facts. She might well say that liability would not be imposed in contract because a contract to contract is not a contract (*Courtney* v *Tolaini* [1975] 1 WLR 297). Equally, liability in tort would probably not be imposed given the nature of the damage; there is normally no duty of care for pure economic loss, and while there are exceptions to this principle, the tendering conditions would probably be interpreted as excluding any duty at the pre-contractual stage (*Caparo Industries plc* v *Dickman* [1990] 2 AC 605). A negotiating party is not normally under a duty to take into account the interests of the other party (*Walford* v *Miles* [1992] 2 AC 128).

Yet, the local authority was found liable to the claimants, and the question arises as to why this was. If the rule of law implies that decisions of the courts will be predictable on the basis of a set of abstract, rationalised and determinable rules and principles, is it not a denial of justice to render a decision that seems to contradict these rules and principles? There is no doubt that counsel for the local authority thought that imposing liability would amount to an injustice. As Bingham LJ noted in his judgment, "Mr Toulson submitted that the warranty contended for by the club was simply a proposition 'tailor-made to produce the desired result'... on the facts of this particular case" and that the "court should not subvert well-understood contractual principles by adopting a woolly pragmatic solution designed to remedy a perceived injustice on the unique facts of this particular case". Even Bingham LJ, who delivered the principal judgment in favour of the claimants, originally thought that this argument was persuasive. However, what changed his mind were the exchanges with counsel during the hearing. As he states, 'During the hearing the questions were raised: what if, in a situation such as the present, the council had opened and thereupon accepted the first tender received, even though the deadline had not expired and other invitees had not yet responded? Or if the council had considered and accepted a tender admittedly received well after the deadline? Mr Toulson answered that although by so acting the council might breach its own standing orders, and might fairly be accussed of discreditable conduct, it would not be in breach of any legal obligation because at that stage there would be none to breach (at 1200–12010)'.

Bingham LJ's reaction to this response was clear: 'This is a conclusion I cannot accept. And if it were accepted there would in my view be an unacceptable discrepancy between the law of contract and the confident assumptions of commercial parties, both tenderers (as reflected in the evidence of Mr Bateson) and invitors (as reflected in the immediate reaction of the council when the mishap came to light)'.

The Lord Justice thus arrives at his conclusion not by applying an abstract and pre-existing rule to the set of litigation facts but by gradually arriving at a conclusion through the posing of arguments. It was the responses by counsel to the judge's questions that convinced him that liability should be imposed. One might say of this argumentation (dialectical) process that it was motivated not so much by the formal application of an existing contractual principle, even if technically speaking the Court of Appeal upheld the trial judge's conclusion that the tendering process on these facts amounted to a collateral contract. It was motivated more by a functional argument taking as its starting point the "confidential assumptions of commercial parties". The function of the law of contract is to give effect to these (reasonable?) assumptions.

This functional approach is then supported by a sleight-of-hand jump within an apparent description of the facts from a descriptive notion to a normative concept. Accordingly, Bingham LJ follows his commercial parties point with a fairly long description of a tendering process to indicate how it is "heavily weighted in favour of the invitor." Halfway through this apparently descriptive paragraph he then says:

> But where, as here, tenders are solicited from selected parties all of them known to the invitor, and where a local authority's invitation prescribes a clear, orderly and familiar procedure – draft contract conditions available for inspection and plainly not open to negotiation, a prescribed common form of tender, the supply of envelopes designed to preserve the absolute anonymity of tenderers and clearly to identify the tender in question, and an absolute deadline – the invitee is in my judgment protected at least to this extent: if he submits a conforming tender before the deadline he is entitled, not as a matter of *mere expectation* but of *contractual right*, to be sure that his tender will after the deadline be opened and considered in conjunction with all other conforming tenders or at least that his tender will be considered if others are (at 1202 emphasis added).

And to add extra support to this shift from 'expectation' to 'right,' he reverts back to an imaginary oral debate. "Had the club, before tendering, enquired of the council whether it could rely on any timely and conforming tender being considered along with others," he said, "I feel quite sure that the answer would have been 'of course.'" For the "law would, I think, be defective if it did not give effect to that." *Ex facto ius oritur* (law arises out of fact), as Baldus might have put it.

123.   QUI NON INTELLIGIT PRINCIPIUM CASUS, NON POTEST INTELLIGERE CASUM

> *He who does not understand the principle of a case is unable to understand a case.*
>
> (Baldus, Comment on D.1.2.1 no 12)

What a case like *Blackpool* illustrates is this: one should perhaps focus less on the perceived substantive law that is seemingly applicable in a liability case and concentrate instead on a variety of fact situations where liability is in issue in order to identify a range of models from which one might be able to see the deployment of different concepts or patterns of concepts and conceptual relations. Thus, in the law of tort, liability can be approached through a number of different conceptual approaches. One might adopt what could be called the descriptive model, in which the facts of a tort problem are matched to a set of formal categories of fact situations, themselves set out as a list of 'torts' (and 'torticles') (Rudden 1991–92). This can be called the causes of action approach, and it is descriptive in that one is essentially matching by way of analogy one fact situation with another (see Diplock LJ in *Letang* v *Cooper* [1965] 1 QB 232, at 242–243). Alternatively, one might adopt an interests model whereby the interests of the defendant in any factual situation are matched against those of the claimant (Cane 1996). This model might be labelled inductive in that one is searching within the facts to induce an apparently descriptive concept ('interest' or 'expectation') in order to transform it into a fully normative concept such as a 'right'. This might well be the best way to characterise the approach used by Bingham LJ in the airport case: he induces out of the facts the notion of an 'expectation' to transform it into a 'right'.

However, the appeal judge could equally have adopted some quite different reasoning approaches. He could, for example, have argued that the whole point of a tendering procedure is that it formally establishes at what point there will be a legally binding contract, namely when the invitor accepts a particular tender. Any dealings before this formal acceptance would thus, logically, be subject to the rule that there is no intention to create legal relations. Parties ought to know where they stand in relation to negotiations. Consequently, one might argue, the proper approach is to see law as a set of abstract, or relatively abstract, principles waiting to be applied in a deductive manner. One starts off from the normative proposition – for example 'a contract to contract is not a contract' – and applies it logically to the facts, perhaps employing a dialectical approach to sharpen up the conceptual edge (pre-contract negotiations contrasted with formal acceptance of an offer). Indeed, one could take this approach to an even more formal level where the normative propositions (rules and principles) are seen as being analogous to mathematical theorems; precedents and statutory texts are simply the basis for a set of axiomatic propositions (see Gray & Gray 2003). Rights, within this model, are not induced out of factual situations via the notion of an interest; they exist in a Platonic world of axiomatic legal concepts and relations (see e.g., Hohfeld 1919).

As we have seen, Bingham LJ did not adopt any of these more formal approaches. He arrived at his conclusion through argument with counsel and through a progressive moving out from one factual situation (ordinary tendering procedure) to another (the extraordinary tendering procedure which formed the facts of the case before him). This indicates that merely studying the common law as a structure of formal rules is inadequate; it fails to embrace the flexibility of different types of reasoning schemes. Logical, functional, and structural approaches are different and can lead to different results. Moreover, it is important to note at the outset when analysing a case the remedy being claimed: is it a claim for a debt, for damages, for rescission, for an injunction, or for what? In *Blackpool,* the claim, as we have seen, was for damages. But imagine that the council had not, when the claimant learned of the fate of its tender, awarded the contract to another tenderer. Could the claimant have obtained an injunction against the council? Could they have brought an action for judicial review? One might finally ask what would have happened if *Blackpool* had been appealed to the House of Lords (now Supreme Court)? Would they have reversed the decision? (One might note that Mr. Toulson in *Blackpool* later became the Supreme Court judge Lord Toulson.)

124.   EX IURE FACTUM ORITUR

Fact arises from law.

(reversal of maxim 122, and based upon *de iure quod ex facto oritur* and *factum, ex quo nullum ius oritur*, Johannes Althusius, *Politica*, Preface, and *Dicæologicæ, Liber tres*, p 23)

The expression *ex iure factum oritur* has been used by more recent writers to express the idea that law does not arise from fact (cf. maxim 122) but that fact arises out of law. The maxim itself, in a slightly different form, has its origin in the work of the Renaissance humanist jurists, some of whom pioneered law as a coherent system; and this was followed by a school of jurists who associated law with mathematics (*mos mathematicus*). This development was an important methodological and epistemological (theory of knowledge) landmark in that law was now seen as an abstract and coherent intellectual system, like mathematics, from which solutions to legal problems were a matter of deduction from axioms. This vision of law was well expressed by the German jurist Johann Gottlieb Heineccius (1681–1741) who wrote:

All the proper sciences reason by way of an intelligence of principles and their cohesion with posited conclusions. And just as those who teach the divine and sublime mathematics do not demand their audience to learn by heart thousands of problems, but instead inculcate and demonstrate definitions, axioms and theorems by which of themselves any problem can be promptly solved. And so it is not for the jurist, I think, to stuff their audience's brains with decisions and cases.... (*Elementa Juris Secundum Ordinem Institutionum* (1725), at Praefatio).

One had moved from an inductive method (*ex facto*) to a deductive one (*ex iure*), opening the way to a progression towards codification in continental Europe. No doubt this codification movement was to prove much less successful in England for a variety of reasons, and the idea of a *mos mathematicus* mentality never really took hold (see maxims 47 and 132). But the influence of the systematisers was not negligible on common law thinking, and it tends to expose itself in discussions about legal formalism.

There is another aspect to the *ex iure* maxim which concerns the facts themselves. In asserting that facts arise out of law, what is meant is that legal facts are not the same as what might be termed brute facts. The point was well expressed by the American jurist Karl Llewellyn (1893–1962). Reflecting on the facts of a case involving a motor vehicle, he said:

> How many of these facts are, as we say, legally relevant? Is it relevant that the road was in the country or in the city; that it was concrete or tarmac or of dirt; that it was a private or a public way? Is it relevant that the defendant was driving a Buick, or a motor car, or a vehicle? Is it important that he looked around as the car swerved? Is it crucial? Would it have been the same if he had been drunk, or had swerved for fun, to see how close he could run by the plaintiff, but had missed his guess? (1951: 48).

What the law does is to define facts that are relevant from facts that are not. The law defines, so to speak, its own particular factual situation, and thus one might argue that they are 'virtual' rather than real facts. They are refined, distilled, or whatever, not by social reality as such, but by the abstract framework of legal thought. They are *ex iure*.

125.   PLANE EX REGULIS COMPONIMUS SYLLOGISMOS

Clearly we compose the syllogism from rules.

(Matthaei Gribaldi Mofa, *De methodo ac ratione studendi, Libri tres*, 1541, p 18)

This *ex iure* view of the legal world was also to effect a shift from 'bottom-up' reasoning to one that was 'top-down'. One did not start with a descriptive set of facts and induce legal notions out of these facts; one started from an abstract principle that formed the major premise in a process of syllogistic logic. The syllogism is the classic method of deductive logic in which one goes from a general proposition ('all men are mortal') to a specific assertion ('Socrates is a man') which automatically generates a conclusion ('Socrates is mortal'). With the circulation of Aristotle's work in the 13th century, the syllogism was adopted by the jurists as a means not just of injecting certainty into legal reasoning but also of extending the case examples in the Roman sources to new situations not envisaged by the Romans. One searched the Roman factual cases for an underlying *regularum seu axiomatum* (as Mofa put it), which would then act as the major premise for new factual situations. Centuries later, the importance of codification was that the codes acted as a set of *axiomata* from which the solution to any legal problem could be logically deduced.

Even in the common law, such thinking can be fundamental. As one House of Lords judge asserted:

> A judicial decision will often be reached by a process of reasoning which can be reduced into a sort of complex syllogism, with the major premise consisting of a pre-existing rule of law (either statutory or judge-made) and with the minor premise consisting of the material facts of the case under immediate consideration. The conclusion is the decision of the case, which may or may not establish new law (Lord Simon in *Lupton* v *FA & AB* [1972] AC 634, 658–659).

A good illustration of this method is to be found in an Australian case. As the judge put it:

> The unanswerable logic of Ms Singh's claim that she is not an alien can be seen in the following polysyllogism (a polysyllogism consists of two or more syllogisms in which the conclusion of one is the premise of the next). An alien is a person who does not owe permanent allegiance to the Queen of Australia. A person who is born in Australia owes an obligation of permanent allegiance to the Queen of Australia. Therefore, a person born in Australia is not an alien. Ms Singh was born in Australia. Therefore, Ms Singh is not an alien (Mc Hugh J in *Singh v Commonwealth of Australia* [2005] 3 LRC 290, para 40)

And the judge continued:

> The Commonwealth cannot defend its claim that Ms Singh is an alien unless it can successfully attack the validity of the premise in the prosyllogism (a prosyllogism is the syllogism that leads to the conclusion that forms the premise of the succeeding syllogism which is called an episyllogism). The Commonwealth cannot succeed without demonstrating at least one of two propositions: first, that it is erroneous to say that an alien is a person who does not owe permanent allegiance to the Queen of Australia; and, second, that it is erroneous to say that a person who is born in Australia owes an obligation of permanent allegiance to the Queen of Australia until it is voluntarily abandoned (para 41)

126. MULTA AUTEM IURE CIVILI CONTRA RATIONEM DISPUTANDI PRO UTILITATE COMMUNI RECEPTA ESSE INNUMERABILIBUS REBUS PROBARI POTEST

Many are the examples that can be proved in civil law that go against rational reasoning and argumentation in favour of the common interest.

(Julian, D.9.2.51.2)

Care, of course, must be taken – as has been seen (maxim 47) – since it would equally appear that the life of the common law has not been logic but experience, as seems to have been the case on occasions in Roman law. Other forms of reasoning and argumentation, besides logic, are regularly employed by common law judges. One particular form of justification is policy. "In previous times," said Lord Denning, "when faced with a new problem, the judges have not openly asked themselves the question: what is the best policy for the law to adopt?" However, he continued, "the question has always been there in the background and has been concealed behind other questions about duty, proximity, foreseeability and so on" (*Dutton v Bognor Regis UDC* [1972] 1 QB 373, 397). Despite the criticism this approach has received, it is common for judges even in the House of Lords and now Supreme Court to appeal on occasions to policy. Thus, in one 'administrative liability' case involving the police, Lord Keith asserted, "in my opinion there is another reason why an action for damages in negligence should not lie against the police in circumstances such as those of the present case, and that is public policy" (*Hill v Chief Constable of West Yorkshire* [1989] AC 53, 63; see also *Elguzouli-Daf v Commissioner of Police of the Metropolis* [1995] QB 335).

Just what is meant by policy is, of course, an interesting question (Waddams 2011: 14). One judge has said that it can be seen as a means of identifying "social interests beyond the purely legal which call for the modification of a normal legal rule" (Lord Simon in *D v NSPCC* [1978] AC 171, 235). In the Court of Appeal decision of *Barclays Bank v O'Brien* ([1993] QB 109), one of the judges used policy as a means of solving a problem that he felt could not be dealt with by recourse to precedent. The precedents were ambiguous and could be used to justify a decision one way or the other. "The choice should", said Scott LJ, "be a matter of policy". This use of policy would give rise to a social question: "Ought the law to treat married women who provide security for their husband's debts, and others in an analogous position, as requiring special protection?" (at 139). Here again, of course, one is looking beyond the text to the interests in play. However, this appeal to an interest through the use of policy does not solve the problem of ambiguity; for, in the House of Lords' decision in *O'Brien*, Lord Browne-Wilkinson focused on a quite different interest. In place of the social interest of wives, he emphasised the economic interest of business enterprise. "If the rights secured to wives by the law render vulnerable loans granted on the security of matrimonial homes," said the Law Lord, "institutions will be unwilling to accept such security, thereby reducing the flow of loan capital to business enterprises." It was for him "essential that a law designed to protect the vulnerable does not render the matrimonial home unacceptable as security to financial institutions" ([1994] 1 AC 180, 188).

Another way of viewing policy is as a matter of social or practical justice. It represents the pragmatic approach of the common law which "has not always developed on strictly logical lines". And "where logic leads down a path that is beset with practical difficulties, the courts have not been frightened to turn aside and seek the pragmatic solution that will best serve the needs of society" (Griffiths LJ in *Ex parte King* [1984] 3 All ER 897, 903). This pragmatic approach can now be seen in terms of policy. One judge has said that we now live in "a less formalist age" and that policy is an issue that arises when more than one "solution is logically defensible". In the area of contract, "good sense, fairness and respect for the reasonable expectations of contracting parties suggests that the best solution" is one which "at least has the merit of promoting more sensible results than any other solution" (Steyn LJ in *Watts v Aldington* (1993) *The Times* 16 December 1993 quoted in *Jameson v CEGB* [1997] 3 WLR 151, 161).

This 'sensible solution' approach was particularly evident in Lord Denning's judgment in the *Spartan Steel* case, where the issue was whether pure economic loss could be recovered from a defendant who had carelessly cut off the electricity supply to the plaintiffs' factory (*Spartan Steel & Alloys Ltd v Martin & Co* [1973] 1 QB 27). "At bottom I think the question of recovering economic loss is one of policy", said the then Master of the Rolls (at 36). For one must consider the nature of the hazard. According to Lord Denning, the cutting off of electricity is a hazard that everyone has to face, and it usually results in economic loss that is not very large. Most people, he claimed, take the risk of such losses upon themselves and "they do not go running round to their solicitor". The policy to be pursued here, accordingly, was one of recognising that this "is a healthy attitude which the law should encourage" (at 38).

Yet another way of viewing the policy approach is from the position of social science method: the approach of Lord Denning in *Spartan Steel* can be seen as a form of functionalism. That is to say, a rule is judged not by its literal meaning but by its envisaged function. Lord Denning, having examined the pure economic loss rule in negligence in terms of its history in the case-law, abandons precedent as such to justify the application of the rule by reference to the fact that when the supply of electricity is cut off, it affects a multitude of persons by putting them to inconvenience and sometimes causing economic loss. However, such "a hazard is regarded by most people as a thing they must put up with – without seeking compensation from anyone." They "do not go running round to their solicitor" and they "do not try to find out whether it was anyone's fault." In other words, the economic loss rule has as its *function* the aim of discouraging litigation, and it is this function that, for Lord Denning, gives the rule its normative force.

This approach of Lord Denning MR in *Spartan Steel* came in for criticism by the then Professor of legal philosophy at the University of Oxford. According to Ronald Dworkin (1931–2013), a judicial decision in a hard case like *Spartan Steel* "should be generated by principle not policy" (Dworkin 1977: 84). An argument of policy, says Dworkin, is one which justifies the advancement or protection of some collective goal of the community as a whole. For example, the argument that a subsidy should be paid to aircraft manufacturers in order to protect the defence of the nation would be an argument of policy. An argument of principle, on the other hand, is one that advances or secures "some individual or group right" (1977: 82). Now if an aircraft manufacturer sues to recover such a subsidy, it would not argue the case on the ground that national defence would be enhanced by the subsidy; the argument would be based strictly on its right to the subsidy (1977: 83). This, asserts Dworkin, is right and proper since judges are not elected and thus are not responsible to the electorate in the same way as the legislator. It is for the legislator to make policy and to pass laws on, inter alia, arguments of policy. As for judges, they "should be as unoriginal as possible" (1977: 84) because it seems "wrong to take property from the individual and hand it to another in order just to improve overall economic efficiency" (1977: 85).

The courts themselves have recognised problems regarding policy arguments, at least to some extent (see *Michael v Chief Constable of South Wales Police* [2015] AC 1732). One Supreme Court judge has, however, argued:

> It should be acknowledged that it is sometimes asserted that that part of the policy considerations which related to the danger of defensive policing lacks hard evidence. That may technically be so, since there has not existed the kind of duty of care which would test it in practice. But like Lord Brown in *Smith* [*Smith v Chief Constable of Sussex Police* [2008] UKHL 50; [2009] AC 225] I for my part would regard that risk as inevitable. It can scarcely be doubted that we see the consequences of defensive behaviour daily in the actions of a great many public authorities. I do not see that it can seriously be doubted that the threat of litigation frequently influences the behaviour of both public and private bodies and individual (Lord Hughes in *Robinson v Chief Constable of West Yorkshire* [2018] UKSC, 4 para 112).

This lack of empirical evidence is a problem that is associated with policy reasoning by judges. Nevertheless, using functional rather than conceptual reasoning is not necessarily to be criticised. In fact, the late Stephen Waddams (1942–2023) – probably the leading academic common law specialist on the law of obligations and legal reasoning up until his death – thought that the Dworkin distinction between principle and policy was always unrealistic. He indicated that most of the principles in the law of contract fashioned by the 19th and 20th century judges always had a functional dimension to them (Waddams 2011).

127. NON POSSUNT OMNES SINGILLATIM AUT LEGIBUS AUT SENATUS CONSULTIS COMPREHENDI: SED CUM IN ALIQUA CAUSA SENTENTIA EORUM MANIFESTA EST, IS QUI IURISDICTIONI PRAEEST AD SIMILIA PROCEDERE ATQUE ITA IUS DICERE DEBET

Legislation or senatorial decrees cannot cover every single thing, but when the basis of the enactment is clear, the judge ought to proceed by way of analogy and should declare the law accordingly.

(Julian, D.1.3.12)

Another form of reasoning is by way of analogy. In fact, if one returns to Lord Simon's statement about the complex syllogism (see maxim 125), the Law lord went on to say this:

> Where the decision does constitute new law, this may or may not be expressly stated as a proposition of law: frequently the new law will appear only from subsequent comparison of, on the one hand, the material facts inherent in the major premise with, on the other, the material facts which constitute the minor premise. As a result of this comparison it will often be apparent that a rule has been extended by an *analogy* expressed or implied.

And he continued:

> I take as an example ... *National Telephone Co v Baker* [1893] 2 Ch 186. Major premise: the rule in *Rylands v Fletcher* (1866) LR 1 Exch 265, (1868) LR 3 HL 330. Minor premise: the defendant brought and stored electricity on his land for his own purpose; it escaped from the land; in so doing it injured the plaintiff's property. Conclusion: the defendant is liable in damages to the plaintiff (or would have been but for statutory protection). Analysis shows that the conclusion establishes a rule of law, which may be stated as 'for the purpose of the rule in *Rylands v Fletcher* electricity is analogous to water' or 'electricity is within the rule in *Rylands v Fletcher*'. That conclusion is now available as the major premise in the next case, in which some substance may be in question which in this context is not perhaps clearly *analogous* to water but is clearly analogous to electricity. In this way, legal

luminaries are constituted which guide the wayfarer across uncharted ways (Lord Simon in *Lupton* v *FA & AB* [1972] AC 634, 658–659 emphasis added).

One can see here how, in addition to the syllogism, the operation of precedent requires an analogy at the level of material facts. The escape of electricity fell within the rule of *Rylands v Fletcher* because electricity was analogous to water. If some future case were to involve, say, the escape of gas, in order for the rule to apply, it would have to be decided that gas was analogous to electricity.

Analogy is particularly important with regard to extending the tort of negligence (duty of care) to new factual situations. The approach is not one of applying an abstract principle like CC art 1240 to a set of facts. The new situation needs to be analogous to the facts of an existing duty of care case (*Caparo Industries plc v Dickman* [1990] 2 AC 605, 635). This point has been explained in more detail by Lord Reed:

> It is normally only in a novel type of case, where established principles do not provide an answer, that the courts need to go beyond those principles in order to decide whether a duty of care should be recognised. Following *Caparo,* the characteristic approach of the common law in such situations is to develop incrementally and by analogy with established authority. The drawing of an analogy depends on identifying the legally significant features of the situations with which the earlier authorities were concerned. The courts also have to exercise judgement when deciding whether a duty of care should be recognised in a novel type of case (*Robinson v Chief Constable of West Yorkshire* [2018] UKSC 4, para 27).

Lady Hale made a similar observation:

> The common law is a dynamic instrument. It develops and adapts to meet new situations as they arise. Therein lies its strength. But therein also lies a danger, the danger of unbridled and unprincipled growth to match what the court perceives to be the merits of the particular case. So it must proceed with caution, incrementally by analogy with existing categories, and consistently with some underlying principle (see *Caparo Industries plc v Dickman* [1990] 2 AC 605) (*Woodland v Swimming Teachers Association* [2014] AC 537, para 28).

There are limits to the use of analogy. While it has a role to play in developing or applying case law, when it comes to legislation, the common law judges are much more restrained. They will not – perhaps unlike the situation in Roman law – extend a statutory provision by analogy. By this, it is meant that they will not take a statutory provision such as section 2(1) of the Animals Act 1971 – which provides that where "any damage is caused by an animal which belongs to a dangerous species, any person who is a keeper of the animal is liable for the damage" – and apply it by analogy to dangerous things that are not animals. The judges would see that as usurping the role of the legislator. This is

not to say that analogy has no reasoning role in the interpretation and application of a legislative text. It can have a role in the interpretation of a statute, as
the following example indicates:

> Mr Bowen submits that, as a matter of construction, s 312(2)(b) ought to be inter-
> preted so that the reference to disability includes someone who has exceptionally
> high intelligence, as C undoubtedly has. He recognises that the word "disability"
> would not naturally be thought to embrace somebody with the advantage of high
> educational ability, but he says that a functional approach to construction should be
> adopted. He relies by *analogy* upon the approach of the House of Lords in the case
> of *Fitzpatrick v Sterling Housing Association* [2001] 1 AC 27, [1999] 4 All ER 705.
> In that case the survivor of a stable and permanent homosexual relationship was
> held to fall within the definition of being a member of the tenant's family for the
> purposes of succeeding to a tenancy. The House of Lords held by a bare majority
> that it was legitimate to give the concept of family a wide meaning, having regard
> to the purpose of the legislation and changes in social attitude. Mr Bowen sub-
> mits, moreover, that, as in *Fitzpatrick*, matters have moved on since legislation was
> passed some nine years ago and that there is a greater appreciation of the needs of
> brighter children. The legislation should be construed so as to recognise and give
> effect to that development (Elias J in *S v Special Educational Needs and Disability
> Tribunal* [2005] EWHC 196, para 25 emphasis added).

The judge did not accept the analogy, but the argument is nevertheless an interesting one in that the analogy focusses less on the meaning of the words of the
legislation and more on the reasoning to be employed. The claimant's counsel was arguing that, by way of analogy, the judge should adopt a functional
approach just as the court did in the *Fitzpatrick* case.

128. CUM IN VERBIS NULLA AMBIGUITAS EST, NON DEBET ADMITTI VOLUNTATIS QUAESTIO

> *When there is no ambiguity in the words, the question of the intention ought
> not to be admitted.*

(Paul, D.32.25.1)

As for the methods of approach regarding statutory interpretation, they are
usually regarded as different from the methods applied in the understanding and application of precedents. Indeed, the importance of precedent as a
principal source of law and a fundamental characteristic of the common law
tradition should also be treated with caution. Whatever may have been the
position in the past, the primary source of law today in the UK is legislation,
and this reflects itself in the case law in that nine out of ten cases heard by the
English appeal courts involve the interpretation of a statutory text. In addition
to interpreting these public law texts, the courts often have to decide upon

the meaning of words or phrases in private texts such as contracts, leases and wills. Traditionally, this interpretative function of the courts in common law jurisdictions has given rise to its own set of methods, rules, presumptions and principles. And these are often contained in a different chapter, in books on legal method, from the methods used for handling case law precedents.

The interpretation of statutes in English law is both a constitutional and a methodological issue. It is constitutional in as much as it is closely tied with the supremacy of Parliament, which requires that judges apply statutes without any power whatsoever to strike them down as unconstitutional. The judges themselves continue to insist upon this constitutional position even after the coming into force of the Human Rights Act 1998 (*In re K (A Child)* [2001] 2 WLR 1141, para 119). However, the judges have reserved to themselves the right to interpret these laws, and it is this reservation that has, in part given rise to a number of methodological issues. For example, it has encouraged the refusal of the courts, until recently, to look beyond the text itself when it came to interpretation, leading not just to a relatively literal approach to texts (compared with civil law systems) but also to a reluctance to examine Parliamentary reports and debates (see generally *Pepper v Hart* [1993] AC 593).

Another factor that has influenced statutory interpretation is history. Before the 19th century, statutes were viewed by judges not as statements of principle but as rules governing particularities; they were, as a result interpreted strictly and confined to their factual circumstances. Thus, as has already been noted, the Animals Act 1971, unlike a precedent such as *Rylands* v *Fletcher* ((1866) LR 1 Ex 265 (Ex); (1868) LR 3 HL 330 (HL)), could never be used as the basis for an analogy for a general rule for liability for dangerous things. In turn, this attitude has encouraged Parliament to draft detailed texts in a style that is often opaque if not impenetrable. In recent years, however, there has been some modification by the judges with respect to their approach to interpretation.

This change of attitude is not at first sight always obvious to perceive. Thus it has relatively recently been stated that "it is an elementary rule in the interpretation and the application of statutory provisions that it is to the words of the legislation that attention must primarily be directed." In other words, "it will be the ordinary meaning of the words which will require to be adopted" and "whatever the intensity of the process the temptation of substituting other expressions for the words of the statute in the course of interpreting it is to be discouraged, however attractive such a course may seem to be by way of explaining what it is thought the legislature is endeavouring to say" (Lord Clyde in *Murray v Foyle Meats Ltd* [2000] 1 AC 51, 58). This is perhaps an advance on what was once said to be one of the basic rules of English statutory interpretation, namely the literal rule. This rule required judges to follow the words of an Act, if they were clear, "even though they lead to manifest absurdity" for "the Court has nothing to do with the question whether the legislator has committed an absurdity" (*R v Judge of the City of London Court* [1892] 1 QB 273, 290). There was, according to this rule, little scope for flexibility (see e.g. *Haigh v Charles W Ireland* [1973] 3 All ER 1137) and some scope for undermining the intention of Parliament (see e.g. *Fisher v Bell* [1961] 1 QB 394).

Accordingly, the methodology associated with the literal rule might be termed a 'shallow' hermeneutical approach in that it takes as its point of focus only the text. This restricts of course the type of reasoning and research that can be applied, for the emphasis is on the words and on a dictionary (*verba*) rather than on the function of the rule. In turn, this lack of partnership between judge and legislator has resulted in two textual characteristics. The first is the detailed and often opaque style of legislation (as already mentioned), and the second is the use of undefined legal concepts. For example, section 2 (1) of the Misrepresentation Act 1967 is both difficult to read, given the long sentences, and, anyway, cannot be properly appreciated without a knowledge of the tort of deceit.

129. SCIRE LEGES NON HOC EST VERBA EARUM TENERE, SED VIM AC POTESTATEM

> *To know legislation is not to hold to the words but to the force underpinning them.*
>
> (Celsus, D.1.3.17)

This literal approach and method have not disappeared, but there have been developments. Some of these developments are as old as the literal rule itself in as much as this rule was just one of three such approaches. The 'golden' and the 'mischief' rule have long been regarded as alternatives. In addition, there has been an important change with respect to external aids: it is now permissible, in certain circumstances, for judges to look at Parliamentary debates in *Hansard* if the statute is ambiguous or obscure (*Pepper v Hart* [1993] AC 593). At a more substantive level, one needs to ask if there have been developments with respect to the type of reasoning used by the judges in statutory interpretation cases.

The first development beyond the literal rule is to be found in a range of 19th-century cases. "We must... in this case", said Jervis CJ, "have recourse to what is called the golden rule of construction... viz., to give the words used by the legislature their plain and natural meaning unless it is manifest from the general scope and intention of the statute that injustice and absurdity would result" (*Mattison v Hart* (1854) 14 CB 357, 385). This approach might be said to be an advance on the shallow hermeneutical method in that it does go someway beyond the 'signifier' (words of the text) to embrace a 'signified' that takes its meaning not from the words of the text but the intention of the legislator. However, if there is no absurdity, then the shallow hermeneutical method applies (see e.g. *Clarke v Kato* [1998] 1 WLR 1647: 'road' does not include car park).

A more profound development, which actually predates the golden rule, is the mischief rule. Lord Diplock has explained its historical context:

> the so-called 'mischief' rule... finds its origin in *Heydon's Case*, 3 Co.Rep. 7a decided under the Tudor monarchy in 1584. The rule was propounded by the judges in an age when statutes were drafted in a form very different from that which they assume today. Those who composed the Parliaments of those days were chary of creating exceptions to the common law; and, when they did so, thought it necessary to incorporate in the statute the reasons which justified the changes in the common law that the statute made. Statutes in the sixteenth century and for long thereafter in addition to the enacting words contained lengthy preambles reciting the particular mischief or defect in the common law that the enacting words were designed to remedy. So, when it was laid down, the 'mischief' rule did not require the court to travel beyond the actual words of the statute itself to identify 'the mischief and defect for which the common law did not provide,' for this would have been stated in the preamble. It was a rule of construction of the actual words appearing in the statute and nothing else.

Lord Diplock then went on to point out that:

> In construing modern statutes which contain no preambles to serve as aids to the construction of enacting words the 'mischief' rule must be used with caution to justify any reference to extraneous documents for this purpose. If the enacting words are plain and unambiguous in themselves there is no need to have recourse to any 'mischief' rule. To speak of mischief and of remedy is to describe the obverse and the reverse of a single coin. The former is that part of the existing law that is changed by the plain words of the Act; the latter is the change that these words made in it (Lord Diplock in *Black-Clawson Ltd v Papierwerke A.G* [1975] AC 591, 637–638).

Nevertheless, as Lord Nicholls has recently explained, the mischief rule has at least allowed the judges to progress beyond the text through the use of external aids. Nowadays, the courts look at external aids for more than merely identifying the mischief the statute is intended to cure; they are now "adopting a purposive approach to the interpretation of statutory language" where the "courts seek to identify and give effect to the purpose of the legislation" (*R v Secretary of State for the Environment, Transport and the Regions, Ex p Spath Holme Ltd* [2001] 2 AC 349, 397). Does this mean that the mischief rule has evolved into a functional approach?

Whatever the situation, one can note from Lord Nicholls' comments that the three rules seem to have given way to a rather different method, that of the "purposive approach". Other judges have confirmed this method as the contemporary approach (see, e.g., Lord Steyn in *R (Quintavalle) v Secretary of State for Health* [2003] 2 WLR 692, para 21; and Leggatt LJ in *R v Central Bedfordshire Council* [2019] 3 All ER 20, paras 19–20). In terms of the three rules, this might be seen as an adoption and extension of the mischief (purpose) rule, but care must be taken since 'purpose' probably embraces a policy reasoning aspect that was not at the root of the original mischief rule.

In fact, policy can sometimes play a more open role in statutory interpretation. In one relatively recent case, Lord Hoffmann opened his judgment by saying:

> My Lords, on the surface, this does not look like a very momentous case. The question is whether Mr and Mrs Oakley's landlord should have provided them with a basin in the WC. The statute which they say made it necessary to install one is ambiguous. The language is capable of bearing such a construction. On the other hand, it is very unlikely that this was what Parliament intended. So the courts have a choice. If they say that Mr and Mrs Oakley should have had a basin, landlords of old houses and flats all over the country will have to install them. Local authorities and housing trusts will have to incur very considerable expense. Under the surface, therefore, the case raises a question of great constitutional importance. When it comes to the expenditure of large sums of public and private money, who should make the decision? If the statute is clear, then of course Parliament has already made the decision and the courts merely enforce it. But when the statute is doubtful, should judges decide? Or should they leave the decision to democratically elected councillors or members of Parliament? (*Birmingham CC v Oakley* [2001] 1 AC 617, 628).

The case depended upon how the word "state" of premises was to be construed, and the majority held that this did not cover a bad design, which may indirectly constitute a health hazard; they thus distinguished between 'state' and 'layout'. As one of the dissenting judges observed, "the distinction between layout and state of the premises is not to be found in the statute, and it is certainly not indicated by the language of the provision or the context." And so it "is on analysis no more than a verbal technique to cut down the generality of the wording of the modern statute" (Lord Steyn, at 628). However, as we have seen, Lord Hoffmann took the view that if they held the authority criminally liable, it would result in local authorities having to spend huge sums of money, an obligation imposed by judges rather than the electorate and, as a matter of policy, this was unacceptable.

Another important development with respect to statutory interpretation is to be found in the Human Rights Act 1998. The Act states in section 3(1) that so "far as it is possible to do so, primary legislation and subordinate legislation must be read and given effect in a way which is compatible with the Convention rights". The provision undoubtedly gives the judges considerable freedom to adopt a purposive approach, and no doubt they are taking advantage of this liberty. Nevertheless, it would be a great mistake to think that the literal rule is dead, even regarding constitutional and human rights provisions. In one post-1998 case, the Privy Council had to decide if torture was permissible under the Bahamas' constitution. Article 17(1) clearly states that no one shall be subjected to torture or inhuman treatment or punishment, but Article 17(2) goes on to say that this will not apply to any punishment "that was lawful" before the date of the new constitution. Astonishingly, a majority of the Privy Council held that flogging, admitted by both sides to be torture, was permissible since it was lawful before the said date. As the dissenters pointed out, "the literal interpretation cannot be the proper interpretation of article 17(2) when due regard is had to its transitional purpose" since such an interpretation "gives this proviso a wider scope than can have been intended by those who framed and adopted the Constitution". It "would deny to citizens the full protection intended to be afforded by article 17(1)" (*Pinder v The Queen* [2003] 1 AC 620, para 69 PC). The majority decision seems astonishing and certainly indicates that the literal approach is alive and well. But the House of Lords (now Supreme Court) and Privy Council tend to contain judges trained for the most part in commercial law, and thus an understanding of the more subtle points of public law and basic rights can prove challenging. Perhaps this is the price one pays for not having a specialised constitutional court.

130.   INTERPRETATIO NOVUM JUS NON INDUCIT

> *Interpretation does not produce new law.*
>
> (Alessandro Turamini, *Opera Omnia*, p 31 no 64)

The problem surrounding the interpretation of written laws is by no means a modern problem and was a preoccupation of the 16th century humanist jurists who paid special attention to the penultimate title of the *Digest* (D.50.16) devoted to the meaning of words (see generally Maclean 1992). What emerged from all the old historical discussions was a series of dichotomies associated with interpretation. One could focus either on the words (*verba*) or on their sense (*ad sensium*) (see Baldus Comment on C.6.28.3 no. 1); on the words or on the intention behind them (*ex mente*) (Baldus on C.6.28.4 no. 19); on the words or on the rationality underpinning them (*rationem esse animam legis*: Alessandro Turamini, *Opera omnia*, p. 33); on the meaning (*mens*) or on the rationality behind the words (*ratio legis*); on the words or on the public interest (*pro utilitate*) in play (see maxim 40); on the original meaning of the text and on its present meaning (*lex semper loquitur*: Bartolus, Comment on C.1.5.5 no. 1); or on the words or on the 'mischief' (*malum*) that the words were aimed at resolving. One can see these dichotomies in play in the words of humanist jurist Pietro Gammero (1480–1528):

> In legal interpretation of legislation the intention (*mens*) of the legislator is the primary consideration and should be avoided on as few occasions as possible even when the words (*verba*) seem to contradict it (D.27.1.13.2); the same is true when the words of the legislation have a meaning (*sensum*) that is contrary to what the legislator wishes (D.1.3.17; Decretal 5.40.6); indeed it is the intention (*intentio*) to which one defers and not the intention of the words (*non autem intentio verbis*) (see Decretal 2.28.41).

And he continued:

> When we do not have the intention (*mentum*) we interpret the words according to the commonly accepted meaning of men (*communi hominum acceptione*) (see D.32.1.52.4 and its gloss, D.50.16.162.1 and D.33.7.18.2). I think that this is in accord with right reason (*recta ratione*) in order that the properties (*proprictates*) of the words are assigned to a commonly understood vocabulary (*communem intellectus vocabulis*) through which a single meaning is possible and promoted (PA Gammero, *Legalis dialectica in qua de modo argumentandi et locis argumentorum* (1522), Book I, § De loco ab interpretatione seu ethimologia).

These dichotomies, some of which go way back to Roman law itself, are as relevant today as they were in the late medieval and Renaissance centuries. The fundamental issue, as Ian Maclean says, is the dichotomy between interpretation and law-making. "The rôle of the interpreter", writes Maclean, "according to all these commentors, is to make the text clear; it can never be to add to the law or supplement it in any way" (1992: 157). Jurists and judges cannot, in other words, usurp the authority of the legislator. Nevertheless, another humanist jurist thought that there were limits to this authority. It had to be restrained by *ratio legis* otherwise a legislator could pass laws legitimising robbery, adultery, or false testament (Turamini, *Opera Omnia*, p. 34 no. 14). In the UK today, Parliament could pass such laws, and the judges would have to apply them, although under the Human Rights Act, they could issue a declaration that a human right had been violated. In some countries, such laws could be struck down by a constitutional court.

131.   THAT A SYSTEM OF LEGAL EDUCATION,
       TO BE OF GENERAL ADVANTAGE, MUST
       COMPREHEND AND MEET THE WANTS NOT
       ONLY OF THE PROFESSIONAL, BUT ALSO OF THE
       UNPROFESSIONAL STUDENT

(Parliamentary Select Committee on Legal Education (1846), Report, 25
August 1846, House of Commons Proceedings 686, p lviii).

Turning from reasoning and method to legal education, the question arises
about what such an education should embrace. However, before discussing this
issue, something must be said about the history of such education because it
has had – and continues to have – an impact both upon what constitutes (and
what ought to constitute) legal knowledge and upon what the status of this
knowledge should be.

Once again, the contrasts with the civil law tradition are striking. In the
civilian world, university law professors have been central in shaping the whole
tradition itself (although some of these professors were in practice as well). In
the English common law world, professors have, until relatively recently, been
at best marginal. In fact, the history of the civil law is largely (but not exclusively) a history of the teaching of Roman law (see Stein 1999). In England and
Wales, there were no such teaching institutions before the 19th century, and
legal education was thus for many centuries in the hands of practitioners, that
is to say, the Inns of Court, which were professional organisations not dissimilar to Oxford or Cambridge colleges.

The Inns began their life as lodgings for the advocates (serjeants-at-law,
later in the 15th century called barristers) who controlled and presented cases
to the Court of Common Pleas, but they developed into colleges that provided
lectures, moots and general discussion. Thus, in the early centuries of the
common law, it was the Inns that offered a legal education, and this was sup-
plemented by attendance in court where judges would, as well as presiding
over cases, explain to students what was going on. As for the universities of
Oxford and Cambridge, they taught only Roman law, a subject of no interest to
those practising the common law; this civilian education was studied mainly
by men going into the Church. As for legal education in England, the position
is explained by Sir John Baker. "At its height", he observes, "the professional
law school was tough and effective; but... it came to an abrupt end in the middle of the seventeenth century, leaving self-help as the principal method of
legal education". In other words, a law student would gather his law "from
such books as he could afford to buy or borrow; and the most useful of these

owed more to the alphabet than to schematic analysis" (Baker 2019: 181). In the middle of the 18th century, Blackstone began to give lectures on the common law at Oxford – lectures that were to become the *Commentaries on the Laws of England* (1765–69) and to acquire a status analogous to the *Institutes* in Roman law – but this development, important as it was, did not stimulate a new dawn in English legal education. Lectures on the common law might well have been given at both Oxford and Cambridge from the 17th century, but they often suffered from a lack of audience. The same was true of lectures on the common law offered elsewhere in the first half of the 19th century.

Change came in the second half of the 19th century. A Select Committee on Legal Education, established by the English Parliament, reported in 1846 that "the present state of legal education in England and Ireland... is extremely unsatisfactory and incomplete, and exhibits a striking contrast and inferiority to such education... at present in operation in all the more civilised states of Europe and America". Indeed, the report concluded that no legal education worthy of the name was to be found in England and Ireland. As the report noted, this stood in stark contrast to the situation in continental Europe where there has been a tradition of legal education from Roman to modern times.

The Report of 1846 was to stimulate a change of attitude with regard to the teaching of law in England (Scotland was quite different) with the result that, today, there are well over one hundred law schools in the UK. The change of attitude was not confined just to institutional development; the universities – at that time primarily Oxford and Cambridge – and the Inns of Court "took steps to provide a legal education of the scientific character required by the Report" (Stein 1980: 79). And this scientific character meant, in effect, the study of Roman law since English law, however strong it might have been in terms of its detailed rules and remedies, was weak on legal theory. As Stein notes, while "English law has remained relatively free of Roman influences, English jurisprudence [legal theory and legal philosophy] has traditionally turned for inspiration to the current continental theories, necessarily based on Roman law" (Stein 1980: 123). At the level of legal education, then, there was from the 19th century until right into the 20th century an almost harmonised vision in Europe of legal science founded on a set of universal concepts fashioned in particular by the German civil lawyers of this period. This harmony at the level of theory was, in the longer term, to be ruptured by a movement in the USA known as American Realism.

The 1846 report, as we have seen, encouraged the development of a corps of law professors, but as Richard Card has noted, the "growth of university legal education was a slow business". By "the end of the nineteenth century... it could fairly be said that the academic study of law was firmly established, but even then there were only ten law schools in England and Wales" and the "number had only increased to 29 by the early 1970s." Moreover, until "the early 1950s they relied to a great extent on staff who were in full-time legal practice" and it was only "from the 1950s that university law schools began the transition to their present character" (SPTL Presidential Address, 2002). High standard and research-orientated legal education is, in short, a very modern phenomenon as far as the English common law is concerned, and this in turn accounts for the lack of what a civil lawyer would see as scientific works. The common law had no Cujas or Donellus, and its first 'Domat' or 'Pothier' was Blackstone, whose success was assured by applying the Roman institutional scheme to the English legal material (Cairns 1984).

One result of this absence of a long historical tradition of professorial doctrine was that when a class of university jurists began to emerge during the 20th century, they were treated for much of the century with a certain indifference, if not disdain, by practitioners and judges. Academic doctrine was cited in judgments often only when the authors were dead, and both the Bar and the Law Society once regarded – indeed some members still regard – the university law school as "a complete waste of time," these professionals preferring "people who have read some other subject at university" (see Birks 1998: 404). Things are to an extent changing: more enlightened senior judges, some with law degrees and even faculty teaching experience, decreed at the end of the 20th century that doctrine as well as cases and statutes should now be presented in argument, and the value of comparative law is equally making itself felt (see e.g., *Fairchild v Glenhaven Funeral Services Ltd* [2003] 1 AC 32). However, the long years of disdain had the effect of edging a section of legal scholarship away from analysis and commentary on the common law itself and into high-level legal theory and beyond; a section of doctrine, in other words, has become divorced from the positive law as found in the cases and statutes (Burrows 2021).

This divorce has been encouraged by the statistical fact that only around half of English law graduates enter the legal profession. A percentage of academic lawyers accordingly see themselves as social scientists as much as jurists, their primary duty being one geared towards providing a liberal university education rather than professional training (Cownie 2004). Other academic lawyers, who see the university degree as a vital part of a technical legal education, regret this situation; it is a retreat into the 'ivory tower' and perhaps ultimately destructive of law itself (see e.g., Birks 1998). Whatever one's views, the divorce has not been without its intellectual effects, the principal one being that what constitutes legal 'knowledge' is arguably much wider in Anglo-American law faculties than in French ones (Jestaz & Jamin 2004: 264–301). Many different currents of thought have developed – feminist jurisprudence, critical legal studies, law and literature, to name just some (Jestaz & Jamin 2004: 287–296) – and this has in turn stimulated thinking and debate in common law faculties. It has to be said that the centre of such innovative thinking has not actually been the United Kingdom but the United States, where the relationship between law schools and the legal profession is not quite the same. Nevertheless, many in the American legal profession have noted an increasing gulf between the law schools and practice (see further Samuel 2022b). One might perhaps draw a historical analogy between the *mos Gallicus* and the *mos Italicus*, the former also being considered in its time as professorial and of little use to practitioners (Jones 1940: 42).

Some see this American legal culture as having its origin in a long-term struggle against formalism and in the attempt to profit from advances made in disciplines other than law. Of these movements, the one that was to prove decisive in terms of a comparative analysis of legal knowledge in the civilian and the common law traditions is arguably American Realism (Jestaz & Jamin 2004: 273–284). This movement, as diverse as it was – Twining calls it "an historical phenomenon" – can essentially be summed up by reference to the title of an article by Felix Cohen (1907–1953), namely "Transcendental Nonsense and the Functional Approach" (Cohen 1935). Law and legal knowledge were to be defined and understood not as a set of abstract norms and systematised concepts but strictly in terms of their function. This shift of scheme of intelligibility generated a mass of academic literature that put the emphasis on legal cases and how they are decided, with such doctrine asserting that legal decisions are not the result of the application of an abstract rule applied to an objective set of facts via the syllogism. Instead, the solutions to cases result from social and psychological factors such as the educational and cultural background of the judge and the way facts are constructed (never objective). This movement was denounced as dangerous and nihilistic, but its longer-term impact on the teaching of law in the common law world was, as Twining points out, "that there is more to the study of law than the study of a system of rules" (Twining 1985: 382). Most Anglo-American teachers – and indeed a good many practitioners – would, like Twining, regard this as a truism, thus giving substance to his observation that "we are all realists now". The end result is a legal literature in the common law world that is much more diversified than *la doctrine* in France (Jestaz & Jamin 2004: 267).

132. THAT IS THE BEAUTY OF THE COMMON LAW; IT IS A MAZE AND NOT A MOTORWAY

(Diplock LJ in *Morris v CW Martin & Co* [1966] 1 QB 716, 731)

Nevertheless, one should not allow the impact of American realism to eclipse other aspects of English doctrine. As we have seen, one effect of the 1846 report was to encourage the teaching of legal science, and this proved important when the forms of action were abolished in 1852. The latter half of the 19th century is marked by frequent references in judgments to Roman, French and German texts, and, indeed, the fashioning of a general theory of contract by the judges during this century can be regarded as something of a 'reception' of civil law, although English contract law does display a distinctive character when compared to civilian contractual thinking (see generally Gordley 2013). The fact was that the abolition of the forms of action had left a vacuum, and this was filled at first by continental ideas and categories which, at that time had the status of science.

This input of civilian legal science had quite profound effects on English doctrine, some of which were to last well into the 20th century. For example, Kevin and Susan Gray (2003) show how writers on land law attempted to raise their subject to the status of an axiomatic science, and Steve Hedley (1999) charts the 19th-century codification movement in England, which resulted, if not in a general civil code, at least in the codification of sale of goods, partnership and a few other specific areas of commercial law. The point to be stressed is that during the late 19th century and the first half of the 20th century, English academic writing on law was very influenced by civil law methods. Even in the middle of the 20th century, the 'good' English law textbook is described as one which is more than just a guide to the case-law: "they seek not only to arrange the cases systematically but to extract from them the general principles of the law and to show how those principles may be developed" (Jolowicz 1963: 314–315). The role of the academic, in other words, is to use the methods of science – induction and deduction – so as to produce a legal knowledge that is validated by its internal coherence and its tendency towards objective legal certainty.

Yet the codification movement itself failed. The reason, according to Hedley, was that the growth of university law faculties, instead of encouraging codification, actually stymied the possibility by doctrinally re-presenting the common law as a coherent system of rules. One might add that even if a civil code had been promulgated, the movement would still, over the longer term, have probably failed, as evidence from the USA (and indeed from the English Sale of Goods Act 1893) suggests. The *mentalité* of the common law judge, and of the 20th century legislator, would have conspired to transform the code, through interpretation and legislative amendment, into just another dense area of law in which the facts of cases, rather than the purity of the original text, would be at the basis of legal knowledge. The alphabet would, over time have come to subvert any axiomatic scheme. For as Gray and Gray conclude (after exhaustive research into land law cases and doctrine), the common law mentality is one where the "*axiomatic* has given way to the *axiological* (in the sense of a pervasive concern with the values which underpin legal phenomena)" and the "concept of law which emerges from this analysis is one founded upon collaborative social practices of intellectual exchange or dialectic; it is born of a more authentic perception of the common law as a species of customary law" (2003: 230). Professor Waddams (2003) reached a similar conclusion (on which see Samuel 2005) and Professor Legrand (1996) argues that all this undermines any idea of a European Civil Code. As for legal education itself, both Professor Cownie (2004) and Professor McCrudden (2006) suggest that all law teachers see themselves to a greater or lesser extent as 'socio-legal' now.

This said, in recent years there has been something of a movement back to legal formalism both in the UK and the US. Markus Dubber notes that there is a trend in the United States that "is all about the rediscovery of law as the subject of legal scholarship and of doctrinalism as a respectable, even important, way of going about the academic study of law" (Dubber 2018: 100). Dan Priel has also noted that there remains a distinct anti-interdisciplinary attitude amongst some – many? – common law academic jurists in common law faculties outside of the United States (Priel 2019).

133. SCIENTIA CONSISTIT IN MEDULLA RATIONIS ET NON IN CORTICE SCRIPTURARUM

Knowledge consists in the marrow of reason and not in the skin of words.

(Baldus, Comment on D.1.3.16 no 5)

What, then, is legal knowledge? Within the civil (continental) legal tradition, the history and transmission of a certain type of legal knowledge via Justinian's *Institutes* and *Digest* have largely determined the epistemological and ontological foundation of legal knowledge. However, the history of common law proves much more ambiguous and allows for a number of rather different models. Is it a system of categories and rules? Is it a system of rights and duties? Is it, as some have often implied, just a collection of institutions and remedies ('chaos with an index')? Or is legal knowledge more than this? Should it be integrated into the social and human sciences in general? Certainly, studying the courts and the procedures is not enough to gain a full knowledge of the English (or common law) mentality. One needs to get beyond the 'skin' and to the 'marrow'.

One form of legal education that has been dominant both in civil law and still to some extent in common law faculties is what is termed a doctrinal approach. As one leading comparatist explains:

Essentially, the doctrinal study of law seeks to provide a systematic presentation of the rules, principles, and concepts that preside over a particular field of law or legal institution. Legal doctrine, as a form of legal research, analyses the relationship between these rules, principles, and concepts, seeking to solve ambiguity and fill gaps in the existing law (Husa 2022: 6).

One only needs to study some of the leading law journals, such as the *Law Quarterly Review,* to appreciate that such a doctrinal approach remains alive and well even if there are many other Anglo-American legal academics and journals pursuing different lines of inquiry (see for example the articles in *Legal Studies* over the past decade or two).

Yet what is a student supposed to learn when studying a course (or module as some institutions describe such courses) on the law of contract, tort, property, or whatever? Writing in 1975, the comparative lawyer René David (1906–1990) had this to say:

> The lecture course (*le cours magistral*) and the tutorials (*les travaux dirigés*) have as their function, in their eyes, to get students to know what they have to know on the day of the examination; they fill this role well enough and it matters little whether or not they be the tools for a satisfactory legal education. One basically learns, within a positivist perspective, the rules of today's law without preoccupying oneself with what will be the law of tomorrow, what will have to be applied in life (quoted in Orianne 1990: 207).

David thought that too much emphasis was being put on memory work in the law faculty to the prejudice of legal reasoning in practice and that what was needed was a reform, if not abolition, of the traditional law exam (see Orianne 1990: 208).

In fact, it would seem that little has changed since the very first of the university law schools started teaching in medieval Italy. James Brundage, speaking not just about law, says that the medieval university faculty had three objectives:

> first, each faculty sought to make sure that its students thoroughly and systematically mastered the authoritative texts of the discipline. In addition, faculties insisted that their students must learn how to analyze problems and frame persuasive arguments, so that they could effectively uphold one side of an issue while refuting the others (Brundage 2008: 248).

One might easily mistake these objectives as coming from a contemporary law school. Nevertheless, it would seem that learning rules within particular legal categories was not a skill to be confined just to the exam room. As has been seen (maxim 4), a judge must decide litigation in accordance with the rules of law that are applicable to it and must assign the facts to their correct legal category. To some extent, this is an exercise demanded of students in their courses and exams, although often the course or module has already determined the legal category in play. Accordingly, said Christian Atias (1947–2015), legal knowledge:

> is based on rules, on classifications and on distinctions between the different domains, on notions and categorisations, on legal dispositions, on the principles formulated by legal decisions considered as being particularly important, on the modes of interpretation, but also on various types of situations, on difficulties (2011: 174).

However:

> This knowledge does not of itself permit one to reason in law. It only provides the base. Its effect is to provide a legal framework into which the reasoning can be inserted; the consequence is that it makes the reasoning relevant and constrained, or at least it facilitates its acceptance by the respondent or listener said to belong to the world of lawyers (*ibid*).

This idea of reasoning in law being inserted into a particular knowledge framework might seem epistemologically evident, but it equally implies that there are limits to the types of reasons that can be employed within this world of lawyers. Christian Atias made this point by saying that lawyers do not invoke certain arguments on the ground that they are not legal arguments. Accordingly, as Atias went on to say, "philosophical, economic and sociological arguments have little chance of being convincing in themselves." Such arguments have to be translated into legal terms (2011: 114). This said, economic and sociological arguments are not entirely irrelevant in French law (Rouvière 2023: 306–325); but one difficulty is an historical tradition in the nineteenth century in which there was a "quasi-refusal for the presence of sociology in the law faculties and ... a closed inward-looking corporate attitude on the part of law teachers" (Audren, Chambost & Halpérin 2020: 206). In the first part of the last century, there was "a professionalisation attaching to the teaching body searching to align themselves with the scientific standards coming from Germany" (2020: 207). Summing up the contemporary position in France, it would seem that not much has changed: 'At present, unlike economic approaches to law which have succeeded in gaining a certain visibility in the academic and political field, neither the sociology of law (despite the existence of a journal such as *Droit et Soiciete*), nor anthropology of law (despite the journal *Droit et Cultures)* have managed to acheieve a serious presence in the education of French lawyers and rare are, amongst the latter, those who are engaged with these subjects' (Audren *et al* 2020: 240).

There may be the occasional exception, but this must not mask "the orientation profoundly positivist of a large part of the legal community little affected by the questions that contemporary social sciences pose" (*ibid*). An Oxford law exam question once asked if law was resilient. In the civil law world, it would seem so, if by resilience one means resistant to epistemological insights from other disciplines.

One should not be surprised, of course, as a university degree was and remains a fundamental requirement on the continent. Consequently, the education regime was almost bound to follow the money, so to speak. In England, a law degree is not essential. Yet contemporary university legal education regimes in England and Wales are, as has been seen, a relatively recent phenomenon, and the new corps of academic lawyers that followed the 1846 report were inevitably going to look to Roman and civilian learning, especially given the report's emphasis on 'legal science'. Where else could one look? This said, the professions in England are becoming more detached from what goes on in law schools. And law schools themselves have to face the fact that more than half of their law students will not go on to become professional lawyers. Legal education is, partly as a result, becoming – perhaps has now become – a legal knowledge topic in itself attracting its own research and scholarship. This development may well result in helping jurists to discover the 'marrow' beyond the 'skin'.

CONCLUDING REMARKS

It has been said that legal scholars are not good at reflecting on their own discipline (Van Gestel & Lienhard 2019: 449) and that legal doctrine "is often too descriptive, too autopoietic, without taking the context of the law sufficiently into account; it lacks a clear methodology and the methods of legal doctrine seem identical to those of legal practice; it is too parochial" (Van Hoecke 2011: 3). One reason for this situation, so it has been argued, is that doctrinal scholars "see themselves as 'practical' scholars who aim to help the courts reach better decisions... a task for which there is no need for any serious knowledge of history, economics, psychology or philosophy" (Priel 2019: 165). There are no legal maxims, rules, or abstract assertions that can counter these problems, save assertions either that law as a university discipline should become more interdisciplinary (Legrand 2015; Husa 2022) or that law as a distinct academic subject should be removed from the university world (Siems 2011). The latter suggestion seems unlikely to happen. At the level of an introduction to law, perhaps all that can be achieved is to encourage a sensibility that law as a discipline should be viewed as open to important historical, comparative and interdisciplinary orientations and that legal reasoning and method are one focal point where these orientations are particularly relevant. The social and human sciences, it could be argued, do have an important contribution to make here (see further Samuel 2024).

Final thoughts

What, finally, can be said about maxims? At one end of the spectrum, they can be seen as little more than lightweight legal fluff designed to add some (perhaps spurious) authority to the dignity of law. At the other end of the spectrum, they can be seen as fundamental legal principles capable of acting as a normative source of law. In between these spectrums, there are a number of different possibilities. One of these possibilities is that, carefully chosen, they can offer some historical windows into the evolution of legal knowledge in Europe from Roman to modern times. Peter Stein's book is an excellent example of this possibility, showing how the *regulae iuris* started out as mere summaries and ended up in the 16th century as legal axioms (Stein 1966). Another possibility is that the *regulae* or *principia* have a comparative dimension capable of exposing how legal knowledge has arisen from both the civil law and common law traditions. This is not to claim that a maxim has necessarily the same meaning to a common lawyer as to a continental one, and so care must be taken when reflecting on the comparative dimension. The preceding chapters are, accordingly, not designed to be sophisticated examples of comparative scholarship. The lightweight comparisons are there to aid understanding for those at an early stage in their legal studies. Yet another spectrum possibility is that many of the *regulae* can, hopefully, be of aid in fostering an appreciation that there have been, over the last two millennia, some outstanding jurists who have made fundamental contributions (often unappreciated today) to doctrinal legal scholarship – at least outstanding when compared to some more recent doctrinal scholarship.

Are there, then, some maxims that are more memorable or fundamental than others? Gaius' institutional plan must rank as one of the most fundamental statements regarding legal taxonomy (maxim 41) – forever imprinted on Europe's civil codes – while Ulpian's definition of justice, as abstract as it is, has been quoted right up to modern times. The distinction between *ius naturale* and *ius positivum* (maxims 45–46), again, has proved fundamental for legal theorists, even if the distinction meant something different in the 12th century than it did for legal philosophers in the last century. Bartolus' definition of ownership (maxim 79) and Ulpian's assertion about possession (maxim 80) are probably the two important starting points for many property lawyers given their continuing relevance, even if Bartolus' definition of ownership is not so easily applicable in English law given the trust. As for the law of obligations, the obligatory force of contract still finds expression through a pithy *principium* (maxim 85) which continues to be quoted today, while in the law of tort the principle of foreseeability is as relevant now as it seemingly was for the Romans (maxim 103). In the domain of restitution, two maxims (112–113) are nothing less than fundamental to the subject. With regard to legal method, the dichotomy between bottom-up (casuistic) (maxim 122) and top-down (axiomatic) (maxims 47, 123–124) reasoning is particularly pertinent for contemporary jurists interested in legal analysis. Finally, one must not forget the great *quod omnes tangit* brocard (maxim 54) that still, surely, resonates within the modern democratic and liberal mind. There are, of course, a range of other maxims in the previous chapters that also remain of importance, while others – some of which might not be considered true maxims (especially if they are not expressed in Latin) – are perhaps more useful as introductions to various legal topics.

Taken together as a collection, a book of maxims or *regulae iuris* also has some relevance in as much as it forms part of a tradition that stretches back to the medieval jurists. This relevance does not necessarily endow such a book with any status or guarantee of quality. In fact, it suggests, if anything, a somewhat lack of originality. However, quite a few of these books of the past have not made too much effort to research the original source of many of these *regulae,* and this is to be regretted because many have their origin in the writings of the medieval jurists, especially the post-glossators (on which see Stein 1999: 43–74; Gordley 2013: 28–81). As Peter Stein put it:

> One of the aims of glossatorial scholarship was to discover the general principles, or brocards, inherent in the Corpus iuris. Some of them were already assembled in the last title of the Digest, dedicated to maxims. Others were detached from their original context and were used as part of an argument on any matter to which they could be made relevant.

This author then went on to say:

> Collections of brocards appear in the last quarter of the twelfth century. They always introduced strings of texts, which either supported or denied the proposition adopted by the brocard. Although apparently a civil law invention, they were taken up with enthusiasm by the canonists. They directed the busy lawyer quickly to the textual authorities, with which he could embellish his argument and impress the judge; often they were used to 'blind the judge with science' (1999: 48).

In identifying the original source (where possible), this collection of brocards takes on and identifies the different historical, cultural and mentality epochs in which the substance of a maxim was asserted. In the medieval era, collections of maxims served a practical purpose in that they were part of an advocate's armoury. Later, during the Renaissance, such works were aimed at establishing law as a coherent science. In the 18th century, especially in France, books of maxims were laying the foundations for a *Code civil* that was already being prepared in projects at the end of this century.

This present collection is certainly not aimed at any codification movement, but it does have the purpose of aiding, not the busy lawyer, but the student of the common law lost in the maze (maxim 132) of conflicting precedents and opaque statutes. Lady Hale once said that she pitied "the practitioners as well as the academics who have to make sense of our judgments in difficult cases" (*Sienkiewicz v Greif (UK) Ltd* [2011] 2 AC 229, para 167). Quite so, one might say. But what, then, of the poor student? Maybe the interesting sayings of the Roman, medieval, Renaissance and 19th-century jurists might help them orientate themselves. It could be a compass rather than a map. Moreover, most of the brocards are very readable, which is not often true of legal literature (although France prides itself on elegance). Still, as the great Baldus (1327–1400) once said, *Sapientia sine eloquentia parum prodest, et eloquentia sine sapientia multum nocet Republicae*, which basically means that knowledge without eloquence does little harm to anyone, but eloquence without knowledge does great harm to everyone. The Brexit debate in the UK indicated only too well that Baldus was not just speaking to his own generation. He was one of the outstanding jurists in the history of European legal thought. And rulers and princes of the time certainly recognised this, for he died a very rich man (just like some lawyers today).

Bibliography

Andrews, N (2000), A New Civil Procedure Code for England: Part Control (2000) 19 *Civil Justice Quarterly* 19

Atias, C (2011), *Devenir juriste: Le sens du droit* (LexisNexis, 2011)

Audren, F, Chambost, A-S & Halpérin, J-L (2020), *Histoires contemporaines du droit* (Dalloz, 2020)

Austin, J (1832), *Province of Jurisprudence Determined* (John Murray, 1832, reprinted Cambridge University Press, 1995)

Baker, J (2002), *An Introduction to English Legal History* (Butterworths, 5th ed., 2019)

Baker, J (2003), *The Oxford History of the Laws of England: Volume VI 1483–1558* (Oxford University Press, 2003)

Baker, J (2019), *An Introduction to English Legal History* (Oxford University Press, 5th ed, 2019)

Bell, J (2006), *Judiciaries within Europe: A Comparative Review* (Cambridge University Press, 2006)

Bellomo, M (1995), *The Common Legal Past of Europe 1000–1800* (The Catholic University of America Press, 1995, trans LG Cochrane)

Bengoetxea, J (1993), *The Legal Reasoning of the European Court of Justice* (Oxford University Press, 1993)

Berman, H (1983), *Law and Revolution: The Formation of the Western Legal Tradition* (Harvard University Press, 1983)

Birks, P (1997), Definition and Division: A Meditation on *Institutes* 3.13, in P Birks (ed), *The Classification of Obligations* (Oxford University Press, 1997) 1

Birks, P (1998), The Academic and the Practitioner (1998) 8 *Legal Studies* 397

Birks, P (2014), *The Roman Law of Obligations* (Oxford University Press, 2014; edited by E Descheemaeker)

Blomeyer, A (1980), Types of Relief Available (Judicial Remedies), *International Encyclopedia of Comparative Law*, Volume XVI, Chapter 4 (JCB Mohr) (completed 1980)

Boyron, S (2010), La *summa divisio* vue d'outre-Manche, in B Bonnet & P Deumier (eds), *De l'intérêt de la summa divisio droit public-droit privé ?* (Dalloz, 2010) 121

Brundage, JA (2008), *The Medieval Origins of the Legal Profession* (University of Chicago Press, 2008)

Burrows, A (Lord) (2021), Judges and Academics, and the Endless Road to Unattainable Perfection, *The Lionel Cohen Lecture 2021* https://www.supremecourt.uk/docs/lionel-cohen-lecture-2021-lord-burrows.pdf

Cadiet, L, Normand, J & Mekki, SA, *Théorie générale du procès* (Presses Universitaires de France, 2nd ed., 2013)

Cairns, J (1984), Blackstone, An English Institutist: Legal Literature and the Rise of the Nation State (1984) 4 *Oxford Journal of Legal Studies* 318

Cane, P (1996), *Tort Law and Economic Interests* (Oxford University Press, 2nd ed., 1996)

Cane, P & Stapleton, J (eds), *The Law of Obligations: Essays in Celebration of John Fleming* (Oxford University Press, 1998)

Canning, J (1987), *The Political Thought of Baldus de Ubaldis* (Cambridge University Press, 1987)

Cappelletti, M (1989), *The Judicial process in Comparative Perspective* (Oxford University Press, 1989)

Cappelletti, M & Garth, B (1986), Introduction – Policies, Trends and Ideas in Civil Procedure, *International Encyclopedia of Comparative Law*, Volume XVI, Chapter 1 (JCB Mohr) (Completed 1986)

Cohen, F (1935), Transcendental Nonsense and the Functional Approach (1935) 35 *Columbia Law Review* 809

Cownie, F (2004), *Legal Academics* (Hart, Oxford, 2004)

Dantoine, J-B (1710), *Les règles du droit civil, dans le méme ordre qu'elles sont disposées au dernier Titre du Digeste* (Leonard Plaignard, Lyon, 1710)

Dantoine, J-B (1772), *Les règles du droit canon, dans le méme ordre qu'elles sont disposées au dernier Titre du cinquième Livre du Sexte, & au dernier Titre du cinquième Livre des Décrétales* (J Dessain, Liege, 1772)

Deakin, S & Markou, C (eds) (2020), *Is Law Computable? Critical Perspectives on Law and Artificial Intelligence* (Hart Publishing, 2020)

Deroussin, D (2012), *Histoire du droit des obligations* (Economica, 2nd ed., 2012)

Descheemaeker, E (2009), *The Division of Wrongs: A Historical Comparative Study* (Oxford University Press, 2009)

Doria, CM (2016), Variazioni in tema di 'regulae iuris' (a mo'di introduzione), in C Cascione, CM Doria & C Nitsch (dir), *Regulae Iuris: Ipotesi di lavoro tra storia e teoria del diritto* (Jovene Editore, 2016) 1

Dubber, M (2018), Legal History as Legal Scholarship: Doctrinalism, Interdisciplinarity, and Critical Analysis of Law, in Dubber, M & Tomlins, C (eds) (2018), *The Oxford Handbook of Legal History* (Oxford University Press, 2018) 99

Dworkin, R (1977), *Taking Rights Seriously* (Duckworth, 1977)

Dworkin, R (1986), *Law's Empire* (Fontana, 1986)

Dworkin, R (1995), Y a-t-il une bonne réponse en matière d'interprétation juridique, in P Amselek (ed.), *Interprétation et droit* (Bruylant/Presses Universitaires d'Aix-Marseille, 1995), 227

Eagleton, T (2022), *Critical Revolutionaries* (Yale University Press, 2022)

Errera, A (2006), *Lineamenti di epistemologia giuridica medievale* (Giappichelli, 2006)

Fabre-Magnan, M (2024), *Droit des obligations: I – Contrat et engagement unilatéral* (Presses Universitaires de France, 7th ed., 2024)

Finnis, J 1980), *Natural Law and Natural Rights* (Oxford University Press, 1980)

Fiss, OM (1984), Against Settlement (1984) 93 *Yale Law Journal* 1073

Fontin, J (2021), Revisiting the Application of Statutes to the Crown: A Historical Constitutional Approach (2021) 3 *Journal of Commonwealth Law* 271

Frommelt, F (1878), *Regulae iuris* (Weiss & Neumesiter, Leipzig, 1878)

Gaius, see Gordon & Robinson (1988)

Galeotti, S (1954), *The Judicial Control of Public Authorities in England and in Italy* (Stevens & Sons, 1954)

Garde, R (1841), *An Analysis of the First Principles, or Elementary Rules, of Pleading* (Maxwell, 2nd ed., 1841)

Glanert, S, Mercescu, A & Samuel, G (2021), *Rethinking Comparative Law* (Edward Elgar, 2021)

Goff, R. (1999), 'The Search for Principle', reprinted in William Swadling and Gareth Jones (eds) (1999), *The Search for Principle: Essays in Honour of Lord Goff of Chieveley* (Oxford: Oxford University Press) 313

Goltzberg, S (2018), *100 principes juridiques* (Presses Universitaires de France, 2018)

Gordley, J (2013), *The Jurists: A Critical History* (Oxford University Press, 2013)

Gordley, J (2022), *Regulae Iuris* and Legal Principles: Whence and Whither? (2022) 37 *Tulane European & Civil Law Forum* 201

Gordon, W & Robinson, O (1988), *The Institutes of Gaius* (Duckworth, 1988)

Goulliart, P-L (1798–1799), *Exposition des règles du droit ancien* (HL Perronneau, Paris, 1798–1799).

Graveson, R (1953), *Status in the Common Law* (Athlone, 1953)

Gray, K & Gray, S (2003), The Rhetoric of Reality, in J Getzler (ed.), *Rationalizing Property, Equity and Trusts* (Butterworths, 2003), 204

Hackney, J (1997), More than a Trace of the Old Philosophy, in P Birks (ed.), *The Classification of Obligations* (Oxford University Press, 1997) 123

Hamblem, N (Lord) (2020), The Commercial Court – Past, Present and Future, COMBAR Lecture

Harris, DR (1961), The Concept of Possession in English Law, in Guest, A (ed.) (1961), *Oxford Essays in Jurisprudence* (Oxford University Press, 1961) 69

Hart, H (1961), *The Concept of Law* (Oxford University Press, 1961)

Hart, H (1994), *The Concept of Law* (Oxford University Press, 2nd ed, 1994)

Hazeltine, HD, Lapsley, G & Winfield, PH (eds) (1936), *Maitland Selected Essays* (Cambridge University Press, 1936)

Hedley, S (1999), How has the Common Law Survived the 20th Century? (1999) 50 *Northern Ireland Legal Quarterly* 283

Herzog, P & Karlen, D (1977), Attacks on Judicial Decisions, *International Encyclopedia of Comparative Law*, Volume XVI, Chapter 8 (JCB Mohr) (completed 1977)

Hohfeld, W (1919) *Fundamental Legal Conceptions* (Yale University Press, 1919; reprint, 1966)

Holmes, OW (1897), The Path of the Law (1897) 10 *Harvard Law Review* 457

Hunter, R, McGlynn, C & Rackley, E (2010), *Feminist Judgments: From Theory to Practice* (Hart, 2010)

Husa, J (2022), *Interdisciplinary Comparative Law: Rubbing Shoulders with the Neighbours or Standing Alone in a Crowd* (Edward Elgar, 2022)

Ibbetson, D (1999), *A Historical Introduction to the Law of Obligations* (Oxford University Press, 1999)

Jestaz, P & Jamin C (2004), *La doctrine* (Dalloz, 2004)

Johnston, D (1999), *Roman Law in Context* (Cambridge University Press, 1999)

Jolowicz, HF (1957), *Roman Foundations of Modern Law* (Oxford University Press, 1957)

Jolowicz, HF (1963), *Lectures on Jurisprudence* (Athlone, 1963)

Jolowicz, JA (ed) (1992), *Droit anglais* (Dalloz, 2nd ed., 1992)

Jolowicz, JA (1996), The Woolf Report and the Adversary System (1996) 15 *Civil Justice Quarterly* 198

Jolowicz, JA (2003), Adversarial and Inquisitorial Models of Civil Procedure (2003) 52 *International and Comparative Law Quarterly* 281

Jones, J (1940), *Historical Introduction to the Theory of Law* (Oxford University Press, 1940)

Justinian, *Digest*, see Mommsen, Krueger & Watson (1985)

Kahn-Freund, O (1949), Introduction, in K Renner, *The Institutions of Private Law and their Social Functions* (Routledge & Kegan Paul, 1949; reprint 1976)

Kirby, M (2007), Judicial Dissent – Common Law and Civil Law Traditions (2007) 123 *Law Quarterly Review* 379

Kohl, A (1982), Romanist Legal Systems, in *International Encyclopedia of Comparative Law*, Volume XVI, Chapter 6, Part II (JCB Mohr) (completed 1982)

Kuttner, S (1936), Sur Les Origines du Terme 'Droit Positif' (1936) 15 *Revue Historique de Droit Français et Étranger* 728

Lasser, M (2004), *Judicial Deliberations: A Comparative Analysis of Judicial Transparency and Legitimacy* (OUP, Oxford, 2004)

Lawson, FH (1972), Common Law, *International Encyclopedia of Comparative Law*, Volume VI (Property and Trusts), Chapter 2 (Structural Variations in Property Law), Part II

Lawson, F (1980), *Remedies of English Law* (Butterworths, 2nd ed., 1980)

Lawson, F & Rudden, B (2002), *The Law of Property* (Oxford University Press, 3rd ed., 2002)

Legrand, P (1996), European Legal Systems are not Converging (1996) 45 *International and Comparative Law Quarterly* 52

Legrand, P (2015), *Le droit comparé* (Presses Universitaires de France, 5th ed., 2015)

Legrand, P (2022), *Negative Comparative Law: A Strong Programme for Weak Thought* (Cambridge University Press, 2022)

Lesaffer, R (2009), *European Legal History: A Cultural and Political Perspective* (Cambridge University Press, 2009)

Lewis, R (2005), Insurance and the Tort System (2005) 25 *Legal Studies* 85

Llewellyn, K (1951), *The Bramble Bush* (Oceana, 1951)

Lobban, M (1991), *The Common Law and English Jurisprudence 1760–1850* (Oxford University Press, 1991)

Maclean, I (1992), *Interpretation and Meaning in the Renaissance* (Cambridge University Press, 1992)

Macmillan, C (2010), *Mistakes in Contract Law* (Hart Publishing, 2011)

Maine, H (Sir) (1890), *Early Law and Custom* (John Murray, 1890 edition)

Maitland, FW (1908), *The Constitutional History of England* (Cambridge University Press, 1908)

Maitland, FW (1909), *The Forms of Action at Common Law* (Cambridge University Press, Reprint 1979) (first published 1909)

Maitland, FW (1936), see Hazeltine, Lapsley & Winfield (1936)

McCrudden, C (2006), Legal Research and the Social Sciences (2006) 122 *Law Quarterly Review* 632

Mestre, J-L (1985), *Introduction historique au droit administratif français* (Presses Universitaires de France, 1985)

Milsom, S (1981), *Historical Foundations of the Common Law* (Butterworths, 2nd ed., 1981)

Mommsen, T, Krueger, P & Watson, A (1985), *The Digest of Justinian* (University of Pennsylvania Press, 1985) (4 Vols)

Munday, R (2002), 'All for One and One for All': The Rise to Prominence of the Composite Judgement in the Civil Division of the Court of Appeal [2002] *Cambridge Law Journal* 321

Ogus, A (2007), The Economic Approach: Competition Between Legal Systems, in E Örücü & D Nelken (eds) (2007), *Comparative Law: A Handbook* (Hart, 2007) 155

Oliver, D (2001), Pourquoi n'y a-t-il pas vraiment de distinction entre droit public et droit privé en Angleterre? [2001] *Revue Internationale de Droit Comparé* 327

Orianne, P (1990), *Apprendre le droit: Éléments pour une pédagogie juridique* (Éditions Labor, 1990)

Patault, A-M (1989), *Introduction historique au droit des biens* (Presses Universitaires de France, 1989)

Paynot-Rouvillois, A (2003), Personne morale, in D Alland & S Rials (eds) (2003), *Dictionnaire de la culture juridique* (Presses Universitaires de France, 2003) 1153

Porter, J (2007), Justice, in J-Y Lacoste (ed.) (2007), *Dictionnaire critique de théologie* (Presses Universitaires de France, 2nd ed., 2007) 741

Pradel, J (1989), *Histoire des doctines pénales* (Presses Universitaires de France, 1989)

Priel, D (2019), Two Forms of Formalism, in A Roberstson & J Goudkamp (eds), *Form and Substance in the Law of Obligations* (Hart Publishing, 2019) 165

Provost, R (ed.) (2017), *Culture in the Domains of Law* (Cambridge University Press, 2017)

Rampelberg, R-M (2005), *Repères romains pour le droit européen des contrats* (LGDJ, 2005)

Roberts, S & Palmer, M (2005), *Dispute Processes: ADR and the Primary Forms of Decision-Making* (Cambridge University Press, 2005)

Roland, H & Boyer, L (1999), *Adages du droit français* (Litec, 4th ed., 1999) (2 volumes)

Rouvière, F (2023), *Argumentation juridique* (Presses Universitaires de France, 2023)

Rudden, B (1991–92), Torticles (1991–92) 6/7 *Tulane Civil Law Forum* 105

Rudden, B (1992), Equity as Alibi, in S Goldstein (ed) (1992), *Equity and Contemporary Legal Development* (The Hebrew University of Jerusalem, 1992) 30

Rüfner, T (2010), The Roman Concept of Ownership and the Medieval Doctrine of *Dominium Utile*, in J Cairns & P du Plessis (eds) (2010), *The Creation of the Ius Commune* (Edinburgh University Press, 2010) 127

Samuel, G (2000), Can Gaius Really be Compared to Darwin? (2000) 49 *International & Comparative Law Quarterly* 297–329

Samuel, G (2004), English Private Law: Old and New Thinking in the Taxonomy Debate (2004) 24 *Oxford Journal of Legal Studies* 335–362

Samuel, G (2005), Can the Common Law be Mapped? (2005) 55 *University of Toronto Law Journal* 271

Samuel, G (2018), *Rethinking Legal Reasoning* (Edward Elgar, 2018)

Samuel, G (2022), *Rethinking Historical Jurisprudence* (Edward Elgar, 2022)

Samuel, G (2022a), Liability for Accidents Revisited (2022) 17 *Journal of Comparative Law* 462

Samuel, G (2022b), What is the Role of a Legal Academic? A response to Lord Burrows (2022) 3 *Amicus Curiae* (Series 2) 305–334 (https://journals.sas.ac.uk/amicus/article/view/5414)

Samuel, G (2024), Can Methods from the Social and Human Sciences Be of Value in Understanding Comparative Law Methodology? (2024) 19 *Journal of Comparative Law* 321

Sériaux, A (2003), Droit naturel, in D Alland & S Rials (eds) (2003), *Dictionnaire de la culture juridique* (Presses Universitaires de France, 2003) 507

Siems, M (2011), A World Without Law Professors, in M van Hoecke (ed.) (2011), *Methodologies of Legal Research: Which Kind of Method for Which Kind of Discipline?* (Hart, 2011) 71

Spencer, J (1998), *La procédure pénale anglaise* (Presses Universitaires de France, 1998)

Stein, P (1966), *Regulae Iuris: From Juristic Rules to Legal Maxims* (Edinburgh University Press, 1966)

Stein, P (1980), *Legal Evolution: The Story of an Idea* (Cambridge University Press, 1980)

Stein, P (1984), *Legal Institutions: The Development of Dispute Settlement* (Butterworths, 1984)

Stein, P (1999), *Roman Law in European History* (Cambridge, 1999)

Susskind, R (1987), *Expert Systems in Law* (Oxford University Press, 1987)

Sutton, R (1929), *Personal Actions at Common Law* (Butterworths & Co, 1929)

Taitslin, A (2019), The Genesis of Concepts of Possession and Ownership in the Civilian Tradition and at Common Law: How Did Common Law Manage Without a Concept of Ownership? Why Roman Law Did Not, in Moréteau, Masferrer & Modéer 341

Teubner, G (1998), Legal Irritants: Good Faith in British Law or How Unifying Law Ends Up in New Divergences (1998) 61 *Modern Law Review* 11

Thatcher, M (1987), Interview, *Women's Own* 31 October 1987

Tierney, B (1982), *Religion, Law, and the Growth of Constitutional Thought 1150–1650* (Cambridge University Press, 1982)

Tiley, J (1968), *A Casebook on Equity and Succession* (Sweet & Maxwell, 1968)

Twining, W (1985), *Karl Llewellyn and the Realist Movement* (Weidenfeld & Nicolson, reprint 1985)

Ullmann, W (1975), *Medieval Political Thought* (Penguin, 1975)

Van Caenegem, R (1971), History of European Civil Procedure, *International Encyclopedia of Comparative Law*, Volume XVI, Chapter 2 (JCB Mohr) (Completed 1971)

Van Caenegem, R (1987), *Judges, Legislators and Professors: Chapters in European Legal History* (Cambridge University Press, 1987)

Van Caenegem, R (1992), *An Historical Introduction to Private Law* (Cambridge University Press, 1992)

Van Caenegem, R (1999), Le rôle de la conscience du juge dans l'histoire du droit anglais, in J-M Carbasse & L Depambour-Tarride (ed) (1999), *La conscience du juge dans la tradition juridique européenne* (Presses Universitaires de France, 1999) 263

Van Gestel, R & Lienhard, A (eds) (2019), *Evaluating Academic Legal Research in Europe* (Edward Elgar, 2019)

Van Hoecke, M (2011), Legal Doctrine: Which Method(s) for What Kind of Discipline?, in M van Hoecke (ed.), *Methodologies of Legal Research: Which Kind of Method for Which Kind of Discipline?* (Hart Publishing, 2011) 1

Verkuil, PR (1975), The Ombudsman and the Limits of the Adversary System (1975) 75 *Columbia Law Review* 845

Villey, M (1986), *Philosophie du droit: I. Définitions et fins du droit* (Dalloz, 4th ed., 1986)

Virgo, G (2021), Equity and Trusts, in Barnard, C, O'Sullivan, J & Virgo, G (2021), *What About Law? Studying Law at University* (Hart, 3rd ed, 20021) 129

Waddams, S (2003), *Dimensions of Private Law: Categories and Concepts in Anglo-American Legal Reasoning* (Cambridge University Press, 2003)

Waddams, S (2011), *Principle and Policy in Contract Law: Competing or Complementary Concepts?* (Cambridge University Press, 2011)

Watson, A (1994), The Importance of "Nutshells" (1994) 42 *American Journal of Comparative Law* 1

Weir, T (1998), The Staggering March of Negligence, in P Cane & J Stapleton (eds) (1998), *The Law of Obligations: Essays in Celebration of John Fleming* (Oxford University Press, 1998) 97

Weir, T (2006), *An Introduction to Tort Law* (Oxford University Press, 2nd ed., 2006)

Williams, I (2016), The Role of Legal Maxims in Early-modern Common Law, in M Del Mar & M Lobban (eds) (2016), *Law in Theory and History: New Essays on a Neglected Dialogue* (Hart, 2016) 188

Wilson, G (1973), *Cases and Materials on The English Legal System* (Sweet & Maxwell, 1973)

Woolf, H (Lord) (1996), *Access to Justice: Final Report to the Lord Chancellor on the Civil Justice System in England and Wales* (HMSO, July 1996)

Zakrzewski, R (2005), *Remedies Reclassified* (Oxford University Press, 2005)

Zander, M (2007), *Cases and Materials on the English Legal System* (Cambridge University Press, 10th ed., 2007)

Index

.